DIVCO
A History of the Truck and Company

by

Robert R. Ebert & John S. Rienzo, Jr.

Published by

Antique Power Inc.

Author Profiles

ROBERT R. EBERT, PH.D.

Mr. Ebert holds the Buckhorn Endowed Chair in Economics at Baldwin-Wallace College in Berea, Ohio, where he has taught since 1967.

He has published several articles on the economics of the automobile and commercial vehicle industries. In 1993, he received the Carl Benz prize from the Society of Automotive Historians, for outstanding periodical article on automotive history, for his work on Studebaker.

JOHN S. RIENZO, JR.

Mr. Rienzo is Librarian for the Divco Club of America and is a Divco collector and enthusiast. His library includes an extensive collection of Divco literature. He is restoring two Divcos: a 1936 Model S and a 1960 Model 15.

He is a member of the Suffolk County (Long Island, New York) Police Department.

First published in 1997
by Antique Power Inc.
P.O. Box 838
Yellow Springs, Ohio 45387

All pictures, illustrations, and photographs in this book are from the authors' private collections unless otherwise indicated.

Printed in the United States by Batson Printing

ISBN 0-9660751-1-0

With appreciation,

the authors dedicate this book

to their wives for their

understanding and patience...

To Marcia Ebert and Joyce Rienzo

Contents

Acknowledgments

It is customary to thank those who have helped in preparing a book for publication. Naming individuals is a hazardous undertaking because inevitably someone is left off the list. Therefore, we offer a simple "thank you" to the dozens of members of the Divco Club of America, former Divco employees and their families, dealers, and customers, and Divco enthusiasts who helped research the Divco story. However, several people are due specific thanks and appreciation: Les Bagley, editor of *The Divco News*, who provided the initial encouragement and continual prodding to keep us at our appointed tasks; Tina M. Alexander, Lisa Burkhart, Nicole R. Price, Michelle Volpe, and Nicole Weinbroer, who provided invaluable research and manuscript preparation help as research assistants in the Economics Department of Baldwin-Wallace College; and Janet C. Joseph, Writing Specialist at Baldwin-Wallace College, who provided editorial assistance. Baldwin-Wallace College provided invaluable encouragement and assistance in the writing of the book, particularly in providing a Gund Foundation Grant to hire a student research assistant. In the end, though, we accept responsibility for the accuracy of the material presented or for errors of omission or commission. It has been a labor of love.

Robert R. Ebert
John S. Rienzo, Jr.

Introduction

Divco was a survivor. For 60 years, Divco survived the trials and tumult of the Depression, a world war, numerous mergers and acquisitions, and a dramatically changing environment for its product, multi-stop delivery trucks. After almost exactly 60 years, Divco production came to an end in early 1986. Even at the end, in one sense, Divco was a survivor because it was a profitable product for its builder. The Divco story is one of trucks, people, and a changing economy. It is a tale of innovation and creativity as well as one of mistakes, oversights, and miscalculations. In the pages that follow, we hope the reader will gain an appreciation for the environment in which Divcos were designed, built, sold, and used and how they came to be "America's Favorite Milk Truck."

Why Divco?

The virtual passing of the house-to-house milk delivery truck during the last twenty years has left a void in what was once a vital role for the motor truck in city life. Once the last major domain of the urban work horse, retail milk delivery was slowly being motorized after World War I, with the battery powered truck playing an important part in this process. However, with the advent of the specially designed Divco motor truck in 1927, the switch from horses to motor vehicles accelerated in the home delivery field.

By the mid-1930s the short-nosed Divco had become a familiar sight in nearly every American city. In its streamlined version, introduced just before the start of World War II, the Divco became recognized as America's quintessential milk delivery truck. Therefore, it is only fitting that an in-depth study of the Divco company and its products be made available. As the reader will see, the history of Divco involves the struggle by a small but dedicated group of people to develop a quality special-purpose vehicle in the face of serious competition and economic stress. Through all the ups and downs of corporate ownership and market changes, the Divco truck maintained a dedicated following which persists to this day.

John B. Montville
August 1, 1997

Divco: The Early Years
(1926-1935)

The Beginnings

George Bacon was born in 1867 in Scranton, Pennsylvania where he grew to adulthood and worked for a while as an electrician.[1] By 1920, Bacon was Chief Engineer of the Detroit Electric Car Company. Detroit Electric had been building various models of electric trucks since 1909. Inspired by the many horse-drawn delivery wagons that could be seen plying the streets of the city, Bacon realized that the electric vehicle concept was a natural for the multi-stop truck market. The electric milk delivery truck he subsequently developed became the immediate predecessor of the Divco so familiar to generations of Americans.

A unique feature of Bacon's electric delivery truck was that it had four driving positions: front, rear, and both sides. The design was inspired by the horse-drawn milk wagons that could be operated with the driver sitting up front, standing on either side, or even standing on the tail gate at the back with the driving reins running through the vehicle and over the load.[2] The four-point control concept of Bacon's electric is shown in the accompanying drawings from patent 1,831,405 applied for on January 14, 1924, granted to George Bacon on November 10, 1931, and assigned to Divco.

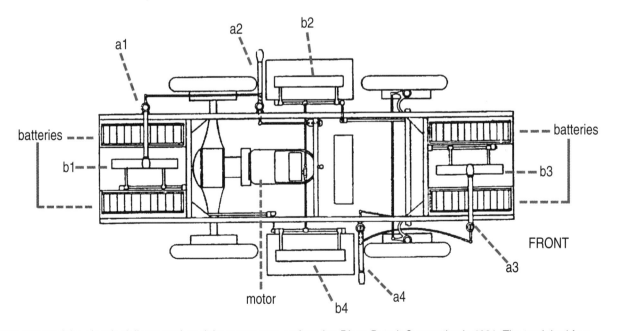

Bacon patented the electric delivery truck and the patent was assigned to Divco-Detroit Corporation in 1931. The truck had four tillers (a1, a2, a3, and a4) for steering and four brake pedals (b1, b2, b3, and b4) for stopping. The brakes were released when the pedal was pressed and applied when the pedal was released.

C. H. L. Flintermann

B. H. Eaton

W. H. Linsell

C. R. Norton

D. M. Ferguson

G. M. Bacon

William Anderson, owner of the Detroit Electric Car Company, was impressed enough with Bacon's electric delivery truck that he showed Bacon's design to Henry Ford. According to Divco documents, Mr. Ford was very impressed with the truck.[3] Tests of the truck by Detroit Creamery revealed some limitations of Bacon's vehicle including excessive battery weight and limited range.[4] However, George Bacon and some associates saw sufficient promise in the concept to form a new company, the Detroit Industrial Vehicle Company (DIVCO), in a small building on Fort Street West in Detroit to manufacture it. The new company soon shifted its efforts away from Bacon's original electric design and produced a truck powered by a Le Roi gasoline engine. The new truck incorporated some of the unique features of Bacon's electric delivery truck, including a complete power plant unit that could be slid out of the front end on rails, thus making repairs easy. Once again, the Detroit Creamery was called on to test an experimental vehicle of Bacon's design, and the gasoline truck did very well. Although there were some failures on the route, when the truck completed the day's deliveries without problems, it always returned in a shorter elapsed time than horse-drawn milk wagons.[5]

The picture of the Merrick Ave. factory greatly exaggerates the size of what was a fairly small plant.

Models A and B

The successful testing of the Le Roi powered vehicle motivated the production of twenty-five experimental trucks known as Model A Divcos. These trucks, featuring 3-point control, at the front or either side, went into service during 1926.

By 1927, Divco trucks were developed well enough to go into production. The Divco-Detroit Corporation was formed in 1927 with capital of $1 million to produce Divco trucks. Divco-Detroit has some impressive names on its letterhead. Carl H. L. Flintermann, formerly Managing Vice President of the Detroit Steel Products Company and Vice President of the Midland Products Corporation, and at that time President of automotive radiator manufacturer Flintlock Corporation, became the president of Divco. Associated with Flintermann were C. R. Norton, former General Sales Manager of the Packard Motor Car Company and Don M. Ferguson, former Chief Engineer for Studebaker.[6] Norton became Directing Vice President and Ferguson became Chief Engineer. One of the sad notes in Divco history is that the first president of Divco, Carl H. L. Flintermann, died in 1931 by his own hand. His obituary stated that his business affairs were in good order but he had complained of a severe headache for months which apparently prompted his suicide in a Jackson, Michigan, hotel.[7]

The new Divco-Detroit Corporation took over a plant at 2435 Merrick Avenue just off Grand River Boulevard in Detroit. The plant previously was occupied by Gemmer Manufacturing Company, a manufacturer of steering gears. An improved Model B Divco was developed by George Bacon. The Model B was powered by a four-cylinder Continental engine with control and steering apparatus at the front and both sides.[8]

In its 60 years of business, Divco had over 30 patents assigned to it. Most were obtained in the first 20 years of Divco production (a list of patents assigned to Divco appears as an appendix to this book). Of particular note in the early years were two patents assigned by George M. Bacon to Divco-Detroit Corporation. Patent number 1,692,535, filed

This picture of a Divco Model B, operated by Detroit Creamery, shows the maneuverability of the early Divcos as well as the versatility of "three-point control."

(Courtesy, James Bibb Collection)

The Dairymens Milk Company of Cleveland, Ohio purchased this fleet of fourteen Model B Divcos in October of 1928.
(Courtesy, Cleveland State University, Cleveland Press Photo Collection)

January 14, 1924, and granted November 20, 1928, was entitled "Steering Mechanism For Motor Vehicles." The main feature of this patent was the four-point (front, back, both sides) control concept. A second early patent assigned by Bacon to Divco-Detroit, number 1,737,489, filed November 21, 1927, and granted November 26, 1929, complements the 4-point control patent. Entitled "Control Mechanism for Motor Vehicles," the patent emphasizes the importance of operation safety and carries the following statements by Bacon:

> *... certain motor vehicles used as delivery cars are provided with controls located on the running boards as auxiliary to the controls adjacent to the driver's seat. This enables the delivery man to shift the car from house to house without the necessity of mounting to the seat. With such exposed controls there is always danger of someone tampering with them as for instance releasing the brake when a vehicle is parked on a grade. I have therefore devised a construction which permits of easily applying and locking the brake but which requires the manipulation of another control member before the brake can be released.*

Although Divco was an innovator in the multi-stop delivery truck business and had important patents to its credit, all did not go smoothly in the early years. The new vehicles encountered many problems because multi-stop service placed special demands on components that were, at that time, not up to the challenge. For example, generators had to be developed which provide sufficient electric current for all electric loads at idle speed even at night. Even though speeds were low, many routes had 300 stops per day which placed tremendous strain on transmissions, clutches, engines and brakes. The three-speed transmissions were tested for over one million shifts before being considered satisfactory for home delivery service.[9]

The production Model B Divcos featured an 86 inch wheelbase with a Continental, 3⅜ bore by 4¼ stroke industrial engine mounted over the front axle. The engine had aluminum pistons and a balanced crankshaft. This engine was designed to require an oil change only every 5000 miles when it was equipped with an oil filter. The forward, left-hand driving position controls were connected with duplicate controls on either side, midway in the chassis, to provide three-point control. The frame was built of five inch channel steel with 1¾ inch flanges reinforced with five cross members. Two sets of 16 by 2¼ inch brakes were mounted on the rear hub. One set was linked to the clutch pedals in such a way that depressing the pedal two inches would release the clutch while further depression applied the brake also. The second set of brakes, used for emergencies, operated from a second pedal.[10]

The body of the Divco Model B was made of oak. It came with full electric lighting (head, two tail, instrument, and dome lights) as standard equipment. The turning circle had a 32 foot diameter. Tests of the truck by creameries over milk routes varying from 10 to 50 miles in length demonstrated that the Model B cost a total of 10 cents per mile to operate.[11]

This Model B was outfitted and ready for an Upper Peninsula of Michigan winter.

The Divco Model G is shown on one side of this promotional coin of the Divco-Detroit Corporation. On the other side, Divco boasts the cost of operating a Divco is only 90 cents per day.

The model B was an innovative truck but it did not sell in large enough quantities to keep Divco-Detroit financially healthy. Serial number records show that 908 Model Bs were built from 1927 through 1930. The company worked on a hand-to-mouth basis, getting some fleet orders for 5, 10, and 25 trucks at rather lengthy intervals.[12] At times, only 4 people were working at the firm and, ultimately, a creditors' committee was formed in January 1931 to operate the company.[13]

In spite of the financial problems and slow sales, some exciting developments occurred at Divco between 1929 and 1931. One development was the introduction of the Model G in 1929. The Divco Model G was an attractive, conventional-looking truck that was a radical departure from the more bus-like Model B. The front driving controls were

The Model G Divcos were conventional looking but had dual controls making the truck operable from the step on either side of the truck.

(Courtesy, American Truck Historical Society)

eliminated and it could be operated from either running board.[14] The Model G had the same 4-cylinder Continental engine that powered the Model B. Although the new model was not enough to pull Divco-Detroit Corporation out of its financial problems, it sold considerably better than the Model B, with 1469 units leaving the factory in 1929, 1930 and 1931. The Model G was the first of several important product innovations that Divco introduced in the 1929-1938 period, including the Model H in 1931 and Model U in late 1937. Before those models were developed, however, a merger was undertaken which laid the foundation for a radical change in the way Divco trucks were designed and engineered.

Divco Buys Step-N-Drive

Divco survived as a truck manufacturer for 60 years. What does it take to survive in an industry? According to Nobel Laureate economist George Stigler, a firm that survives and is efficient "is one that meets any and all problems the entrepreneur actually faces: strained labor relations, rapid innovation, government regulation ... and what not."[15] Such firms may be large or small and the kinds of firms that survive in a given industry may change over time.[16] In its first decade Divco contended with major challenges in its struggle for survival, including the deteriorating economic conditions that followed the financial crisis of 1929 and rapid change and innovation in the delivery truck industry. Divco recognized the need to innovate, particularly with respect to driver convenience and accessibility.

Driver convenience was the principal idea behind a patent application filed on December 10, 1928, by two Divco engineers, Edwin Maurer and Donald Ferguson. U.S. Patent 1,831,360, granted on November 10, 1931, showed the essential design features for a new multi-stop delivery truck that eventually became Divco Model H. The full patent application is lengthy. Two illustrations from the patent reveal what is described in the patent application as "a driver's compartment provided with a depressed floor portion located substantially below the floor level of the vehicle but above the running gear of the same so as to form an unobstructed transverse passage-way through the vehicle." The depressed floor feature became the basis for the Divco drop-frame.

The truck in Patent 1,831,360 was described as "an invention [that] provides for simplifying the method of manufacture ... by introducing a body constructed and designed to carry the loads of the

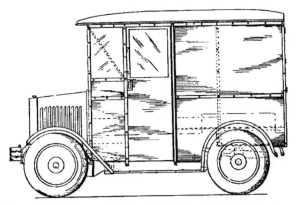

The essential design features of the Divco Model H are shown in this image taken from the patent granted to Divco engineers Edwin Maurer and Donald Ferguson.

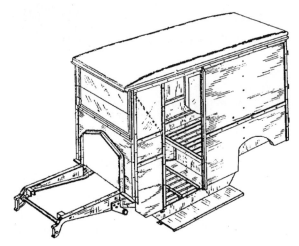

The Maurer and Ferguson design had a transverse passageway and unibody construction. Divco never put the unibody concept into production.

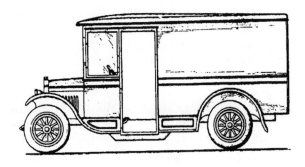

Divco bought Step-N-Drive to gain control of the patents for drop-frame construction. This drawing from a Step-N-Drive patent shows the basic features of the Step-N-Drive body.

vehicle without the assistance of the customary chassis frame." The proposed new Divco had unibody construction with a pair of auxiliary frame sills in the front to support the engine. Divco never put a unibody truck into production, but its desire to provide easy accessibility for drivers by having a low platform is clear from the patent. The production Model H had the low platform, but with an actual frame of one-piece drop-frame construction. This provided a low-platform transverse aisle enabling the driver to pass through from either side even with a collapsible seat in position.[17] The Model H is described further in the next section.

To proceed with its desire for a transverse aisle in its trucks, Divco confronted a dilemma. A competitor, the Step-N-Drive Corporation of Buffalo, New York, had some patents Divco wanted. The Step-N-Drive was a special delivery body that could be mounted on either a Ford or Chevrolet chassis. Step-N-Drive units were sold through the dealer organizations of those firms.[18] Standard Ford and Chevrolet chassis were modified to accept the Step-N-Drive body by cutting away side members of the chassis and substituting a drop portion for the cut-away frame sections. In the *Ford Dealer News* the Step-N-Drive was promoted by Ford as the lowest priced specialty house-to-house delivery vehicle on the market when fitted with a Ford chassis. In 1931, 18 major dairy fleets were listed as operating Step-N-Drive trucks.[19]

Although Divco-Detroit Corporation was struggling financially through the late 1920s and early 1930s, the company purchased Step-N-Drive in September of 1930, just a few months before the Divco creditors committee was formed. In acquiring Step-N-Drive, Divco acquired the patent rights to a vehicle that enabled a driver to enter it from the level of a roadway with a single step.

On January 4, 1928, when Step-N-Drive was still an independent firm, the founder of the company, Edward C. Oberkircher, and Charles G. Kaelin of Buffalo filed a patent application for a motor driven vehicle. The patent states the vehicle had a dropped portion between the motor of the vehicle and the rear axle "whereby it is possible to conveniently enter the vehicle and, after driving the vehicle, to conveniently leave the same, all while in an upright position." The accompanying illustration from the patent shows the basic Step-N-Drive features. Control over the rights to the Step-and-Drive low-platform vehicle along with its own patents gave Divco legal protection for the introduction of the drop-frame Model H.

Initially, Divco announced that Divco-Detroit and Step-N-Drive would continue to operate separately with the existing personnel in the Detroit and Buffalo plants.[20] However, the financial problems at Divco and the darkening national economic scene caused Divco to reconsider that policy. In early 1931, manufacturing operations of Step-N-Drive were moved to Detroit. John Nicol, President of Divco-Detroit, said the consolidation of manufacturing in the Detroit plant would promote efficiencies. Separate sales forces for Step-N-Drive and Divco were maintained, but both were located in Detroit and E. C. Oberkircher was made Vice President for Sales of Step-N-Drive.[21] Step-N-Drive was operated as, and advertised its products as, a separate division of Divco-Detroit Corporation.[22]

The Model H

In 1931, Divco-Detroit Corporation was ready to introduce the first Divco truck with a drop-frame. Armed with the Step-N-Drive technology and some innovative ideas of its own, Divco launched the Model H. Kenneth R. Herman, Chief Engineer, appears to have made a major contribution to Model H development. Herman came to Divco-Detroit Corporation in early 1927 as Assistant Engineer. His previous experience included being a designer for the Oakland Motor Car Company and Chief Engineer and Production Manager for the Kimball Truck Company of Los Angeles. Herman was promoted to the position of Chief Engineer at Divco in 1929.[23] Herman's design for a drop-frame chassis with one-piece sill bars for the Model H formed the basis for another Divco patent. Filed January 5, 1931, almost simultaneously with the introduction of the Model H, Patent 1,972, 224 was granted September 4, 1934. A principal object of the invention was "to provide a vehicle of the house-to-house delivery type with a strong and durable chassis containing full-length one-piece chassis sill bars so constructed and arranged as to provide a transverse aisle extending completely across the vehicle ... having continuous one-piece sill bars extending above the aisles, each provided with drop center intermediate portions ...." The drawings on page 9 illustrate both the transverse aisle and drop-frame. The drop-frame was an important innovation featured on Divcos built from 1931 until the end of production in 1986.

The Model H marked a departure from the designs of George Bacon, whose trucks could be controlled from multiple locations. The Model H was

Step-N-Drive bodies were available on Ford (top) and Chevrolet (bottom) truck chassis.
(Courtesy John B. Montville)

controlled from a standard left-hand drive location but was an extremely convenient truck for the driver to operate because it could be driven from either a standing or sitting position. There were throttle controls on the floor board, steering column, and shift lever. The Divco Model H continued to feature the patented combination clutch and brake pedal with automatic brake lock which had been on earlier Divcos. The principal feature of the truck was the easy access to either side due to the low platform with drop-frame. The Model H was powered by a 4-cylinder Continental engine with a specially designed intake manifold to reduce fuel consumption during idling.

By the time the Model H was introduced in early 1931, Divco had built 2428 trucks according to company serial number records. The company news releases in early 1931 announcing the Model H boasted that 1800 Divcos were being operated by over 260 owners in the U.S. and Canada. Some of the Divcos already had over 100,000 miles on them and were being "double-shifted"—that is, used for both day and night deliveries.[24] When the Model H was introduced in 1931 Divco could honestly boast its trucks had a reputation for reliability and durability.

INCREASE YOUR PROFITS! MOTORIZE!

YOU, MR. MILK DEALER, WILL MOTORIZE YOUR MILK ROUTES

because you can increase your profits. Nothing interests you as much as increasing your profits.

YOU WILL BUY STEP-N-DRIVE TRUCKS

either Ford or Chevrolet, when you are convinced that Step-N-Drive Drop Center Trucks will reduce your delivery costs.

Delivery costs per point consist of the cost of operating the vehicle plus the driver's pay. Obviously, by delivering more points for the same cost, the *cost per point* is less.

Step-N-Drive Trucks are consistently doing this!

Prove this for yourself. Go to your Ford or Chevrolet dealer. Buy 2 Step-N-Drive trucks and deliver the business of 3 of your average horse routes. Then you will want Step-N-Drive trucks for all your routes.

NEW LOW PRICE

$1190

FORD OR CHEVROLET
Prime Paint at Detroit

STEP-N-DRIVE DIVISION

DiVco-Detroit Corporation
2435 Merrick Ave., Detroit, Mich.

Please mention MILK PLANT MONTHLY when writing to advertisers.

After Divco bought Step-N-Drive, production was consolidated at Merrick Avenue in Detroit. Note the Step-N-Drive logo in this ad from the Milk Plant Monthly *features the drop-frame design.*

(Courtesy John B. Montville)

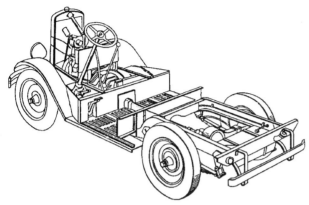

The Model H Divco introduced in 1931 had a transverse aisle and drop frame as shown in this patent drawing.

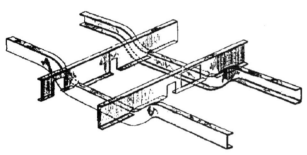

This drawing from the Herman patent gives a close look at the design of the first Divco drop-frame.

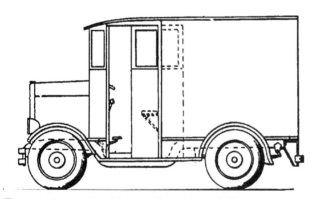

The patent granted to Divco engineer Kenneth Herman shows the basic design features of the Model H.

By early 1931, Divco owned Step-N-Drive and had the new Model H on the road. But the company was far from financially secure. The creditors committee began to function the same month that the Model H was introduced and the consolidation of Step-N-Drive into the Detroit plant occurred. The creditors committee operated Divco-Detroit Corporation until April, 1932, at which time the company was sold at an auction. [25]

Borden's was an early customer for the Divco Model H.
(Courtesy, John B. Montville)

Continental-Divco Company

The successful bidder in the April 30, 1932, auction for the Divco operations was the Continental Motors Corporation of Detroit. Continental's winning bid of $90,000 exceeded a bid of $86,000 by the Autocar Truck Company.[26] Continental traced its history back to 1902 when it was started in Chicago as the Autocar Equipment Company. The name Continental Motors Corporation was adopted in 1917. In 1932, Continental supplied four auto makers, 30 truck builders (including Continental-Divco), three aircraft manufacturers, and two agricultural equipment builders with its line of internal combustion engines.[27] The purchase of Divco was a strategic move for Continental. In early 1932, Continental entered both the truck business (by purchasing Divco) and the automobile business by acquiring the assets of the bankrupt De Vaux-Hall Motors Corporation. In the deal Continental also acquired the lease of a plant in Grand Rapids, Michigan. The auto-producing subsidiary became the Continental Automobile Company which manufactured a low-priced automobile under the "Continental" name-plate. Continental's auto experiment was short-lived. The Continental Automobile Company was dissolved in 1933.[28]

At the time of the Divco purchase, Continental was a large firm. It had plants located in Detroit, Grand Rapids, and Muskegon, Michigan, with about 1.5 million square feet of manufacturing space. The impact of the Depression resulted in production declines at Continental and a decline in employment from 3500 in 1929 to 950 in 1932.[29] The reduced

FEATURES OF THE
NEW MODEL "H" DIVCO

"Here is a one-piece drop frame ¼ inch thick with a 6 inch channel and a 2 inch flange - - - sturdy, strong and low."

"This low aisle permits a clear passage through from either side even with the driver's collapsible seat in position."

"4-wheel mechanical self-energizing brakes are used on this job. In addition there is a hand emergency brake."

"A steering wheel, a combination clutch-brake pedal with safety lock and accelerators on the shifting lever, steering wheel, and floor board, are real features."

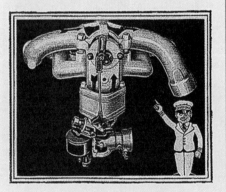

"This automatic take-up on the timing chain eliminates noise, unnecessary wear and usual adjustments. Nickel chromium in our cylinder block multiplies its life several times."

"DiVco's special manifold warms the gas mixture thereby providing minimum fuel consumption while idling and reducing engine wear due to oil dilution by raw fuel."

DIVCO-DETROIT CORPORATION

"Divco Dan," who would appear periodically in Divco ads for almost 40 years, is shown pointing out important features of the Model H in this page from the Model H catalog.

(Courtesy John B. Montville)

10

production levels left Continental with excess capacity. By acquiring Divco, Continental kept one of its own customers in business which helped maintain the volume of Continental engine production. Continental made use of its excess capacity by building Divco trucks in its own facilities, moving Divco production from Merrick Avenue to the Continental plant at 12801 East Jefferson Avenue, in Detroit. Though the plant no longer was operated by Continental, it was still easily recognizable in 1995 by the word "Continental" fixed into the brickwork of the smoke stack.

The new staff retained many members of the former Divco management. John Nicol, President and General Manager of Divco-Detroit since 1930, ran Divco through ownership and organizational changes well into the post-World War II era. Nicol joined Divco in 1927. He was a graduate of the University of Michigan who entered the auto business in 1915, when he opened a distributorship for Federal trucks. Immediately before joining Divco, Nicol was Branch Manager for General Motors Truck Company at Chicago and Indianapolis. [31] One of his successors as President of Divco was George Edward Muma, the Continental-Divco Service Manager. Messers McKeough, Eaton and Brown also were Divco-Detroit carryovers. Continental exercised administrative control but had the wisdom to maintain a staff that knew the home delivery truck market and knew how to build and sell Divcos.

One person whose name did not appear on the list of executives at Continental-Divco was George Bacon. Bacon was 65 years old at the time of the formation of Continental-Divco in 1932 and probably elected to retire. No evidence exists that he was involved with Divco after the affiliation with Continental Motors. George Bacon died of natural causes on January 23, 1938 at age 71. His body was cremated by the White Chapel Memorial Association of Detroit.

Continental Motors was optimistic about the prospects for the Continental-Divco subsidiary which it claimed did a "fair volume of business" in 1932. It expected Continental-Divco to increase its volume "in the near future."[32] Indicative of Continental's desire to expand Divco operations was an announcement in May of 1932, that it opened a new complete sales, parts, and service branch in Medford, Massachusetts. The new branch was the eighth Continental-Divco outlet. The other branches were located in New York, Philadelphia, Cleveland, Cincinnati, Chicago, Minneapolis, and Los Angeles. In addition, Continental-Divco

Officer	Position at Continental-Divco	Position at Continental Motors
W. R. Angell	President	President
Roger Sherman	Vice President	Vice President
Wallace Zwiener	Treasurer	Comptroller
Craig Keith	Secretary	Secretary/Treasurer
John Nicol	Vice President & General Manager	-----------
J. K. McKeough	Sales Manager	-----------
B. H. Eaton	Purchasing Agent	-----------
Harry Brown	Factory Engineer	-----------
Edward Muma	Service Manager	-----------

The new management of Continental-Divco clearly reflected Continental control of the Divco operation. Above is a list of the Continental-Divco officers and their ties to Continental Motor Corporation.[30]

announced it was putting a new 6-cylinder truck, the Model K, into production.[33]

By late 1932, Continental-Divco had implemented an aggressive marketing policy. The prices of both the Model H and Model K were reduced. An ad for Continental-Divco in the October 1932 issue of *The Milk Dealer* magazine stated the reduction in prices was made possible by improved efficiencies at the manufacturing subsidiary of Continental Motors. That claim makes economic sense: Continental was a much larger firm than the old Divco-Detroit Corporation; therefore, Continental had the economic power to command favorable prices for component parts from vendors. By utilizing Continental's buying power and consolidating Divco output in the Continental plants, more modern and efficient (low cost) production was made possible.

In addition to the efficiencies created by the Continental-Divco combination the economic realities of the early 1930s contributed to pressures for price reductions. The general price level declined by 20% between 1929 and 1932.[34] Continental-Divco responded to these price pressures by reducing the 4-cylinder Model H price by 15% from $1,525 to $1,295, and lowering the 6-cylinder Model K price 8% from $1,725 to $1,595. Despite the price reductions, sales of the Model H and Model K were not strong. Production records indicate that 702 Model H Divcos were built in 1931, 1932, and 1933 and only 47 Model Ks were built from 1932 through 1934.

In October 1931, a Divco ad in *The Milk Dealer* announced introduction of the New Model J, "The Big Brother of the Famous Model H." The Model J was to have a long body, a six-cylinder engine, and a top speed of 35 m.p.h. The Model J was advertised as suitable for long or heavy routes whereas the four-cylinder Model H, with a top speed of 18 m.p.h., was for average routes. The ad shows only line drawings of a Model J, and no production records, serial number records or parts book entries can be found for the Model J. If more than a prototype ever was built, there is no evidence of it.

Continental-Divco continued to evolve its product line with Models M, Q, and R between 1932 and 1935. The direction the product development was taking became evident in Design Patent 89,574 for a "House-to-House Delivery Vehicle Body" filed December 9, 1932, granted to John Nicol and assigned to Continental-Divco on April 4, 1933. The accompanying illustrations from the patent show designs that were used on the Model R and on the very important Model S introduced in 1935.

The Model S was a lighter and lower-priced Divco developed to meet the demand for a smaller vehicle embodying all the features of delivery efficiency and economy, yet having the sturdy long-life construction features of traditional Divcos. The advertising claimed that the Model S had operating costs 20 percent lower than any previous Divco and was considerably cheaper than single-horse delivery; the new model could idle seven hours on a gallon of gasoline, had an all-steel body, a one-piece drop-frame, and was available as Model S-3 (39 case capacity) or Model S-4 (47 case capacity).

John Nicol responded to concerns that the Model S was just a cheapened Divco in this reply to an inquiry from M. J. Duryea of Longmeadow, Massachusetts:

The Model S Divco lists at $1140.00 f.o.b. factory, Detroit, Michigan equipped with a 39-case body.

In producing this new vehicle, we have not cheapened the quality of former Divcos, but have set a low price, basing this price on manufacturing economy through considerably larger purchases of material, and of an estimated large increase in sales, reducing production costs.

We have, by considerable engineering work, been able to reduce the weight of our vehicle by some 500 pounds and have made some decided improvements in the operating efficiency of our motor. All told, we believe the lighter weight and improved efficiency of the motor will result in 20 percent lower operating cost than was delivered by former Divco models, and the operating cost of former Divco models has been extremely satisfactory to Divco operators.[35]

The Model J never was put into production, but this ad in the October 1931 edition of The Milk Dealer *announces the Model J for longer and heavier routes.*

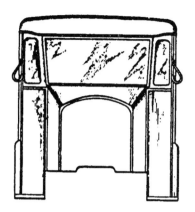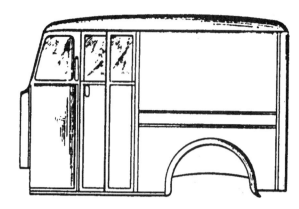

The Design Patent for this body style was granted to John Nicol in 1933. This style became the foundation for the Model R , the Model Q, and the less expensive Model S Divcos.

The Model S was the most important but last major achievement of Continental-Divco. From a financial standpoint, Divco was a disappointment for its parent firm, Continental Motors. The losses sustained by Divco were not huge, but it did not earn a consistent profit, either. Following are the financial results reported for the Continental-Divco subsidiary in the 1933-1935 period.[36]

The improved financial results for 1935 and the following production records indicate that the

Continental-Divco Financial Results

1933:	-$70,681	(loss)
1934:	-$9,961	(loss)
1935:	$17,853	(profit)

Model S was a marketing success when introduced in 1935, so Continental-Divco finally began to

Becker Dairy Farms used this 1937 Divco Model S to deliver milk in Roseland, New Jersey.
(Courtesy, Oliver Ogden)

make a profit on the strength of the new model. Production totals for Divco during the Continental-Divco era by model are given below from company serial number records.

Production Totals during the Continental-Divco Era

Model H	=	702
Model K	=	47
Model M	=	203
Model Q	=	103
Model R	=	497
Model S3	=	1469
Model S4	=	611

Note: Model S trucks built by Divco-Twin are not included. Model H totals include trucks built by Divco-Detroit Corporation before the take-over by Continental.

Although Continental-Divco became profitable in 1935, its parent firm faced serious financial problems. After making a profit of $733,495 in 1929, Continental Motors lost money each year from 1930 through 1935. Total accumulated losses were $13 million.

In 1931, Continental acknowledged that 1930 was a disappointing year but boasted it was in an excellent cash position with $3.3 million on hand and a ratio of current assets to liabilities of 11.76 to 1. The company had no bonds, notes, preferred stock, or bank loans outstanding.[37] However, by 1935, after 6 years of losses, Continental was nearly $1 million in debt to the Reconstruction Finance Corporation[38] for a loan that was obtained to secure desperately needed working capital.[39] It is not surprising, therefore, that in 1936 Continental decided to dispose of its Divco operations in what was a complex financial transaction involving the Twin Coach Company. Continental needed some cash and, undoubtedly, was eager to be rid of a division that had been an overall money loser.

Continental-Divco built the Divco trucks in this factory on E. Jefferson Avenue in Detroit. By 1995, when these pictures were taken, all that was reminiscent of the Continental-Divco days was the name "Continental" in the smoke stack.

Divco Derails Dobbin and Takes on the Competition

Why buy a Divco? Surely, that was a question many house-to-house delivery fleet managers asked in the 1920s and 1930s. In fact, it was a question some fleet operators were still asking in the 1960s. The horse-drawn milk wagon and motor truck were both purchased by businesses to earn profits for their owners. From the standpoint of fleet managers in the 1920s and 1930s, Dobbin and Divco had to justify their existence on the bottom line of company earnings.

During the 1930s, Divco became a major combatant in a competitive war against the horse-drawn milk wagon. Divco certainly knew who it was competing against—old Dobbin. Potential customers were told to capitalize on the advertising value, strong customer appeal, route building values, and efficient low-cost delivery of Divco trucks in comparison with horse-drawn milk wagons. Divco used economic arguments in its advertising to the retail milk market emerging in the 1930s, comparing the nostalgic and commercial attributes of the horse with the costs and benefits of owning a motor truck.

In an August 1936 ad in *The Milk Dealer*, Divco claimed its trucks were cheaper to operate than competitive trucks or horses. Data from three dairies were given on a direct operating cost basis which included gas, oil, tires, maintenance, and repair. Table 2-1 shows Divco's claims.

In an earlier ad in June 1935, Continental-Divco claimed that the Franklin Co-Operative Creamery Association of Minneapolis found single horse routes cost $2.38 per day and team routes cost $4.76 per day in February 1935. Franklin's full costs including overhead of operating its 27 Divcos were only $1.72 per day per truck, whereas 17 other gasoline trucks cost $2.67 per day and 22 electric trucks cost $2.09 per day.

Were Divco's claims legitimate, or was the company engaging in advertising puffery? Was there

---

Table 2-1:
Comparative Costs of Truck Operation

	Miles Per Route	Direct Operating Costs Per Day
New York Dairy		
(Data for 1 Year)		
Divco	9.1	$.749
Electric Trucks	8.9	1.004
Other Gas Trucks	9.7	1.329
Minneapolis Dairy		
(Data for 1 Year)		
Divco	17.0	$.69
Electric Trucks	15.0	1.00
Other Gas Trucks	20.0	1.40
Horses	N.A.	2.22
Los Angeles Dairy		
(Data for 3 Years)		
Divco	N.A.	$.983
Gas Truck 2	N.A.	1.398
Gas Truck 3	N.A.	1.524
Gas Truck 4	N.A.	1.719
Gas Truck 5	N.A.	1.725
Gas Truck 6	N.A.	1.831

Source: "Divco-Twin Operating Costs," advertisement, The Milk Dealer, August 1936.

Table 2-2:

Horse & Wagon / Motor Truck Cost Comparison
Commercial Car Journal, 1932

| | MILES PER DAY | | | | |
	10	15	20	25	30
HORSE AND WAGON					
Single Horse/Wagon[1]					
(Dairy)					
Cost Per Day	$2.2502	$2.2502	$2.2502	N.A.	N.A.
Cost Per Mile	$.225	$.150	$.113	N.A.	N.A.
Team & Wagon					
(Dairy)					
Cost Per Day	$4.3471	$4.3471	$4.3471	$4.3471	$4.3471
Cost Per Mile	$.435	$.289	$.2174	$.1739	$.1449
HOUSE-TO-HOUSE DELIVERY TRUCKS					
Truck A [2]					
(Dairy)					
Cost Per Day	$1.338	$1.493	$1.647	$1.802	$1.956
Cost Per Mile	$.134	$.10	$.082	$.072	$.065
Truck B [3]					
(Bakery)					
Cost Per Day	$1.490	$1.783	$2.012	$2.279	$2.438
Cost Per Mile	$.149	$.177	$.10	$.091	$.081

[1] Single horse drawn wagons seldom exceeded 20 miles per day.
[2] Truck A: average of 25 fleets in 25 cities
[3] Truck B: 40 trucks in the study

Source: "Multistop Units Dub Dobbin a Dud," Commercial Car Journal, vol. 43, no. 2, April 1932, p. 19.
(Calculation errors corrected from original article.)

substance to the claim that trucks were cheaper to operate than horses and wagons? The Horse and Mule Association of America (HMAA) certainly did not think the truck was worth its costs: horse and mule advocates vigorously defended the low cost of using a horse and wagon. In an October 1936 ad in *The Milk Dealer,* the HMAA claimed a study in Bloomington, Springfield, Decatur, Urbana, Champaign, and Danville, Illinois showed that delivery costs were equivalent to 3.48% of dollar sales on horse and wagon routes but 8.01% of sales on gas truck routes! In a large double-paged ad in *The Milk Dealer* in December 1936, results of a study covering 10 Eastern, 11 Midwestern and 8 Southern states for 1935 and 1936 were reported. The HMAA claimed that when all costs (feeding,

Divco boasted its trucks were less expensive to operate than horses or competitive trucks in this June 1935 ad in The Milk Dealer.
(Courtesy Cleveland Public Library)

bedding, labor, depreciation, wagon repairs, etc.) were considered, the cost of delivery on a 20 mile route with a horse and wagon was between $0.0418 and $0.0487 per dollar of sales. On a supposed full cost basis including depreciation, insurance, gas and oil, repairs, etc., the HMAA claimed motor trucks on 20 mile routes in the 29 states had a cost per dollar of sales of $0.0755 to $0.1097.

In a 1936 article in *The Milk Dealer*, Regis Lefebure, a Senior Field Representative for the Horse and Mule Association, elaborated on the findings of the 29-state study. A total of 126 milk companies operating 15,628 gasoline and electric truck routes and 27,766 horse and wagon routes were included in the research. The overall conclusion was that dairies found it profitable to use single horses on routes of 20 miles in length, electric trucks on routes of 20 to 30 miles and gasoline trucks beyond the electric truck zone. Dairies with small branch operations found it more economical and efficient to use horses on routes up to 20 miles and gasoline trucks outside the horse zone.[1] The Horse and Mule Association had an obvious vested interest in making a case for using the horse and wagon on shorter milk routes.

The motor truck industry obviously had an interests in making a case for its product. A 1932 study reported in The *Commercial Car Journal (CCJ)* yielded the results shown in Table 2-2. (Note: the original article had some minor arithmetic errors which are corrected in Table 2-2. Those errors have no material effect on the conclusions.) The *CCJ* study looked at single horse and wagon units, team and wagon units and 2 types of house-to-house delivery trucks—dairy and bakery. The study showed an overwhelming cost per mile advantage for trucks. The study did not identify truck makes; therefore, it is not possible to identify which trucks were gasoline powered, electric, or a combination of gasoline-electric.

The *CCJ* study noted that getting precise comparisons between the cost of using motor trucks and horses was difficult, because many variables entered into the house-to-house delivery cost analysis which made arriving at generalized averages rather complicated. For example, truck mileage on routes in some cities averaged considerably less than in other cities, because road and grade conditions differed by geographic area. Also, the number of stops per route varied, maintenance programs were different among the

RIGHT: *The Horse and Mule Association of America tried to show that horses and wagons were more economical than trucks in a series of ads in* The Milk Dealer *during the 1930s.*
(Courtesy Cleveland Public Library)

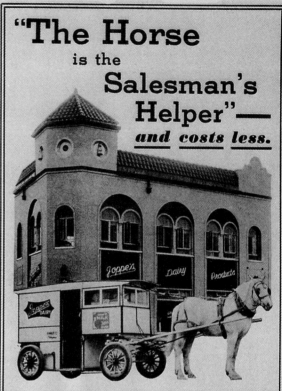

The Model S Divco was priced lower than its predecessors, but could boast of traditional Divco dependability.
(Courtesy, American Truck Historical Society)

firms, and depreciation factors were not uniform. Horse-drawn equipment was depreciated on a 5 to 10-year basis, depending on the dairy; motor trucks for dairies were on a 5-year depreciation basis, and bakery trucks were on a 10-year depreciation schedule. (Dairy trucks were depreciated more rapidly because they carried considerably heavier loads and often operated in more unfavorable conditions than bakery trucks.[2]) Costs in the *CCJ* study were given on a per day and per mile basis. While these were the most generally accepted methods of cost analysis, the dairy industry also calculated the cost of delivering a standard unit, known as a "point." One "point"

consisted of 1 quart of milk or its monetary equivalent in cream, butter, or other dairy products. In a 1933 follow-up to its 1932 study, the *Commercial Car Journal* examined 15-mile dairy routes in New York, Chicago, Cleveland, and New England and compared the costs per point per day. The study found that a motorized truck could deliver 450 points per day compared to 350 points per day for a horse and wagon. After considering all costs of depreciation, feed, gas and oil, maintenance, etc., trucks cost $2.19 per day, and the single horse and wagon only $1.96 per day in 1933 in these markets. However, the costs per point were $0.0049 for the truck and

$0.0056 for the horse. It may not seem like $0.0007 per point is much of an advantage for the truck. But in a sizable dairy operation selling 10 million points per year, $.0007 per point would mean an added profit of $7000—not a trivial amount of money during the Great Depression. If the dairy selling 10 million points per year had been making a $50,000 profit, the addition of another $7000 meant a 14 percent increase in profits![3]

The studies cited by the Horse and Mule Association and the *Commercial Car Journal*, of course, reached different conclusions, particularly for the shorter routes, because different methods of calculation were employed. The HMAA used cost per dollar of sales, while the *CCJ* used cost per mile and per point. It is virtually impossible to reconcile all the issues associated with these differing conclusions because a retrospective long-term comparative study of horses vs. trucks cannot be undertaken in the late 20th century.

If markets work at all efficiently, though, the demand for horses and wagons and motorized delivery trucks should reflect the expected rate of return on what are essentially pieces of capital equipment. Whether or not a dairy, bakery, or parcel delivery service was willing to buy a truck rather than use a horse and wagon ultimately depended on the expected rate of return on investment from these pieces of equipment. By the end of the 1930s, the trend was clear: the efficiency and cost advantages of the truck were overwhelming.

Farewell to Dobbin

By the outbreak of World War II, the fate of Dobbin was sealed. Divcos and other house-to-house motorized delivery trucks were passing fewer and fewer horses on the street, and more and more horses in the pasture. The Horse and Mule Association of America must have come to the realization that trying to persuade dairies to stay with the horse and wagon was a losing cause. The last ad we could find by the HMAA in *The Milk Dealer* magazine was in 1937. By 1937, the truck manufacturers emphasized the advantages of their vehicles over competitive truck makers, not over the horse and wagon. The April 1941 Divco-Twin ad from *Fortune* magazine, "What Ever Happened to the Old Milk Wagon Horse?" certainly puts the horse in an historical, not current, milk delivery context. Old Dobbin had one more moment of glory before totally fading from the scene. During World War II, when gasoline and rubber were scarce, some dairies replaced aging trucks and horse equipment with horses and wagons. Both Batavia Body Company and DeKalb Commercial Body Corporation (formerly DeKalb Wagon Company) took out full-page ads in *The Milk Dealer* in 1942 and 1943. The themes were "Solve your Tire and Gas Problems" with a Batavia horse-drawn milk wagon, and "Keep Your Routes Going" with a DeKalb wagon. The end of the war, however, resulted in a resumption of the trend to motorization. The advantages were quite clear, as pointed out by the *Commercial Car Journal* in the 1930s. (See Table 2-3)

Table 2-3:

Advantages of House-to-House Delivery Trucks Over the Horse

1. **Provides Economical Delivery**
   a. lower operating costs
   b. lower maintenance costs

2. **Develops More Business**
   a. larger territories
   b. more customers per route

3. **Attracts Capable Drivers**
   a. gives job more dignity
   b. drivers can make more money
   c. routes can be traveled faster
   d. more time for solicitations

4. **Provides Driver Comfort**
   a. easy riding
   b. winter protection
   c. reduces in-and-out fatigue

5. **Saves Time**
   a. quick access to cases
   b. no climbing
   c. short wheelbase and turning radius
   d. easy parking

6. **Promotes Safety**
   a. reduces slipping hazard
   b. good visibility
   c. firm driving position
   d. handy controls
   e. easy maneuverability

7. **Has Customer Appeal**
   a. neat, clean appearance
   b. drivers can keep tidier
   c. no noise, dirt, or odor

8. **Advertising Value**
   a. gives character to business
   b. a traveling billboard

Source: "Multi-Stop Units Dub Dobbin a Dud," Commercial Car Journal, vol. 43, no. 2, April 1932, p. 20.

This Divco-Twin ad from the April, 1941 issue of Fortune *says "good bye" to Dobbin while giving a brief history of Divco. Shown are the Model B, Model G, and Model U.*

Truck manufacturers approached the house-to-house delivery market with a variety of products that were functionally attractive. Trucks were built for the specialized segments of house-to-house delivery including dairies, bakeries, laundries, and parcel delivery. The heart of the multi-stop delivery truck was its simplified driving controls combined with a low floor which reduced driver fatigue. The combination of easy entry and exit, more power, and easy controls made the retail delivery truck a motorized store: customers could easily enter the truck and select whatever products were desired from bread to milk. The motorized store could cover more territory and at a lower overall cost than a horse and wagon.

Yet, even once the advantages of the motorized truck became clear, the disappearance of the horse and wagon in house-to-house delivery was not complete. Almost a quarter of a century after the end of World War II, a certain amount of nostalgia was associated with the final departure of the horse from milk routes. In a company publication in 1946, Matt T. Daly, Vice President of Borden's in New York, noted that many city folks whose hearts were on the farm would miss the Borden horse and milk wagon. However, he observed that the average consumer wanted prompt delivery service from all types of retail establishments, which meant motorized trucks would take over for the horse.[4]

Horses and wagons required more scarce city parking space than trucks. Large cities found there was not enough space on the increasingly crowded urban and suburban streets for horses and wagons. Neither was there the necessary room in the cities for the storage and care of horses and horse-drawn equipment. Horse feed, blacksmith and wagon shops, and the horses and wagons required space far exceeding that needed for garaging an equal number of route-delivery trucks.

The rapidity of the transition to trucks is evident in the experience of Borden's. In 1928, Borden's Farm Products of New York operated 3,025 horse drawn routes which required 3,697 horses. (Some wagons were drawn by teams. Horses had to rest every few days, and about 100 horses were sick each day.) Borden's of New York purchased 500 horses and sold $23,000 worth of manure per year! By 1946, Borden's of New York operated only 168 horsedrawn routes with 181 horses, which dropped to 52 routes and 65 horses in 1947.[5]

All routes of Borden's of New York were motorized by 1948.[6]

One of the "famous" holdouts for horses was Abbotts Dairies of Philadelphia. The peculiar nature of the routes covered by Abbotts in South Philadelphia provided an incentive for them to keep horse-drawn wagons on some routes: South Philadelphia had narrow streets with a heavy density of row houses so that a small route of only 3 by 5 city blocks could account for 600 quarts per day. Abbotts began converting to trucks in 1927 but held onto horse-drawn routes in some neighborhoods of Philadelphia until 1964.

When Abbotts finally made the 100% conversion to motor trucks in 1964, it received national attention in *Business Week* and *The Milk Dealer*. The two events that finally caused Abbotts to retire its horses were that its blacksmith retired and stable costs were rising. When the decision was made to withdraw the horses and wagons, Abbotts was concerned that retiring the horses too rapidly would upset the children who had befriended the horses in the Philadelphia neighborhoods. As a result, the horses were withdrawn from service slowly, in easy stages month by month. What replaced old Dobbin at Abbotts in Philadelphia? A fleet of Divcos, of course![7]

Meet the Competition

Divco was not alone in challenging the horse for the multi-stop, house-to-house delivery truck business. From the start of production in 1926, Divco faced many competitors. Table 2-4 gives a listing of firms known to have built multi-stop delivery trucks, their chassis, or their bodies during the 60 years of Divco history. (The list was

Table 2-4:
Representative List of Manufacturers of Multi-Stop Delivery Trucks and Bodies

Truck Manufacturers
- Chevrolet Motor Div. of General Motors (Detroit, Michigan)
- Diamond T (Chicago, Illinois)
- Divco (Detroit, Michigan)
- Dodge Division of Chrysler (Detroit, Michigan)
- Federal Motor Truck Co. (Detroit, Michigan)
- Ford Motor Co. (Detroit, Michigan)
- GMC Truck and Coach Division of General Motors (Pontiac, Michigan)
- Indiana Motor Truck Co. (Cleveland, Ohio)
- International Harvester Co. (Chicago, Illinois)
- Kenworth Motor Truck Corp. (Seattle, Washington)
- Mack (Allentown, Pennsylvania)
- Reo Motor Car Co. (Lansing, Michigan)
- Step-N-Drive Truck Corp. (Divco Owned) (originally Buffalo, New York)
- Studebaker Corp. (South Bend, Indiana)
- Stutz (later Auburn built) Pak-Age-Car (Indianapolis, Indiana)
- Thorne Motor Corp. (Chicago, Illinois)
- Twin Coach Corp. (Kent, Ohio) (Trucks combined with Divco in 1936)
- Walker Vehicle Company (Chicago, Illinois)
- Ward Motor Vehicle Co. (Mt. Vernon, New York)
- White Motor Co. (Cleveland, Ohio)
- Yellow Truck and Coach - Part of GMC (Detroit, Michigan)

Body Builders
- Baker-Raulang Co. (Cleveland, Ohio)
- Batavia Body Co. (Batavia, Illinois)
- Boyertown Body Works (Boyertown, Pennsylvania)
- DeKalb Commercial Body Corp. (DeKalb, Illinois)
- Grumman Olson Bodies (New York, New York)
- Hackney Bros. Body Co. (Wilson, North Carolina)
- Herman Body Co. (St. Louis, Missouri)
- Montpelier Manufacturing Co. (Montpelier, Ohio)
- Murphy Body Works (Wilson, North Carolina)
- Schnabel Company (Pittsburgh, Pennsylvania)
- York-Hoover Corporation (York, Pennsylvania)
- Vanette (Detroit, and later Delaware, Ohio)

The White Horse delivery truck built by the White Motor Company in the late 1930s and early 1940s was a serious competitor for Divco.

assembled from a variety of publications and advertisements. Given that the industry had a large number of participants and was widely scattered geographically, we undoubtedly missed some builders of trucks and bodies.) No attempt is made here to give a thorough history of even the major competitors of Divco; instead what follows is a brief survey. We give particular attention to several makes which disappeared by World War II, but which had as their primary business the manufacturing of multi-stop delivery trucks. Included in this group are Thorne, Twin Coach, Pak-Age-Car, Walker, and Ward.

Chrysler (Dodge trucks), Ford, and General Motors (GMC, Yellow Truck and Coach, and Chevrolet trucks) also competed in the multi-stop segment of the industry. The multi-stop delivery truck was only a small part of the truck products offered by these firms, however. Typically, they supplied chassis

for which the various body manufacturers produced delivery truck bodies. The body manufacturers, including Herman, Montpelier, Hackney and others often showed Big Three and other trucks in their ads.

Two other major truck manufacturers that built vehicles for the multi-stop market were White and International. White introduced the "White Horse" delivery truck in 1939. The White Horse had an air-cooled, Franklin-designed, 4-cylinder engine mounted transversely on the rear axle along with the clutch and transmission.[8] The White Horse was a serious competitor for Divco: Over 3,000 were sold in the first 2 years, only about 150 fewer than Divco sold in 1939 and 1940.[9] White re-entered the delivery truck market in the 1960s with the PDQ delivery vans which were the only multi-stop, forward-control, diesel-powered trucks with the chassis and body built by the same manufacturer.

The 1931 Ward-Electric delivery truck (like the one shown here) competed with Divco. Ward accused Divco of infringing on its patents related to drop-frame construction.

International marketed its Metro model, available as a chassis for custom bodies, for over 30 years. The first International Metro was introduced in 1938 using bodies built by the Metropolitan Body Company of Bridgeport, Connecticut.[10] In 1965, International continued in direct competition with Divco with the introduction of an all-new line of Metro multi-stop trucks in the 4,000 pound to 23,000 pound Gross Vehicle Weight class. Depending on the model, the line introduced in 1965 was available with 4-cylinder, 6-cylinder, or V-8 engines.[11] Through the years, International also produced Metroette delivery trucks which had the chassis and front end of an International pickup truck with a multi-stop delivery body.

When Divco introduced its three-point control truck in 1926, it had to compete with several independent producers of multi-stop trucks as well as the Big Three. The Big Three sold chassis to the multi-stop market that were usable in a number of commercial vehicle applications. The independent firms including Divco, Thorne, Walker, Ward, Pak-Age-Car, and Twin Coach, however, built vehicles marketed exclusively to the multi-stop delivery industry.

Among Divco's competitors were firms that built electric delivery trucks including Walker and Ward. Ward, which started building delivery trucks in the early 1900s, made a major effort to enter the house-to-house delivery truck market in 1915 with a light-duty electric vehicle called the Ward Special. The Ward delivery truck of 1919 featured a hinged dashboard that swung away for easy access and exit; a front step also served as a bumper.[12] Patent number 1,649,630 was issued to Charles A. Ward on November 15, 1927 for an electric-powered truck with a chassis of standard construction. The chassis side frame members ran the whole length of the truck. On each side of the truck was a step to enable the driver to enter and exit easily. Controls were located so that the truck could be operated by a driver standing on the step.

In late 1928, Ward alleged that the structure of Divco trucks infringed on Ward patent 1,649,630.[13]

Another competitor of Divco was Walker. Divco and Walker pooled their patents following the infringement accusations by Ward. This late 1930s Walker Gas-Electric delivery truck was called the "Dynamotive" model.

(Courtesy John B.Montville)

Given the time of the patent infringement complaint by Ward, the Divco trucks in question undoubtedly were the Model Bs. Several letters dealing with the patent infringement issue were exchanged between Ward and Divco, Ward's attorneys and Divco, and Ward's attorneys and Ward management during 1929.[14] In December, 1928, Ward also charged the Walker Vehicle Co. with infringement of patent 1,649,630.[15] Walker believed it may have invented a truck of Ward's design prior to Ward seeking a patent.[16] Correspondence on the matter continued through most of 1929 among attorneys representing Ward and Walker.

On October 15, 1929, John Nicol, Vice President and General Manager of Divco, suggested a patent pool be established among Divco, Ward, and Walker.[17] Prior to suggesting the patent pool, Divco indicated it believed it had nothing to fear regarding infringement of the Ward patent and claimed Divco manufactured a vehicle embodying the Ward patent

over 2 years prior to the filing of the Ward patent.[18] Ward rejected the idea of a patent pool and apparently hoped to obtain royalty payments from Divco and Walker.[19]

Ward apparently took no further action against Divco in the matter. Divco and Walker decided to cooperate on a patent pool. Patent 1,619,775, granted March 1, 1927 to Eddy R. Whitney of Philadelphia, was reissued March 4, 1930 as Patent Re: 17,610, and assigned one-half to Walker and one-half to Divco. Whitney had been associated with the C-T Electric Truck Company which was absorbed by Walker in 1928. The Whitney patent was for a delivery truck that had a transverse aisle made from building the main frame in two sections with a depression between the sections. The term "drop-frame" was not used in the patent, but, in essence, that is what the Whitney design was. The driver of the truck could operate it from either a sitting or standing position. The power for the truck was from an electric motor.

The 1929 Thorne gas-electric delivery truck was another early competitor of Divco.

The pooling of this patent between Walker and Divco, and Divco's purchase of Step-N-Drive in 1930, established the legal framework from which Divco was able to design and build the drop-frame Model H in 1931.

Although Walker was Divco's partner in the Whitney patent, Walker was also a competitor. The Walker Vehicle Company of Chicago was a division of the Yale and Towne Manufacturing Company which also produced industrial lift trucks. In addition to building electric trucks, in 1938 Walker introduced a model called the Dynamotive, a gas-electric combination truck that featured a gasoline engine of conventional design coupled to a direct current generator that furnished the electric power for a direct current series-type electric motor mounted transversely in the rear axle. The Walker design eliminated the need for a battery pack and a transmission and, most importantly, a drive shaft, making the drop-frame construction possible.[20]

Another independent manufacturer that competed with Divco in the multi-stop truck market was Thorne. The motivation for the Thorne gas-electric trucks was recalled by Niblack "Bill" Thorne as follows:

Two gasoline-propelled delivery vans appeared in 1927: Divco and Step-N-Drive. They had an engine-clutch-transmission drivetrain with a drive shaft that cut the vehicle in half and put the driver on a high seat above the hump. It was uncomfortable, tiresome, and slow for him to climb on the seat, go through the gears to the next stop and jump off again. Furthermore, the equipment couldn't take the frequent stop-start abuse, and durability suffered.[21]

Pak-Age-Car originally was an independent firm that later became part of Stutz and then Auburn but was marketed in the late 1930s and early 1940s by Diamond T.

(Courtesy, John B. Montville)

Niblack Thorne and his brother Ward formed The Thorne Motor Corporation in 1928 in Chicago. The gas-electric truck they built had a gasoline engine which was directly coupled to an electric generator and provided the voltage to drive a motor on the rear axle. Driver controls were simple: the throttle produced infinitely variable power which could propel the truck from a crawl to a jack-rabbit start. A major benefit to the system was that there was just a pair of cables under the floor and no driveshaft, so the middle of the truck could be curb high and flat. Thorne offered both the low-frame model and a straight-frame chassis.[22]

However, the Divco competitor in the multi-stop delivery truck market that had the most complex history was the Pak-Age-Car which was made by or associated with four separate firms in a 15-year period. The Pak-Age-Car, introduced in 1927 at the National Retail Delivery Association Convention, featured an engine and transmission at the rear of the chassis.[23]

From 1926 to 1932, the Pak-Age-Car was produced by Pak-Age-Car Company of Chicago. In 1932 Pak-Age-Car was acquired by the Stutz Motor Car Company of America. Stutz auto production had all but ceased in the early 1930s (only 122 Stutz cars were built in 1932 and six in 1934), so the firm looked for growth in the multi-stop truck market. A combination of the Depression, mounting financial losses, lack of capitalization, and stiff competition made producing the Pak-Age-Car in any quantity difficult for Stutz. Under Stutz ownership, production of Pak-Age-Car trucks was minimal and sporadic. Production of the Pak-Age-Car commenced under Stutz on March 20, 1933, and that year 74 Pak-Age-Cars were built. In 1935, Stutz announced that manufacturing autos was no longer part of the company's program but that manufacture and sale of the Pak-Age-Car was part of the program. In 1938, when no acceptable financial reorganization plan was forthcoming, a federal court ordered the insolvent Stutz liquidated.[24]

27

The liquidation of Stutz was not the end of Pak-Age-Car, however. In August 1938, as part of the Stutz liquidation, another struggling former automobile maker, Auburn Automobile Company, bought the rights to manufacture the Pak-Age-Car. By 1938, Auburn ceased automobile production and sold the plants it had used to build the Auburn, Cord, and Duesenberg autos but commenced production of the Pak-Age-Car through a subsidiary known as Pak-Age-Car Corporation at its Connersville, Indiana, plant. Production of Pak-Age-Car trucks continued through the bankruptcy and reorganization of Auburn, which became incorporated as the Auburn Central Manufacturing Corporation in 1940 and was controlled by Aviation Corporation. The Pak-Age-Cars built by Auburn had rear mounted, Lycoming four cylinder engines. Lycoming at the time was part of the Auburn organization.[25] The Diamond T Motor Car Company became the distributor of the Pak-Age-Car for Auburn. Diamond T had an extensive dealership organization to market its trucks. The Pak-Age-Car was a convenient way for Diamond T to provide a multi-stop delivery truck for its dealers without having to design, tool, and produce one. Likewise, it provided a "ready-made" dealer network for Auburn's output of Pak-Age-Cars. Diamond T distributed the Pak-Age-Car from March of 1939 through the outbreak of World War II.[26] Precise production figures for Pak-Age-Car are not available. However, the *Complete Encyclopedia of Commercial Vehicles* states overall production of Pak-Age-Cars was about 3,500.[27] The war ended production of the Pak-Age-Car.

The independent producer of multi-stop delivery trucks that had the most impact on Divco was Twin Coach. William B. and Frank R. Fageol organized Twin Coach in 1927 to produce heavy-duty urban transit buses—a product for which it was known into the 1950s. In 1929 Twin Coach of Kent, Ohio, introduced a line of delivery trucks.[28] By 1933, Twin Coach cooperated in a patent cross-licensing agreement with Divco. Apparently, Divco claimed that some control features of Twin Coach stand-drive delivery trucks interfered with Divco patents. The matter was settled by Divco and Twin Coach licensing to each other features covered in their patents.[29] Further cooperation between Twin Coach and Divco occurred in 1936 when Twin Coach discontinued manufacture of delivery trucks and sold the delivery truck portion of its business to the newly-formed Divco-Twin Truck Company for about 17% of Divco-Twin stock.[30] The advent of the Divco-Twin Truck Company was a complex transaction:

Continental Motors Corporation sold all of its stock in its Continental-Divco subsidiary to investment bankers, and Twin Coach organized and "spun off" a separate company, Divco-Twin, of which it (Twin Coach) owned 17 percent.[31] (A detailed discussion of the formation and organization of Divco-Twin is found in Chapter 3.)

In the frantic fight to replace old Dobbin, how did the competitors of Divco do? The Big Three, International, and White all survived World War II and built trucks that continued to compete with Divco in the 1945 to 1986 era. For these firms, the multi-stop delivery truck was a side line because chassis and units sold in the multi-stop market were marginal or extra income for the full-line truck producers. The multi-stop delivery truck absorbed very little of the firms' total overhead.

However, for Divco, Thorne, Walker, Ward, and Pak-Age-Car, the multi-stop delivery truck was the whole market. These firms survived or failed on the basis of a single line of trucks. In that market, Divco did very well. In the late 1930s and early 1940s when the truck was replacing the horse and wagon, Divco produced from 1,500 to 2,000 trucks per year. Pak-Age-Car was the only independent and exclusive builder of multi-stop delivery trucks competing with Divco that built a substantial number of vehicles. Most of the 3,500 Pak-Age-Cars were built after Diamond T took over distribution rights.

By the 1940s, it was clear that the era of horse-drawn, house-to-house delivery wagons was coming to an end. During the decade and a half before World War II, Divcos established a reputation as reliable and durable trucks capable of lasting a decade. Divco boasted in its advertising that it was the "ten year truck" at a time when competitive makes often lasted only four or five years. While Divco did not cause the disappearance of the horse-drawn delivery wagon, it did provide dairies, bakeries, and other businesses with viable and reliable alternatives to the horse. Against its competition, Divco did very well, and it became the only independent multi-stop delivery truck producer to survive and build trucks after World War II.

Divco-Twin and the Model U
(1936-1944)

It was streamlined, modern-looking, had a drop-frame, an all steel body, and a snub nose. For more than two generations of Americans, it defined the term "milk truck." It was the Divco Model U. Though distinctly Divco, the new Model U was a product of a new company—the Divco-Twin Truck Company.

The Divco-Twin Truck Company

In 1935, Continental-Divco made a slim $17,853 profit for Continental Motors Corporation—better than the losses of the previous years, but not good enough. The pressure was on Divco to produce better results for its parent company. Vice President and General Manager John Nicol headed for the East Coast to call upon dairies and, hopefully, to generate new business. He came back with orders for 500 trucks! While in the East he also laid the groundwork for a change of ownership of Continental-Divco.[1]

The creation of the Divco-Twin Truck Company is linked to the history of the Twin Coach Company, founded in 1927 by William and Frank Fageol. Twin Coach began production

of house-to-house delivery in 1929.[2] Twin Coach delivery trucks, which bore some resemblance to a small bus and to the Model B Divcos, had unit body and frame construction and sliding doors.[3] Twin Coach's experience building delivery vehicles made it a logical partner for Divco.

On February 25, 1936, Continental Motors Corporation advised the New York Stock Exchange that it had agreed to sell its entire interest in Continental-Divco for cash by April 15, 1936.[4] The sale was formally announced on April 17, 1936.

DIVCO-TWIN *Model* **U**

The Divco-Twin Company introduced the Model U for the 1938 model year. The Model U defined the term "milk truck" for Americans for nearly 50 years.

Purchasers of all the stock of Continental-Divco and the delivery truck part of the Twin Coach business were F.R. (Frank) Fageol of Kent, Ohio and the two New York investment banking firms of Reynolds & Company and Laurence M. Marks & Co.[5] The transaction involved Twin Coach owning 17 percent of Divco-Twin's capital stock.[6] The sale of Divco yielded $175,000 in much needed cash for Continental.[7] Frank Fageol, Chairman and President of Twin Coach, became Chairman of Divco-Twin, and William Fageol, Vice President of Twin Coach, became a director of Divco-Twin. John Nicol became the new President of the Divco-Twin Truck Company, while Laurence Marks of the New York banking firm that helped finance the creation of Divco-Twin also became a director of the company.[8]

Legally, the Divco-Twin Truck Company was a successor to Continental-Divco Co. Beginning in 1933 and extending through 1966, Divco-Twin and its successors Divco Corporation and Divco-Wayne Corporation were described by Moody's Manual of Investments as "Divco-Twin Truck Company: Incorporated in Michigan, May 2, 1932 as Continental-Divco Co." Legally, then, all that changed was the name and ownership of the company—a new firm was not created.

Sales, service, and parts outlets for Divco and the Twin Coach delivery truck division were combined following the merger. To expand the market for Divco-Twin trucks in Canada, a sales subsidiary was formed as the Divco-Twin Truck Company of Canada Limited.

Twin Coach built a delivery truck that looked like a small bus. Carl and Sherry Abell of Medina, Ohio, own this beautifully restored 1933 Twin Coach. This truck was originally used by Helms Bakery of Los Angeles, California, for house-to-house delivery. Elm Farm, which currently appears on the Twin Coach, was the name of the dairy owned by the Abell family.

The Divco-Twin manufacturing operations were consolidated in the plant formerly run by Continental-Divco at 12801 East Jefferson Avenue in Detroit. The announcement of the merger stated:

In the past, the Continental-Divco Co. and the delivery unit division of the Twin Coach Co. developed the most economical motor vehicles used in the delivery of retail milk, house-to-house delivery of baked goods, and parcel delivery, and with the ample finances now provided, will enter the entire door-to-door delivery field. Their patents cover the operation of any vehicle from a standing or sitting position.[9]

Although there was an ownership stake in Divco-Twin by Twin Coach as well as some management overlap, the 2 companies were separate legal and operating entities. The independence of Divco-Twin Truck Company was underscored by the listing of 220,000 shares of the company's common stock on the New York Curb Exchange (later called the American Stock Exchange) on May 26, 1937.[10]

In 1936 and 1937, the Divco-Twin product line included both the Divco Model S and Twin Coach versions of house-to-house delivery trucks. After introduction of the Model U, the Twin Coach version was discontinued. However, the Twin Coach style lived on, even after World War II, in the form of a special body purchased by Helms bakery from the Standard Body Company of Los Angeles and mounted on a chassis provided by Divco.[11]

The first two years after the merger brought prosperity to the Divco-Twin Truck Company. From sales of $576,433 and profits of $17,853 in 1935, sales increased to $1,292,907 in 1936 and $1,552,239 in 1937. Profits in 1936 were $100,226 and $110,185 in 1937.[12] By 1937, Divco-Twin, doing well financially with a respected product, was ready to launch a revolution in the multistop delivery truck business.

The Model U

The Model U was the most important single product in the history of Divco. For the next 48 years the styling of the Model U defined the term "milk truck" for millions of Americans. What and/or who generated the design and features of this unique truck? Divco corporate records with specific accounts of decisions and activities that created "America's Favorite Milk Truck" have not survived. They may well have been disposed of through the changes in

This picture shows an early Divco-Twin Model U in service as "America's Favorite Milk Truck."

(Courtesy, American Truck Historical Society)

This Ford 1-ton chassis conversion was done by Transportation Engineers, Inc., of Dearborn, Michigan and was called the Ford "Dearborn Line." It appeared in 1938, the same year as the Divco Model U.

(Courtesy John B. Montville)

ownership of Divco. The principal persons involved in management at Divco-Twin Truck Company are no longer with us to offer firsthand accounts of development of the Model U. Yet, it is not difficult to engage in some informed speculation about the "whys and hows" of the development of the Model U.

The Model U was developed while Divco-Twin was emerging from the difficult years of the Depression and was being confronted by some formidable competition. Divco-Twin's competitors included Pak-Age-Car which was the only other independent and exclusive builder of multi-stop delivery trucks that produced a substantial number of vehicles in the late 1930s. However, several serious contenders in the market were large firms with deep pockets— White, International, General Motors, Ford, and Dodge. To survive and thrive, Divco needed something revolutionary to get the attention of potential customers. Getting attention was something the Divco Model U certainly did! And under that distinctive body was a truck built on solid Divco principles of durability and reliability. It was destined for success as customers were offered a combination of an attention-getting delivery truck and a vehicle that delivered all it promised in mechanical durability.

If any single person was entitled to lay claim to conceiving the Model U, it was John Nicol, born in Detroit in 1880. After attending the University of Michigan, he worked for the Detroit, Ypsilanti, Ann Arbor, and Jackson Railway from 1902 to 1905. From 1905 to 1907, he was an engineer and salesperson for New Process Refrigerating Company. For the next

five years, he was General Manager of the Tacoma Water Supply Company. After working for W.N. Coler and Company from 1912 to 1915 as Superintendent of Construction, Nicol organized his own distributorship for Federal trucks known as the John Nicol Company. He gained more truck industry experience when he became manager of the General Motors Truck Company in the Northwest in 1923. In 1927 Nicol joined Divco-Detroit Corporation as its President and General Manager. After Continental's buy out of Divco, he became Vice President and General Manager of Continental-Divco. With the creation of the Divco-Twin Truck Company, Nicol once again became President and General Manager of the firm.[13]

In addition to being an experienced truck industry executive, Nicol was an inventor and designer. Between 1933 and 1944, eight patents issued to Divco bore his name (see the appendix for a list of Divco patents). These patents were assigned by him to Continental-Divco and later Divco-Twin. Design Patent 109,521, issued May 3, 1938, bears John Nicol's name. The application for the patent was filed October 9, 1937, which was virtually simultaneous with the public announcement of the Model U. The patent is very short, but it is a "Design for a Delivery Vehicle" that shows the unmistakable design of what became the famous Divco snubnosed Model U. While Nicol appears to be the principal developer of the Model U, he undoubtedly was assisted in designing and engineering the snubnosed delivery truck by his engineering staff under L.D. Mead, who had succeeded Kenneth Herman as

UNITED STATES PATENT OFFICE

109,521

DESIGN FOR A DELIVERY VEHICLE

John Nicol, Detroit, Mich., assignor to Divco-
Twin Truck Company, Detroit, Mich., a corporation of Michigan

Application October 9, 1937, Serial No. 72,102

Term of patent 14 years

To all whom it may concern:

Be it known, that I, John Nicol, a citizen of the United States, residing at Detroit, in the county of Wayne and State of Michigan, have invented a new, original, and ornamental Design for a Delivery Vehicle, of which the following is a specification, reference being had to the accompanying drawing, forming a part thereof.

Figure 1 is a side elevational view of the vehicle of my new design showing the doors in closed position. The side of the vehicle opposite that shown in Figure 1 is substantially identical with the side shown in Figure 1 except that the fuel tank cap shown at the lower right hand side of Figure 1 is not present.

Figure 2 is a perspective view of the vehicle as seen from the front with the doors open.

Figure 3 is a perspective view of the vehicle as seen from the rear.

I claim:

The ornamental design for a delivery vehicle, substantially as shown and described.

JOHN NICOL,

Chief Engineer at Divco in 1931. Mead had been a design engineer for trucks and buses at Studebaker and Pierce-Arrow, a chassis engineer for Dodge-Graham, Assistant Engineer of Barley Motor Company in Kalamazoo, Michigan, (which built the Roamer car), and Chief Engineer of the Lewis Spring and Axle Company of Jackson, Michigan, before going to Divco.[14]

When the Model U was introduced, the Divco-Twin press releases described the unique features that ultimately endeared it to customers and the public in general:

> *Styling has been improved and the lines flow front to back. Lights are built in and the windshield is slanted backward with the driver seated close behind it for better vision. Side windows are of the rotating type. A book pocket is provided and an instrument panel is wide enough to provide space for an open route book, while there is storage space under the front floor for the driver's personal equipment. The through-aisle is lower and operating devices are clear of it.*[15]

The new Divco-Twin Model U was revolutionary and quite distinctive when compared to its much more traditional-appearing predecessors and other multi-stop delivery truck of its time. (Table 3-1 lists basic specifications of the first of the snub-nosed Divcos.)

Clearly, streamlined designs inspired John Nicol and other Divco-Twin designers and marketing people as they developed the Model U. In addition to emphasizing the Divco drop-frame construction, the factory literature introducing the Model U also made a point of emphasizing the all-steel, streamlined body. The 1930s was an era of designer fascination with streamlining: cars from the 1934 Chrysler Airflows to the 1936 Hupmobiles featured streamlined designs. The new Divco styling appears to have been influenced by the Chrysler Airflow and may be viewed as a logical extension to commercial vehicle designs of the streamlining trend.

The Model U development costs were very modest when compared to the hundreds of millions and even billions of dollars spent to develop new models of modern cars and trucks. In its *1938 Annual Report* (covering the period November 1, 1937 to October 31, 1938), Divco-Twin reported expenditures of $71,844.92 for new machinery, dies, tools, and patterns, most of which, undoubtedly, was attributable to development of and production of the Model U and related models UB and UL (discussed later).

Table 3-1:
Divco-Twin Model U
General Specifications

Model U: Introduced for 1938

Engine (Standard)

Design: L-Head (Continental) 4 cylinders
Bore: 3³⁄₁₆ inches;   Stroke: 4⅜ inches
Compression Ratio: 6.07 to 1
Cubic Inches Displacement: 140
Horsepower, A.M.A. Rating: 16.26
Horsepower, Brake: 38 at 2800 RPM
Governed engine speed: 2200 RPM
Governed road speed: 25 M.P.H.

Engine (Optional at extra cost - specially adapted to service in hilly country and on long-haul routes which require more speed.)

Design: L-Head (Continental) 4 cylinders
Bore: 3⁷⁄₁₆ inches;   Stroke: 4⅜ inches
Compression Ratio: 5.73 to 1
Cubic Inch Displacement: 162.4
Horsepower, A.M.A. Rating: 18.91
Horsepower, Brake: 41
Governed engine speed: 2590
Governed road speed with 6.6 axle ratio: 35 M.P.H.

Measurements

Overall length: 177 inches
Wheelbase: 100¾ inches
Width: 76 inches
Height: 90 inches
Rated Capacity: 1 ton
Chassis plus Body Weight: 3950 pounds
Milk Case Capacity: 50
Turning Radius: 18 feet

Source: Divco-Twin Truck Company literature

After a year of development effort, the Divco-Twin Model U went into production in late January, 1938.[16]

The sales literature for the Model U emphasized the fact that Divco-Twin's only business was multi-stop delivery trucks. For example, a 1939 catalog for the Model U stated; "We have been able to develop these remarkable vehicles to their present advanced stage by specialization, devoting our facilities to the house-to-house field exclusively instead of trying to build a truck that would fit into every field."[17] In designing the Model U, Divco-Twin considered not only design aesthetics but also driver comfort, convenience, and efficiency. Table 3-2 gives a list of the efficiency, convenience, and comfort features incorporated into the Model U. The rugged durability of Divco-Twins was emphasized with the company claiming per vehicle costs of $1.50 per day for 10 to 20 mile routes and $1.75 per day including all operation, maintenance, and depreciation charges for routes of 20 to 30 miles per day.[18] A major factor in the economy of the Divco-Twin Model U was its ability to idle 7 hours on 1 gallon of gasoline.[19]

The Model U was a truck styling sensation, but more important for Divco-Twin, it was a marketing success, with 1229 being registered in 1938. By comparison, the first regularly reported registration data for Divco or Divco-Twin Model S trucks in the automotive press was in 1936, when 964 Divco-Twin trucks were registered, and in 1937, when registrations were 1125 units.[20] But, although Divco-Twin enjoyed market success in 1938 with production and registrations up and the dollar value of sales increasing to $1.57 million from $1.55 million in 1937, its profits declined to $70,414 in 1938. As a result, the shareholders' common stock dividend was decreased to 10 cents per share.[21] In 1937, when profits exceeded $110,000, the dividend was $.30 per common share.[22] Profits declined in spite of the sales increases because Divco-Twin incurred most of the costs of introducing the Model U during 1938. Divco's fiscal year ended October 31, 1937, so most of the promotion costs for the new model were incurred in fiscal year 1938. In addition, the U.S. economy went into a recession in 1938; therefore, the full sales potential of the new model Divcos was delayed until more prosperous economic times returned.

Hoover Road

To the Divco enthusiast or historian, few addresses have greater significance than 22000 Hoover Road, in Warren, Michigan. In most of its publications and advertising, Divco lists its address as Detroit. The actual location, though, was the Detroit suburb of Warren. While regular Divco production was undertaken in other locations, it was at the Hoover Road plant that Divco enjoyed its "glory years." Divco trucks were built for 60 years, almost 30 of them at Hoover Road.

Table 3-2
Divco-Twin Model U Efficiency Features

- Wide, roomy low-through aisle with doors on each side of truck. Aisle is a low step from the ground. This accessibility eliminates temptation for driver to "slide out from under the wheel" on the dangerous traffic side of road.

- Drives from standing or sitting position.

- Aisle is clear at all times.

- Wide driving vision.

- Easy handling. All driving controls conveniently located. Throttle can be operated from three different points: (1) Foot Accelerator, (2) Hand Throttle on Gear-Shift Lever, (3) Pull-Throttle on Instrument Panel.

- Easy riding. Air wheel truck tires.

- Ventilating cab windows.

- Large loading space in front of aisle.

- Folding side doors operated semi-automatically.

- Adjustable seat with back. Easily moved out of way when not needed.

- Adjustable steering wheel.

- Strong springs. Helper springs. Balanced load distribution.

- Large brakes. Convenient service brake.

- Convenient tool compartment, also used for storing rubber coat, etc.

- Convenient pocket over the windshield for route records.

- Large space for open route book on level instrument panel.

- All-steel body. Steel roof insulated with same approved insulation as used in modern refrigeration.

- Beautifully streamlined modern body styling.

Source: "Divco-Twin Presents a Sensational New Model U," Detroit: Divco-Twin Truck Company, 1938 (sales literature).

The original Hoover Road Divco-Twin factory, opened in 1939, is shown in this aerial photograph.
(Courtesy, Historical Collections, Baker Library, Harvard Business School)

Shown here is the first assembly line at the Hoover Road plant where Divcos were built in a conventional assembly line fashion.
(Courtesy, Historical Collections, Baker Library, Harvard Business School)

Divco-Twin sales were strong in 1938 and the company was optimistic about its future and concerned it may not have enough production capacity to meet the increased demand for its snub-nosed delivery trucks. The solution to the problem was to construct a new plant. In its *1938 Annual Report,* Divco-Twin stated that it spent $7500 for plans for a proposed new factory building. Divco-Twin then applied for a Reconstruction Finance Corporation (RFC) loan to finance the building of the new plant.

The Reconstruction Finance Corporation was established by the administration of Herbert Hoover in 1932 to help deal with the problems of the Depression. The RFC was empowered to lend to corporations, banks, states, railroads, and public and private agencies. The administration of Franklin D. Roosevelt later used the RFC as a major tool to encourage industrial recovery.[23] Divco-Twin turned to the RFC for money because the prevailing economic conditions made 1939 a poor year for a fairly new concern (Divco was 12 years old) with only a couple of really successful years behind it to try to borrow money from the commercial market for plant expansion. A banker might well have questioned the wisdom of expanding capacity in a business environment that was struggling to recover from a decade of depression. The RFC, apparently, however, was willing to take a risk on Divco-Twin and lent it $325,000 for the new factory. The risk paid off for both the RFC and Divco-Twin. Divco sales rose to 1,481 trucks in 1939, 1,622 in 1940, and 2,306 in 1941. Profits increased as well, from only $70,414 in profits in 1938, to $202,605 in 1939, $347,281 in 1940, and $477,796 in 1941. Divco-Twin operations were successful enough by 1940 that the banks were willing to take a chance on the company. In 1940, Divco-Twin repaid the RFC loan through payments

made from earnings and a 3% bank loan for $275,000.[24] By October 31, 1940 (the end of its fiscal year), Divco-Twin reduced the balance of the bank loan to $210,000.[25]

Divco-Twin was proud of its new Hoover Road facility. In its literature introducing the Divco-Twin Model ULM, Divco-Twin boasted, "Located at 22000 Hoover Road, Detroit, the new Divco plant was designed especially for the production of Divco-Twin vehicles. It is equipped with modern machinery and the most advanced equipment, including body manufacturing facilities." In a Milk Dealer ad from October 1939, Divco-Twin indicated that it had been constrained by a lack of capacity prior to building the Hoover Road plant. It stated that many times in the past the demand for Divco-Twin vehicles could not be met, but the new 136,000 square feet of production space removed this handicap. The E. Jefferson Avenue plant had only 53,500 square feet of space.[26] From these statements, it may be inferred that Divco-Twin reached its effective capacity at the old E. Jefferson plant in 1938 when registrations of Divcos reached 1,229 units. The move to Hoover Road set the stage for a production boom at Divco after World War II. Another benefit of the move was that Divco-Twin was now in a plant it owned. The E. Jefferson Avenue plant had been leased, undoubtedly from Continental Motors who built Divco trucks there and who owned the plant for many years.[27]

Although Divco-Twin built the Hoover Road facility to expand its capacity, it had a realistic understanding of its role as a builder of specialized delivery vehicles. Divco neither desired nor was prepared to compete with the major truck builders like Chrysler, Ford, and General Motors. The Hoover Road plant was designed and equipped to take advantage of Divco's position as a specialist, limited production firm. In the *1939 Annual Report*, John Nicol stated:

> *The market for house-to-house stand-drive delivery vehicles is rapidly expanding. However, the volume of business available is not sufficient to induce the large automobile companies to set up the special production lines required for this special type of vehicle. This factor, the demonstrated efficiency of the Divco-Twin Truck, and the strong patent position of the company, have combined to enable it to achieve the dominant position in this particular branch of the truck industry.*[28]

The importance of Divco-Twin understanding its specialty producer status and the implications of that status for the efficiency of its operations following the expansion of the Hoover Road plant are topics for further discussion in Chapter 4.

Expanding the Product Line

By 1939, Divco-Twin was in a position to capitalize on its added capacity and to exploit its position as America's premier builder of delivery trucks. A first

Divco introduced the Model UL on the 127 1/2 inch wheelbase to appeal to delivery businesses other than dairies. This is a Model UL sold to a laundry company by Tri-City Divco of Rock Island, Illinois.

(Courtesy, Barbara Bussard)

step was to expand the Model U line of trucks, and a second step was to expand Divco's activities into the building of delivery truck bodies.

The Model U was a success, but Divco-Twin recognized that it needed to expand its model line to attract a wider range of delivery truck customers. In late summer 1938, the Model UB was introduced as a variation of the basic Model U, now called UM (for milk delivery). The Model UB was aimed specifically at bakeries delivering relatively light weight goods house-to-house. With lighter axles, transmission, and wheels, the maximum load for which it was designed was just 600 pounds.[29]

At the same time that the Model UB was introduced, a longer wheelbase version, the Model UL with a 9-foot panel body and longer 127½-inch

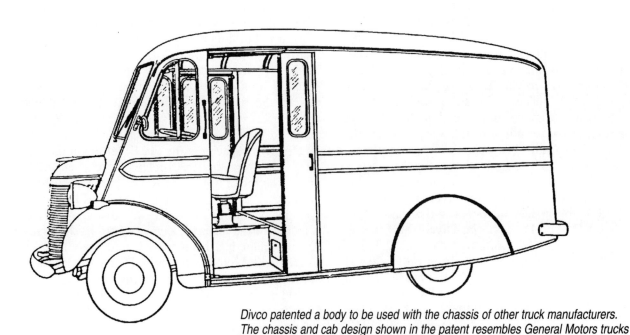

Divco patented a body to be used with the chassis of other truck manufacturers. The chassis and cab design shown in the patent resembles General Motors trucks of the late 1930s which used Divco-built bodies.

wheelbase, was brought to market. The Model UL was targeted at wholesale bakeries, laundries, dry cleaners, department stores, and parcel delivery companies. Divco-Twin had great expectations for its new line of trucks. In its *1938 Annual Report*, Divco-Twin stated, "We should enjoy a very good business on this model as our potential sales will be in several more vocations than they have been formerly."[30] The extended wheelbase model had still another derivative—the Model ULM. This model had a capacity of 100 quart-cases of milk and was aimed at the semi-wholesale milk delivery industry. The Model ULM was also available with a refrigerated body.[31]

The Divco-Twin pre-World War II product line-up was complete with Models UM, UB, UL, and ULM. The company, though, was looking for other ways to utilize its capacity and know-how in the delivery truck business. This desire to make full and efficient use of its facilities led Divco-Twin into the business of building bodies for other truck manufacturers.

The *1939 Divco-Twin Annual Report* included a full page entitled "Special Body in Production for General Motors Corporation." The text of the page stated in part:

Your company recently executed a contract with the General Motors Corporation wherein we are to manufacture for them a large quantity of our recently designed over-engine bodies, using their hood and radiator, which gives them an individually styled delivery truck. These bodies are for use on Chevrolet and General Motors trucks of one-half ton capacity. This special body construction is a new departure in our business. Since moving into our new manufacturing plant, we have available the most modern facilities and equipment for the manufacture of our special type of all-steel bodies.[32]

This new venture for Divco-Twin was backed up by U.S. patent 2,298,773, filed June 13, 1940, and granted October 13, 1942. The patent was assigned by John Nicol to Divco-Twin Truck Company. The patent stated that earlier delivery trucks with bodies mounted on stock chassis required a special subframe beneath the front end of the chassis to permit the mounting of the body. That arrangement was costly and complicated and required rearrangement of the steering gear, brake, and clutch controls. The Divco-Twin invention provided an inexpensive method of assembly by making it possible to assemble a special relatively wide, elongated, large-capac-

These two pictures from the 1940 Divco-Twin Truck Company Annual Report *show Divco-Twin bodies on a GMC (top) and Mack (bottom) chassis.*

(Courtesy of the Detroit Public Library, National Automotive History Collection)

ity truck body on a chassis retaining the original front fenders. Figure 1 from the patent (see page 36) illustrates the basic nature of the Divco-Twin built body. A drawing used in the *1939 Divco-Twin Annual Report* shows a General Motors truck almost identical to the one shown in the patent.

In its annual report for 1940, Divco-Twin states that it had an excellent backlog of unfilled orders as of November 1, 1940, totaling $694,069, which was 27.5 percent of all sales in 1940. It further stated that the backlogged orders "include orders for Divco-Twin Trucks as well as orders for bodies from other truck manufacturers."[33] The body business was important enough that page 7 of the *1940 Annual Report* shows GMC and Mack delivery trucks with Divco-Twin built bodies and a list of firms for which Divco-Twin built bodies. Included in the list are General Motors Corporation, Mack, and Yellow

The GMC 1/2 ton light duty delivery truck used the Divco-Twin made body. Note the similarity of the GMC in this picture from a 1940 GMC catalog and the truck used in the Divco-Twin Patent (shown on page 36).

Truck and Coach Manufacturing Company (which was part of General Motors).

It has not been possible to determine how many Divco-Twin made bodies found their way onto the chassis of other truck builders, but it is doubtful that Divco-Twin was the exclusive body supplier for the other truck builders. For example, John Montville, in his landmark work on Mack, states Mack built some of its own delivery bodies at its body shop in its Long Island City plant. The picture of the Mack MR (Mack Retailer) in his book reveals a body quite different than the Divco-Twin design.[34]

Defending the Product Line

From the introduction of the Model U to the bodies built for other manufacturers, Divco-Twin advertised that its product innovations were covered by patents. Divco literature in the 1930s and 1940s frequently listed the patents held by Divco-Twin. (See appendix F for a list of the patents granted to Divco.) During the 1930s, Divco aggressively defended its patent rights. In 1931, Divco charged a number of concerns with patent infringement including infringement of a Canadian patent by a division of General Motors.[35] However, we have not discovered information regarding the resolution of the allegation against General Motors.

In other patent action in 1931, Divco filed suit against the Ford Motor Company alleging infringement of two patents to which Divco had rights, patent number 1,210,762 and Reissue patent 17,610.[36] Patent 1,210,762 was granted to Melvin B. Church of Grand Rapids, Michigan, on January 2, 1917 and, apparently, later licensed to Divco. The Church patent was for a house-to-house delivery vehicle with a stand or step for the driver at the side near the front of the vehicle. The steering mechanism was accessible to the driver from either the seat or from the side step which, of course, was the steering concept used on the Divco Models A and B. The Reissue Patent 17,610 originally was issued to Eddy R. Whitney of the Commercial Truck Company of Philadelphia,

Table 3-3:
Patent Litigation Divco Income and Expenses

Year	Income from Royalties and Patent Litigation	Expenses of Patent Litigation	Net Patent Income	Net Patent Income as % of Net Profit
1937	N.A.	N.A.	$4,195.42	3.8%
1938	$5,300.00	$5,667.59	$-367.59	—
1939	10,174.75	7,421.72	2,753.03	1.4%
1940	14,658.57	7,698.34	6,960.23	2.0%
1941	20,000.00	10,515.45	9,484.55	2.0%
1942	11,666.68	1,810.48	9,856.20	4.9%

Sources: Annual Reports, Divco-Twin Truck Company, 1937 to 1942.

Pennsylvania, on March 1, 1927 and then assigned to Walker and Divco in the 1930 patent pool between the two companies discussed in Chapter two.

The Divco action against Ford was motivated by the introduction of Ford trucks with a drop-frame design. In March 1931, Ford introduced a drop-floor version of its Deluxe Delivery truck. Then in August 1931, Ford brought out a Model AA 112.1 inch wheelbase drop-frame chassis on which was mounted a Baker-Raulang-built body. The latter truck was called the Ford Type 315-A Standrive Delivery.[37]

After Continental assumed control of Divco, there was speculation the suit against Ford would be dropped because Continental was a supplier to Ford.[38] Continental, though, pressed the suit because it believed it had very strong patent rights and was determined to force the patent issue against anyone making a drop-frame house-to-house delivery truck.[39] By late October 1932, Continental and Ford were negotiating an out-of-court settlement.[40] Full details of any settlement of the Ford vs Continental-Divco patent dispute are unavailable, but Ford discontinued production of the drop-frame, stand-drive trucks in 1933. Ford claimed the reason for ending the manufacture of the stand-drive model was not because of the patent suit but, rather, because mak-

ing specialty trucks did not fit in with Ford's quantity production methods.[41]

Continental-Divco also filed a suit against International Harvester in 1932, charging infringement of nine Continental-Divco patents, including the Church and Whitney patents.[42] Continental-Divco alleged that International Harvester infringed on its patents for building vehicles driven by an operator in a standing position. The suit was settled in 1937 when International Harvester discontinued production of its stand-drive vehicle and agreed to compensate Divco-Twin for past patent infringement.[43]

In 1932, Divco accused the Baker-Raulang Company and Truck Engineering Company of Cleveland, Ohio of infringement of the Divco patents covering stand-drive trucks.[44] Baker-Raulang and Truck Engineering acknowledged the validity of the Divco patents in 1938 and discontinued the manufacture of vehicles driven by an operator in a standing position. As part of the patent-infringement settlement, Divco-Twin granted Baker-Raulang a license under patents owned by Divco-Twin for the manufacture of vehicles other than the stand-drive type.[45]

When White Motor Company introduced the "White Horse" delivery truck in 1939 (see Chapter 2), it licensed the right to build trucks that could be

Any Delivery Truck You Buy Today Will Have to Last *a long Time !*

● HUNDREDS of firms that operate and maintain a fleet of house-to-house delivery trucks will now have a big advantage over less fortunate competitors. They enter the uncertain war years equipped with fleets of Divco-Twin long-life trucks. They can look forward to TEN YEARS of trouble-free, rock-bottom delivery costs. They will save thousands of dollars on costly gasoline alone during these years because of Divco-Twin's unusual fuel economy. They will not be forced to rebuild their trucks, gradually replacing working parts that wear out in a year or two. They will not be "caught short" in an uncertain market three or four years hence when their short-life trucks become useless and must be replaced. The difference between a Divco-Twin and a conventional built truck is the difference between a profitable, long-time, self-liquidating investment and a short term speculation that looks attractive at first and results in a loss later. If your business is handicapped with a short-life, profit-eating fleet, we urge you to investigate DIVCO-TWIN.

The World's Most Economical Delivery Vehicles for—

RETAIL MILK ROUTES

SEMI-WHOLESALE MILK ROUTES

BAKERY ROUTES

LAUNDRY

DRY CLEANERS

FLORISTS

PARCEL DELIVERY

DEPARTMENT STORES

THE PATENTED

ROUTE DELIVERY VEHICLES

D I V C O - T W I N   T R U C K   C O M P A N Y   •   D E T R O I T

Divco durability was legendary by the early 1940s. This ad from the February 1942 issue of Fortune *was a subtle warning that Divco durability would be important during World War II.*

operated from either a standing or sitting position from Divco.[46] Seventeen other truck manufacturers and body builders stopped making the stand-drive or low through-aisle delivery trucks and compensated Divco for past infringements.[47] The actions Divco undertook to defend its patents resulted in patent litigation income, royalty income, and litigation expenses for the Divco-Twin Truck Company. Table 3-3 summarizes the financial impact of the patent actions on Divco-Twin from 1937 to 1942. Following 1942, the detailed financial effects of patent litigation were not given in the company's annual reports. The dollar amounts shown in Table 3-3 are not large, even by the standards of the 1930s. Therefore, we conclude that Divco-Twin, through accusing numerous firms of patent infringement, followed a strategy of trying to discourage competition by the threat of legal action.

As the 1930s came to an end and the war clouds of the 1940s began to gather, Divco-Twin was in a strong market position. It produced attractive and advanced products that had an excellent reputation for durability and reliability as well as patent protection.

War!

The world changed on September 1, 1939, when Adolph Hitler's Nazi German troops invaded Poland. By May 1940, France and the Low Countries were invaded and President Franklin Roosevelt called for a large military buildup program in the U.S. The President of General Motors, William E. Knudsen, was made chair of the National Defense Commission and later Director of the War Production Board. On May 27, 1941, a state of national emergency was declared by President Roosevelt which led, eventually, to an agreement to reduce 1942 automobile production by 50 percent. The cars that were produced substituted plastics for some metal trim, eliminated white sidewall tires (to conserve rubber and zinc oxide used in their manufacture) and substituted iron pistons for aluminum ones. The last 225,000 cars produced for the 1942 model year had "black-out" trim with brightwork used only for bumpers and bumper guards. Production of automobiles in the U.S. ended on February 10, 1942, after the declaration of war, and was not resumed until late 1945. For over 3 years, the production resources of the auto industry were devoted to the manufacture of military goods.[48]

Divco-Twin did its part for the war effort. After the declaration of war, Divco-Twin began to warn its customers and stockholders about what was coming. For example, an ad appeared in the February 1942 issue of Fortune magazine that mentioned that owners of Divco-Twin long-life trucks will have an advantage over competitors in the uncertain war years. In the *1941 Annual Report* issued in January 1942, President John Nicol reports that the company was "redoubling its efforts to secure suitable defense work in order to be of the greatest service to the nation and assure maximum use of the company's facilities."[49]

Sales of Divco-Twin trucks came under government supervision in the beginning of 1942. Dollar sales of Divco-Twin dropped from $4 million in 1941 (a record) to $1.8 million in 1942. Profits also declined from $477,796 in 1941 to $122,185 in 1942 as Divco-Twin began to wind down truck production and gear-up for the war effort. Sales in 1942 included $450,244.76 worth of Divco-Twin trucks sold to the Defense Supplies Corporation. These sales were at cost to the Government by Divco-Twin, which meant Divco made no profits on them. The trucks were stored in indoor storage under Divco-Twin supervision in cooperation with the government conservation program.[50]

Divco-Twin held orders from customers for virtually all of the trucks turned over to the government conservation program, for sales made prior to restrictions being placed on truck sales. Therefore, Divco-Twin secured an option to repurchase the trucks from the Defense Supplies Corporation. Those options could be exercised only as trucks were released for sale under the government rationing program.[51]

The Divco-Twin plant was suitable mainly for assembly work, so the fabrication and assembly of airplane parts became the principle defense activity of Divco-Twin during the war. Divco operated under a cost-plus-a-fixed-fee agreement as a subcontractor to Curtiss-Wright Corporation for the production of airplane parts. By late 1942, conversion of the Divco-Twin plant to the production of aircraft parts was completed.[52]

The financial objectives of the Divco-Twin management during 1942 included maintaining a sound and liquid financial position to enable the company to take advantage of opportunities that would arise at the end of the war. To that end, the mortgage on the Hoover Road plant was retired. In addition, a contingency reserve of $10,000 was allocated for the cost of reconversion to peacetime production at the end of the war.[53]

Divco-Twin sales totaled $3.1 million in 1943 and profits were $154,034.06. About 34% of those earnings resulted from the resale of all the Divco-Twin

No. 1

THINGS TO Remember WHEN PEACE COMES

GAS

DIVCO'S great Fuel Economy saved you thousands of gallons of war-needed *Gasoline* . . .

THE Divco-Twin 4-cylinder engine has always been a gas-saver. In war-time, this great economy is doubly important to you. It brings your fuel costs to rock-bottom level; it helps our war effort by conserving needed gasoline. Carefully kept records of many fleet owners prove that the economical Divco-Twin 4-cylinder engine saves as much as 1½ to 2 gallons of gasoline per truck, per day. In any average size dairy fleet this economy means many thousands of gallons of gasoline saved down through the years. Take good care of your Divco-Twin engine. Service it regularly and properly.

THE PATENTED

Divco-Twin

• 10 YEAR DELIVERY ECONOMY •

DIVCO-TWIN TRUCK COMPANY • DETROIT

Starting in 1943, Divco ran a series of eleven ads reminding customers about the reliability and thriftiness of Divco trucks. Shown here is ad No. 1 from the February 1943 edition of The Milk Dealer.

(Courtesy Cleveland Public Library)

No. 7

THINGS TO Remember WHEN PEACE COMES

365 DAYS EACH YEAR
those faithful **DIVCOS** *roll!*

NOTICE

The Name of the

DIVCO-TWIN TRUCK COMPANY

Has Been Changed to

DIVCO CORPORATION

22000 Hoover Road • Detroit, Michigan

Mail Address

Post Office Box No. 8, Harper Station, Detroit 13

COME Hell or High Water, the faithful DIVCO Dawn Patrol rolls at 5 o'clock every morning! Let the wintry snowdrifts pile high—let the thermometer drop below zero—let the blasting cold bite into every working part—yet those sturdy, dependable DIVCOS roll the routes year after year after year! In these critical war years, when hardly a week passes but some important piece of equipment fails you, it is heartening that your Divco delivery system continues to faithfully carry the milk. What wouldn't you give for a few more Divcos *right now?*

THE
PATENTED **DIVCO**

• **10 YEAR DELIVERY ECONOMY** •

February, 1944

53

"Things to Remember" ad No. 7 in the February 1944 edition of The Milk Dealer *reminded customers of the faithful durability of Divcos, and also announced the name change of the company to the Divco Corporation.*

(Courtesy Cleveland Public Library)

DIVCO IS NOW MANUFACTURING A LIMITED NUMBER OF TRUCKS FOR MILK DELIVERY . . .

As World War II approached an end, Divco was allowed to resume truck production on a limited basis as announced in this December 1944 ad from The Milk Dealer.

(Courtesy Cleveland Public Library)

trucks held in the Defense Supplies Corporation pool. The company also continued to serve as a subcontractor to Curtiss-Wright. In 1943, Divco added $30,000 to its reconversion reserves, which brought the fund to a total of $40,000.[54]

Reconversion to peacetime was already on the minds of Divco-Twin management in 1943. In February, Divco-Twin launched a series of advertisements on the theme of "Things to Remember When Peace Comes." Until resumption of truck production in late 1944, eleven of these ads ran which emphasized Divco economy and durability. Because of the termination of its truck production for the war effort, Divco-Twin had hundreds of customer orders on hand that could not be filled; those orders served as a pool for future production. To estimate future business even more precisely, Divco-Twin wrote every dairy in the United States to determine how many would be interested in purchasing Divco-Twin trucks if production resumed in 1944. The survey results combined with the orders on hand led Divco-Twin to conclude that, when truck manufacturing could be resumed, its business would be greatly increased compared to the prewar years.[55]

Military production began to wind down at Divco in 1944 with the conclusion of the subcontracting work for Curtiss-Wright. Sales were $1.4 million in 1944, and profits totaled $135,439. Sales included the Curtiss-Wright work, reconversion of 457 2½ ton trucks (not Divcos) for overseas duty for the Detroit Ordinance District, and part of an order for 500 Divco trucks for the use of Navy Department personnel. Model UM Divcos began to come down the assembly line again on December 1, 1944. To get one of these trucks, a potential buyer had to present a Certificate of Transfer from the Office of Defense Transportation along with a formal purchase order. Divco confidently predicted that the lifting of war restrictions would enable it to increase production to the full capacity of the factory.[56]

Reconversion to civilian production was one major change at Divco in 1944. Another change was the name of the company. On January 19, 1944, at its annual meeting, the stockholders of Divco-Twin Truck Company voted to change the name of the company to Divco Corporation.[57] The end of World War II in 1945, the resumption of truck production, and a new corporate name put Divco on the threshold of its glory years.

One of Divco's selling points was the ease with which the body could be repaired. Rear fenders were interchangeable and side panels could be easily replaced, but it looks like this Wisconsin owner is going to need some quick repairs.

The costs of operating and maintaining a route delivery fleet are going UP-UP-UP! Future conditions will demand the utmost in economy. Short-lived, "profit-eating" trucks will be a handicap. Over 1500 concerns now deliver with the 10-YEAR-BUILT **DIVCO-TWIN**. By their own records, these firms have save thousands through rock-bottom operating costs, long vehicle life, lowest maintenance costs!

Hilltop Farms
DAIRY PRODUCTS

THE PATENTED
Divco-Twin
THE WORLD'S MOST ECONOMICAL ROUTE DELIVERY VEHICLES

DIVCO-TWIN TRUCK COMPANY ▪ DETROIT

This Divco-Twin ad, from the December 1941 issue of Fortune, *stresses product durability and economic prudence.*

Divco Comes of Age
(The Divco Corporation: 1944-1956)

The Divco Corporation, successor to the Divco-Detroit Corporation founded in 1927, was just a seventeen-year-old adolescent in 1944 but within four years the company truly came of age. The late 1940s were the glory years for Divco, with a plant expansion and record production and profits. After 1948, though, the first evidence of the decline of Divco became clear. During the late 1940s and early 1950s Divco reaped a bountiful harvest from its past investments and product development, but also began to hear the warning alarms of the onset of its decline.

Reconversion

Divco entered the war years in very good financial shape. Record sales of $4 million and profits of nearly a half-million dollars were made in 1941. (See Appendix A, Divco Vital Statistics — Detroit for more detail). Stockholders benefited from those earnings with a 50 cent per share dividend. But the war was not a financial bonanza for Divco. Although the company remained in solid financial condition, sales and profits were lower in 1942, 1943, and 1944 than in 1941.[1] Divco-Twin exercised financial prudence and only paid out about half of its earning in dividends in 1941 and throughout the war. That prudence paid off as the war came to an end and funds were needed for reconversion, product improvements, and facility expansion.

Divco received an allocation from the War Production Board for materials and permission to build a limited number of Divco trucks beginning in late 1944. Production of the standard Model UM began on December 1, 1944, and the Model ULM was added to output in late January 1945. John Nicol, President of Divco, confidently predicted

that "when the war restrictions are lifted, we plan on manufacturing trucks to the full capacity of the factory, as there is a very large demand for house-to-house delivery trucks throughout the United States. Our business should be exceedingly good for several years."[2] It became clear during 1945 that Nicol's the optimism was well-founded. This was the first full year of operation under reconversion conditions. It was a very successful year with sales exceeding $3.5 million, profits the second best in its history at $383,778, and at the end of the year, orders on hand for $13,500,000 worth of trucks. This was more than triple the sales in 1941 and 1940 and almost twice the value of sales that would be realized in 1946.

Expansion at Hoover Road

From the statements of management, it is clear that Divco viewed the key to postwar success as having sufficient production capacity. The seven-year-old Hoover Road plant was already inadequate to meet the pent-up demand. To respond to what appeared to be a booming market, the Board of Directors authorized spending $600,000 for a plant addition and new manufacturing equipment to double production capacity.[3]

Divco signed contracts for enlargement of its Hoover Road plant in the fall of 1945. The expansion program involved adding to the 1939 plant and building a new service building north of the main plant. The service building was designed to provide space for expansion of the parts business. Two new railroad loading docks and a relatively inexpensive Quonset materials storage building for storage of tires and finished sheet metal parts also were constructed. The use of the Quonset building for storage freed up space in the assembly plant which improved its efficiency.

The expansion was achieved, but with some problems. Divco hoped to begin production in the expanded plant in July 1946. But in January 1947 the building still was not in full production due to delays in shipments of presses, conveyors, motors, and machinery. Adding to the construction difficulties were government building restrictions that delayed building of the service building. In late 1946 necessary authorization was received and by May 1947 the facilities were finally completed.[5] The final cost of the expansion was substantially greater than the original $600,000 approved by the board in 1945. The board increased the authorization to $1,300,000, all of which was paid out of earnings. No new financing was required by Divco for the expansion.[6]

While Divco always remained primarily a truck assembler, the new additions enabled it to take charge of more of its own production. In the postwar environment of materials and parts shortages, Divco found that it was nearly impossible to get necessary parts machined on the outside on a timely basis. Therefore, the new additions included installation of Divco's own machine shop.[7] Divco also installed its own press shop. One of the highlights of the new

Divco expanded the Hoover Road facility after World War II by building a new service building (upper left) and Quonset hut storage facilities (lower right).

(Courtesy of the Detroit Public Library, National Automotive History Collection)

The Lake Erie stamping press installed by Divco in 1947 was 24 feet high, weighed 165 tons, and delivered an impact of 800 tons. In one operation the press shaped a one-piece side panel and rear fender for a Model UM.

(Courtesy of the Detroit Public Library, National Automotive History Collection)

equipment in the expansion was a 165 ton, 24 foot high body stamping press that delivered an impact of 800 tons. The press, built by Lake Erie Engineering Corporation of Buffalo, New York, shaped a complete one-piece side panel and rear fender for a Model UM in one operation. The new press increased manufacturing efficiency by reducing manufacturing time. It also improved product quality by using a single stamping for the side and the rear fender, eliminating the use of a separate rear fender and joints where moisture and rust could occur.[8] The new Divco conveyor assembly line installed as part of the expansion was a novel innovation. Earlier Divco models produced at Hoover Road were built on a conventional assembly line in a "head-on" manner. The Divcos came down the new line positioned sideways which enabled the accommodation of all Divco models. The new "sideways" line carried 28 trucks at a time and the company claimed it permitted increased production efficiency.[9]

Divco production fluctuated rather widely at Hoover Road (see Appendix A, Divco Vital Statistics—Detroit for detail). Peak pre-war production was 2,799 in 1941. Divco built 4,392 trucks in the original Hoover Road plant in 1946, before the additions were completed. That production level was exceeded only four times, in 1947, 1948, 1950, and 1951 after the expansion. In the sellers' market of

How Big is Big Enough?

Two prominent economists studied the U.S. auto industry in the 1940s, 1950s, 1960s, and 1970s. In a landmark analysis of American industry, Joe S. Bain of the University of California at Berkeley undertook an extensive survey of automotive industry plant managers and executives in the 1950s. He concluded that an integrated motor vehicle manufacturer (an integrated manufacturer makes most of its own parts) could be profitable producing 100,000 to 150,000 units per year.[10]

Later, Lawrence White, in a 1971 study of the motor vehicle industry from 1945 to 1970, estimated the level of output needed to take full advantage of economies of scale in an automotive assembly plant (economies of scale exist when the cost per unit built can be reduced by increasing output). White concluded that a fully integrated automobile producer, that is,

a firm that builds most of its major component parts from engines to bodies needed to operate its assembly plants at the rate of 200,000 to 250,000 cars per year to be efficient and to minimize costs per unit.[11] But in a 1972 study, R. G. D. Rhys of the University of Cardiff in Wales distinguished between giant mass producers and specialty producers of commercial vehicles. Specialty commercial vehicle producers make vehicles for very specific conditions, functions, and markets for which mass producers may have difficulty adjusting and customizing their work. Rhys concluded that by purchasing reasonably priced components from efficient suppliers and utilizing assembly methods which avoided overcapitalization (and high fixed costs) yet economized on labor, a small specialty truck producer like Divco was able to be profitable in the 1950s.[12]

All sheet metal parts and chassis frames are washed, rinsed, Bonderized, sealed and prime painted through this new seven-stage metal finishing tunnel.

This picture from the 1947 Divco Corporation Annual Report *shows the new metal finishing tunnel in the expanded Hoover Road plant.*

(Courtesy of the Detroit Public Library, National Automotive History Collection)

This new conveyor line carries 28 vehicles traveling down the line sideways and accomodates both models, permitting greatly increased, efficient truck production.

The new "sideways" assembly line installed at Hoover Road is shown in this picture from the 1947 Divco Corporation Annual Report. Note the production orders taped to the side of the trucks.

(Courtesy of the Detroit Public Library, National Automotive History Collection)

MASTER MANUFACTURING ORDER

FORM 303—HECTO

SALES ORDER NO. 11,788

SHIP	Twin Pines Farm Dairy, Inc.	Wayne	DATE ENTERED September 16, 1947

8648 Fenkell, Detroit 21, Michigan

CUSTOMER'S ORDER NO. P.O. 847

INVOICE TO

Same

SALESMAN Fultz

SHIPPING SCHEDULE S.A.P.

CUSTOMER'S ROUTING

Customer Pick-Up

4 MODEL UM-7

Less 10%

		BODY SPECIFICATIONS	
		NO. 1 STANDARD—SOLID BACK WITH NO WINDOWS	
		NO. 2—SOLID BACK WITH WINDOWS	
		NO. 3—FULL-WIDTH OPENING REAR DOORS	
1	335	NO. 4—HALF-WIDTH OPENING REAR DOORS ✓	
		SPECIAL EQUIPMENT	
1	448A	SPECIAL 162 CUBIC INCH ENGINE, WITH 6.6:1 AXLE RATIO ✓	852
		SPECIAL 162 CUBIC INCH ENGINE, WITH 7.2:1 AXLE RATIO	
1	461	GOVERNOR ✓	
1	326	SAFETY GLASS ✓	
1	827	SPARE WHEEL ASSEMBLY ✓	
1	828	SPARE WHEEL CARRIER ✓	
1	133C	RIGHT HAND WINDSHIELD WIPER ✓	
1	134	RIGHT HAND REAR VIEW MIRROR ✓	
1	138	OIL FILTER—REPLACEABLE CARTRIDGE ✓	
		FRONT AND REAR BUMPERS—CHROME PLATED	
1	140	RADIATOR BUMPER GUARD ✓ ☒ PLAIN ☐ CHROME PLATED	
1	101	Square Bottles--Steel Floor ✓	
1	273	FIRESTONE ✓	

CREDIT APPROVED

AUTHORIZED BY *Ray A. Long*

	TOTAL (INCLUDING FEDERAL EXCISE
	STATE SALES, USE OR EXCISE TAX
	DELIVERY CHARGES

TRUCKS	DATE SHIPPED	SERIAL NO.	MOTOR NO.	TERM
1				
2				
3				
4		40936 ✓		
5				
6				
7				
8				
9				
10				
11				
12				
13				
14				

This Master Manufacturing Order (one of the items taped to the trucks in the previous photograph) is for a Model UM-7 for Twin-Pines Dairy dated September 16, 1947. Note that the manufacturing order was signed by Ray A. Long, who was a Divco Vice President in 1947 but later became President of the company.

DIVCO CORPORATION
TRUCK RECORD

SHIPPED TO	Twin Pines Farm Dairy, Incorporated		SERIAL NO.	40936 ✓
ADDRESS	8648 Fenkell,		ENGINE NO.	FH162-A33624 ✓
	Detroit 21, Michigan		SALES ORDER NO.	11,788 ✓
			SHIPPED VIA	dPU ✓
TYPE TRUCK	UM-7		DATE SHIPPED	10-3-47

PART NAME	SPECIAL EQUIP. NO.	SPECIFICATION	PART SERIAL NO. ETC.	PART NAME	SPECIAL EQUIP. NO.	SPECIFICATION	PART SERIAL NO. ETC.
CHASSIS							
AXLE FRONT	STD		C432276	AXLE REAR		5-33	C-554442
SPRINGS FRONT	STD			SPRINGS REAR	STD		
TIRES FRONT	273	6 Ply Firestone 7:00x16		TIRES REAR	273	8 Ply Firestone 7:50x16	
SPARE WHEEL CARRIER	828			SPARE WHEEL	827		
ENGINE							
SIZE		F-4162	A33624	GENERATOR			4694
CARBURETOR			206	STARTER			77 8
TRANSMISSION			71872	DISTRIBUTOR			7B27
GOVERNOR	461		039079	AIR CLEANER			
OIL FILTER	138 ✓			CLUTCH FRICTION			87
SPEDOMETER GEAR NO.							
fly wheel			3110				
OIL				RADIATOR			
ENGINE							OK
TRANSMISSION				HEATER			
REAR AXLE				DEFROSTER			
BUMPERS							
FRONT BUMPER	STD	BLACK		REAR BUMPER	STD	BLACK	
FRONT GUARD	1-140	BLACK		REAR GUARD			
BODY				TYPE BACK	#335	#4 ND	
CASE RACK R.H.		101 Sq. Btls-Steel Floor		CASE RACK L.H.		101 Sq. Btls-Steel Floor	
QUIRK CABINET RH				QUIRK CABINET LH			
WINDSHIELD WIPER R.H.	133C			REAR VIEW MIRROR R.H.	134 ✓		

The Divco Corporation Truck Record, also taped to the trucks on the assembly line, shows that Model UM-7, serial number 40936 was shipped to Twin Pines Dairy on October 3, 1947.

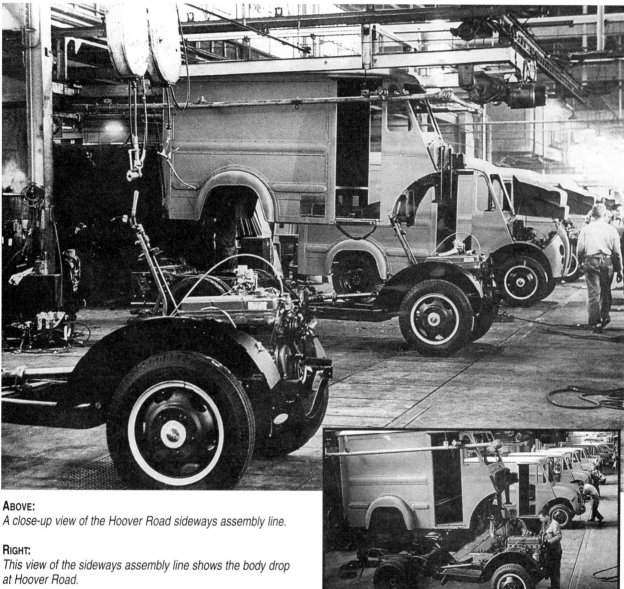

ABOVE:
A close-up view of the Hoover Road sideways assembly line.

RIGHT:
This view of the sideways assembly line shows the body drop at Hoover Road.

1948, Divco production peaked at 6,385. Production never again reached 4,000 units per year after 1951. In the *1945 Annual Report* and *1946 Annual Report*, Divco boasted that it had backlogs of $13.5 million and $15 million, respectively. Output of 3,632 Divcos in 1949 and 5,069 trucks in 1950 indicate that the plant expansion pretty well took care of the backlog problem.

Expanding the Hoover Road plant after the war increased Divco capacity by 150 percent.[13] What, then, was the actual capacity at Hoover Road? In 1946, in what was essentially the original Hoover Road building, Divco strained to produce almost 4400 trucks which may have been close to capacity.

A 150% increase meant Divco had the capacity to produce 6,600 additional trucks, bringing total capacity to about 11,000 by 1947. Output of 24 trucks per day, five days per week, on a 50 week-per-year schedule would have yielded production of 6,000 units annually or almost exactly the 1948 output. Interviews with former Hoover Road employees indicate that peak output on a one-shift basis was 24 trucks per day.[14] On a two-shift basis, production could have reached 12,000 Divcos per year if there had been sufficient demand. The statements of management in annual reports and former employees are consistent: Divco, had it had the orders, could have produced between 11,000 and 12,000 trucks per year.

Shown here is the shipping department and balcony storage for service parts in the service parts building. The balcony was used for storage of large and bulky parts including sheet metal items.

Normal production was about 16 Divcos per day, according to former employees, but fluctuated from as low as eight trucks to as high as 24. From 1948 on, therefore, Divco had excess capacity.

Was Hoover Road an economically viable operation? Did it make economic and business sense? The expansion of the Hoover Road plant must be analyzed from both a short-term production standpoint and from a long-term economic viability perspective.

From the production standpoint, the capacity certainly was needed in 1945. But by the early 1950s, the postwar sellers' market had come to an end. From that time until the end of production at Hoover Road, the capacity of the original 1939 plant would have been adequate to serve the production needs of Divco.

The long term economic viability of the plant is a more complex issue. From the perspective of the economics of the motor vehicle industry, Hoover Road

was a very small facility. With peak annual output of 6385 trucks occurring in 1948, Divco was miniscule compared to the larger and presumably more efficient major car and truck producers like Chevrolet (302,000 trucks in 1948), Ford (over 225,000), and International (125,000). Even Studebaker sold over 50,000 trucks.[15] Although Divco was small, its circumstances were quite different than the large, integrated producers. Divco, in spite of its body building capabilities, was anything but fully integrated. It purchased a major share of important chassis component parts and other standard parts used in its trucks. Divco dealt with more than 330 suppliers who furnished it with over 2,900 items, including engines, axles, clutches, frame members, transmissions, wheels and hubs, steering gears, tires, carburetors, glass, seats, electrical equipment, numerous standard and screw machine parts, and miscellaneous other parts.[16] Over the years, Divco purchased engines from Continental, Hercules, Nash, Detroit Diesel, Perkins and Ford.

It made economic sense for Divco to be an assembler and not to be significantly integrated vertically. At low levels of production it would have been expensive to tool up and produce most of its own components. By buying parts from specialty manufacturers, Divco could take advantage of the economies of scale of parts suppliers who furnish similar components to several customers. Divco was also able to draw on the product development and innovation capabilities of decentralized suppliers without having to commit its own scarce financial resources to the development of components.[17] One of the risks that Divco had to assume was that of suppliers being unreliable. There was a danger that the flow of components needed to keep the assembly line working would be interrupted. To minimize the risk of hold-ups in the flow of production due to unreliable suppliers, Divco arranged for alternative sources of supply for most parts. Having alternative supplier sources provided the added benefit of competitive bidding on purchases which helped Divco hold down costs.[18]

Divco made a profit every one of the 28 years it produced trucks at Hoover Road. From 1939 to the ending of Divco production there in 1967, there was not a single year of financial losses. Indeed, throughout its history, Divco operations were consistent with Rhys' theories (see sidebar on page 49). In the *1939 Divco-Twin Annual Report*, John Nicol viewed this as a competitive advantage that Divco held over the mass producers and in the *1948 Divco Corporation Annual Report* he reaffirmed Divco would not enter the general commercial vehicle market. Divco was successful and maintained profitability by positioning itself as a specialty builder of house-to-house delivery trucks.

Though excess capacity at Hoover Road was not a fatal problem for Divco, it is unfortunate that the company was not able to fully utilize the fruits of its post-war investment. The decline in Divco's primary markets is discussed in Chapter six. That decline, and Divco's inability to expand successfully into new segments of the multistop truck market sealed the fate of Hoover Road and Divco. But Divco rode the crest of its glory years while at the Hoover plant and some great trucks were to emerge from that Hoover Road assembly line.

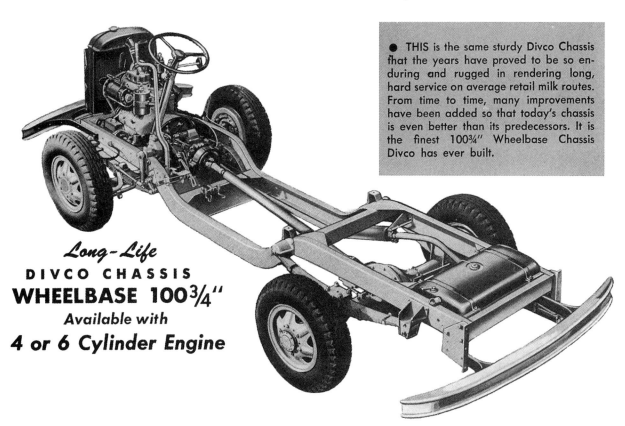

● THIS is the same sturdy Divco Chassis that the years have proved to be so enduring and rugged in rendering long, hard service on average retail milk routes. From time to time, many improvements have been added so that today's chassis is even better than its predecessors. It is the finest 100¾″ Wheelbase Chassis Divco has ever built.

Long-Life
DIVCO CHASSIS
WHEELBASE 100¾″
Available with
4 or 6 Cylinder Engine

The sturdy Divco drop-frame chassis, as used on the Model U and all subsequent trucks.

Start Now

TO PUT YOUR FUTURE DELIVERY FLEET ON A LONG TIME ECONOMY BASIS!

1 STANDARDIZE

On One Type of Vehicle!

As you begin to accumulate your future delivery fleet, don't experiment. Don't buy any and every kind of truck that happens to be available. Don't end up with a garage-full of misfits and profit-eaters. Instead, standardize on a vehicle built especially for milk route delivery—with a record for economy!

2 DIVCO-IZE

For Time-Tested, Low-Cost Delivery!

The patented DIVCO is built exclusively for low-cost milk route delivery. In two models: (1) 50 qt. cases; (2) 100 qt. cases. Both are perfected vehicles that have stood the test of time, with a record of long-time economy that has never been equalled.

3 ECONOMIZE

On Fuel, Maintenance, Repairs, Route Time!

Divco low-cost operation will save you hundreds of gallons of gasoline, per year, per truck. Maintenance and repair expense is negligible. This is a TEN YEAR VEHICLE. Patented features save time on routes. STANDARDIZE and ECONOMIZE. Buy only DIVCOS!

DIVCO
LOW COST
ROUTE DELIVERY

"(1) Standardize, (2) Divco-ize, (3) Economize" was an advertising theme for Divco after World War II, as demonstrated in this ad from the December 1946 issue of The Milk Dealer.

(Courtesy Cleveland Public Library)

Standardize, Divco-ize, Economize

"Standardize, Divco-ize, Economize," was an advertising slogan of Divco in the immediate postwar period, and the product flowing from Hoover Road gave Divco customers the opportunity to do all three. Reconversion to civilian production from defense meant that initial postwar offerings by all vehicle manufacturers were limited. Materials shortages, plant reconversions, and, at times, labor problems and strikes combined to hamper production by the entire industry. It is not surprising, then, that the initial Divco postwar production was limited in its scope of models.

On December 1, 1944, the first snub-nosed Model UMs built since early 1942 went into production. Then, in late January 1945, the model offerings were supplemented by the Model ULM. By 1947 improvements to the Model ULM included a new one-piece side panel, rear fender, and trim moldings. Other new features included sealed beam headlights; special body undercoating; and a seven-stage cleaning, metal finishing and Bonderizing process.[19]

In its late 1940s advertising, Divco reminded customers and potential customers of the legendary durability and reliability of Divco trucks. It felt justified in urging dairies, bakeries, dry cleaners, and anyone else needing a delivery truck to "Standardize, Divco-ize, Economize." Fleet buyers were informed in Divco advertising that the best way to operate an efficient fleet of trucks was to accumulate an all-Divco fleet. In so doing, they were assured they would save on gasoline, garage service, routine maintenance, and route time.

In 1948, Divco introduced its first new postwar model, the UM-8E, which was designed specifically for longer suburban routes where stops are far apart. On the new model the governed speed was stepped up to 46 miles per hour, front shock absorbers were provided for a smoother ride, and only sit-drive was available. It had a payload of 52 quart cases of square bottles.[20]

Encouraged by record sales ($13.4 million and 6,385 trucks) and profits ($1.7 million) in 1948, Divco continued its product development in 1949 with the introduction of Model UM9-E6 with a six cylinder, 229.6 cid Hercules engine (the same engine that was standard on the ULM). This new model had the same 52 case capacity as the UM-8E, but more power and speed to serve better the more scattered

suburban and off-highway routes. Another Divco model was introduced in 1950 and featured the new Divco numerical model designation system. The new Model 31 was built on a 115-inch wheelbase, carried 100 cases of square milk bottles, and had the six cylinder engine and sit-drive. The Model 31 was aimed at heavy retail routes. Table 4-1 gives a breakdown of the Divco line of five models in three wheelbase configurations for 1951 as introduced in October 1950, all with the new numerical model designations.

Divco was presented with a unique advertising opportunity when it introduced the Model 31 and its 1951 trucks. Universal-International Studios produced a comedy film entitled *The Milkman*. Stars of the movie were Jimmy Durante, Donald O'Connor, and a fleet of Divco trucks. In the film, Jimmy Durante, as Breezy Albright the milkman, had a trick Divco that stopped and started when he whistled. It was a great opportunity for Divco to publicize the popularity of its snub-nosed milk trucks. Divco ran ads in dairy publications playing up the link between "America's Favorite Milk Truck" and Hollywood.

Despite the Korean War and its production restrictions and materials shortages, Divco continued to develop products that gave its customers reasons to "Standardize, Divco-ize, and Economize." A major area of product development for Divco was in the field of refrigerated trucks. The concept was not new. For example, in 1935, the C.J. Weiland and Son Dairy of Chicago operated a fleet of M-2 International delivery trucks that carried 50 pounds of dry ice in a bunker as a refrigerant. The truck, doors, and ice bunker had a three-inch layer of insulating material.[21] The *Commercial Car Journal* listed 18 manufacturers of refrigerated truck bodies in 1933. However, most of these were heavy trucks for wholesale and longer distance hauling rather than house-to-house delivery.[22]

In late 1949, Divco introduced Model ULM-6LT (low temperature) into the refrigerated truck market. The ULM-6LT was aimed at the ice cream and frozen foods market. Divco announced that it had contracted with a "reputable and experienced body builder" for insulating Divco bodies to make them ready for installation of refrigerating equipment. Fiberglass insulation was installed in the floor, sides, roof, and front and rear bulkheads.[23]

The success of the ULM-6LT Divco apparently was limited because output figures are not given for it in the Divco Master Parts Book serial number listings. In fact, tracking the number of refrigerated Divcos that were built is a problem because, after the

Table 4-1
Divco Models as of 1951

Model	Wheelbase	Engine	Drive	Case Capacity*	Application
11 (former UM)	100¾"	4cyl.	stand/sit	57	Average city routes with grouped stops
13 (former UM-E)	100¾"	4 cyl	sit	52	City routes with scattered stops
14	100¾" (former UM9-E6)	6 cyl.	stand or sit	52	Suburban and off-highway routes
31 (new)	115"	6 cyl.	sit	100	Heavier than average retail routes
21 (former ULM)	127½"	6 cyl.	sit	116	Semi-wholesale-retail routes

*Cases of square milk bottles
Source: Divco Advertising

change to a numerical model designation system beginning with 1950 models, refrigeration equipment simply was listed as optional equipment on most models. No special serial number code was used for refrigerated trucks, making it difficult to estimate production.

Borden's, Carnation, and National Dairy Corporation (Sealtest) affiliates were consistently the biggest fleet buyers of Divco trucks. Shown here are Borden refrigerated trucks with ammonia holdover plates being recharged.

Development of refrigerated trucks by Divco continued in the early 1950s. Divco considered the development of its own refrigerated trucks a major product innovation and devoted two pages to announcing the new models in the *1953 Annual Report*. Divco brought its three new insulated and refrigerated models to market and placed them in regular production in its own plant in January, 1954.[24] In mid-1954, the Divco line was expanded to include six refrigerated and insulated models built on three wheelbases. Two types of refrigeration were available: ammonia, with a valve connection, and freon with a compressor condenser unit. Trucks with the ammonia system were hooked up to an ammonia line to be charged overnight at the garage or dairy plant. Where adequate ammonia equipment was available, it was the cheapest method of refrigeration. Trucks with a freon and compressor system were used where ammonia refrigeration lines were not available. Both of the Divco refrigeration systems employed holdover plates. These were metal envelopes enclosing continuous coils of steel tubing through which the refrigerant passed. The holdover plates in the ceiling of the cold chamber maintained a low temperature during route delivery.[25]

NOW...5 GREAT DIVCO Models

MODELS TO FIT ALL TYPES OF MILK ROUTES—

- **3 Different Wheelbases**
- **3 Different Payload Capacities**
- **Stand-Drive and Sit-Drive Models**
- **4-Cylinder and 6-Cylinder Engines**

MODEL 11
Combination Stand-Sit Drive
WHEELBASE 100¾"
CAPACITY 57 SQ. BOTTLE QT. CASES
For Average City Routes with Grouped Stops
4 CYLINDER ENGINE

MODEL 13
Sit-Drive Only
WHEELBASE 100¾"
CAPACITY 52 SQ. BOTTLE QT. CASES
For City Routes with Scattered Stops
4 CYLINDER ENGINE

MODEL 14
Available Stand or Sit-Drive
WHEELBASE 100¾"
CAPACITY 52 SQ. BOTTLE QT. CASES
For Suburban and Off-Highway Routes
6 CYLINDER ENGINE

MODEL 31 (New)
Sit-Drive Only
WHEELBASE 115"
CAPACITY 100 SQ. BOTTLE QT. CASES
For Heavier Than Average Retail Routes
6 CYLINDER ENGINE

MODEL 21
Sit-Drive Only
WHEELBASE 127½"
CAPACITY 116 SQ. BOTTLE QT. CASES
6 CYLINDER ENGINE
For Semi Wholesale-Retail Routes
DUAL REAR WHEELS

● DIVCO now offers you an enlarged line of models — each deliberately designed to fit a specific route condition. It will pay you to analyze your various routes and, in some cases, substitute a different Divco model. Doing so will greatly increase your route efficiency, allow more time for collections and soliciting, and further increase the usual Divco economy of operation. See all these models at the Dairy Show. Let us show you how each one can fit into your delivery system. Your best move, in the uncertain years ahead, is to completely DIVCO-ize!

MODEL 11
MODEL 13

MODEL 14

MODEL 31

MODEL 21

VISIT DIVCO
Stage No. 1 DAIRY SHOW
ATLANTIC CITY—OCT. 16 to 21

DIVCO CORPORATION—MAIL ADDRESS: P. O. BOX 3807, PARK GROVE STATION, DETROIT 5, MICH.

In 1950, Divco changed its model designations to a numerical system and boasted in this October 1950 ad in The Milk Dealer that it offered a complete line of five models.

(Courtesy Cleveland Public Library)

Divco stated in the *1953 Annual Report* that it introduced and produced its own refrigerated models because the expanding population in large suburban communities caused food delivery firms to increase the length of delivery routes. The longer routes increased the demand for insulated and refrigerated trucks which maintained foods at lower temperatures for longer periods of time.[26]

Another product innovation introduced in 1954 was the Divcomatic transmission. The Divco Corporation *1954 Annual Report* claimed that introduction of the Divcomatic culminated 15 years of research and experimentation. The Divcomatic was a Warner 3-speed automatic transmission adapted to some, but not all, of the engines available on Divco trucks. Through the years, the Divcomatic was an option on Snub-nose and Dividend models equipped with the Super 4-cylinder, 162 cid Continental engine, and the Standard 6-cylinder, 229.6 cid QXD-3 Hercules, and later, the Standard 6-cylinder 236.7 cid QXLD-3 Hercules engines. The Divcomatic was phased out in 1966. In an October 4 memo to Divco dealers, regional sales managers and service representatives, John C. Priebes, Divco Truck Division Sales Manager, announced the automatic transmission was no

longer available as an option. However, beginning in July 1966, Divco equipped 15 experimental trucks with Ford automatic transmissions. Divco was gradually phasing in the use of Ford engines; first in 1964, the F223 and F262 six cylinder engines were introduced and in 1965 the Ford F240 and F300 6-cylinder engines were offered. The Ford automatic transmission was a logical match for those engines. In a February 9, 1967 memo, the Divco sales department announced that it was ready to make the Ford automatic transmission available for purchase in the field. The Ford transmission was listed as an option in catalogs for Model 206, 300, and 306 Divcos through the end of production in Delaware, Ohio. However, an interruption in the availability of the automatic occurred in late 1971 due to problems with procurement of parts, according to a September 27, 1971 memo to dealers from George Foster, Retail Sales Director.

The refrigerated trucks and automatic transmission models were only part of an expanded Divco line of snub-nosed vehicles. What started as a single Model U for 1938 consisted of a product line of 14 models on three wheelbases by 1954. As purchasers "Divco-ized," it was possible to customize a Divco to the particular and unique needs of individual cus-

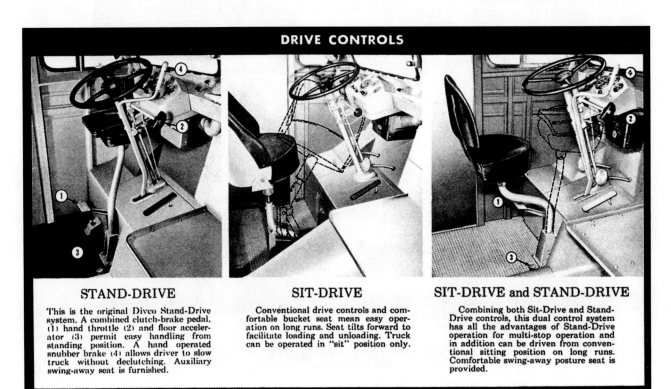

DRIVE CONTROLS

STAND-DRIVE

This is the original Divco Stand-Drive system. A combined clutch-brake pedal. (1) hand throttle (2) and floor accelerator (3) permit easy handling from standing position. A hand operated snubber brake (4) allows driver to slow truck without declutching. Auxiliary swing-away seat is furnished.

SIT-DRIVE

Conventional drive controls and comfortable bucket seat mean easy operation on long runs. Seat tilts forward to facilitate loading and unloading. Truck can be operated in "sit" position only.

SIT-DRIVE and STAND-DRIVE

Combining both Sit-Drive and Stand-Drive controls, this dual control system has all the advantages of Stand-Drive operation for multi-stop operation and in addition can be driven from conventional sitting position on long runs. Comfortable swing-away posture seat is provided.

"Stand-Drive," "Sit-Drive," and "Sit-Drive and Stand-Drive" were either standard or optional equipment depending on the model. The "Stand-Drive" and "Sit and Stand Drive" were major features of the Divco trucks for many years.

tomers while maintaining a family of common parts for major truck components. Also, buyers often required financing to buy the Divco trucks. To assist customers and dealers, Divco formed a wholly-owned subsidiary in 1953 to facilitate long-term financing and leasing of trucks.[27]

Dark Clouds

By the early 1950s, the seller's market ended for the motor vehicle industry and for Divco because the wartime pent-up demand for cars and trucks was satisfied. Divcos now had to be sold truck by truck, on value, features, and dependability. At the end of the fiscal year on October 31, 1950, the Divco backlog was $2.8 million and on October 31, 1951, it had declined to $2.1 million, less than one-seventh of what it had been at the end of 1946.[28]

Sales at Divco declined from the record $13.4 million of 1948 to $8 million in 1949 and rose to only $9.9 million in 1950. Profits also weakened from $1.7 million in 1948 to $739,786 in 1949 and $1,047,736 in 1950. The decline in profits reflected the involvement of the United States in the Korean War which caused truck production to be limited under National Production Authority regulations. Another factor in reducing net profits was that taxes were increased. Divco's average corporate tax rate went from 40% in 1950 to just under 50% in 1951. In addition, Divco received contracts for parts and sub-assemblies for military tanks and incurred the costs of preparing for defense production. During the Korean War, defense business, which began in May 1951,[29] accounted for about 14% of sales.[30]

The expansion of the product line that took place in the late 1940s and early 1950s was an attempt to broaden the market for Divco trucks because the traditional Divco market was in decline. (Trends in the house-to-house delivery market that began to have a significant impact on Divco by the mid-1950s are the subject of Chapter 6.) Divco output declined to 2959 trucks in 1954 and and profits dropped from over $1 million in 1950 to $385,144 in 1954. Management explained that the sales and profit pressures on Divco resulted from lower sales volume following the unusual demand for trucks in late 1950 and 1951 brought on by the Korean War. Interruptions to manufacturing caused by the 54-day steel strike in 1952 also had a negative effect on earnings.[31]

Even though it was confronted with the challenges of declining sales and Korean War production, Divco felt it was appropriate to celebrate its 25th anniversary in 1952. At the Dairy Industry National Convention the week of September 22, 1952, Divco showed several of its newest trucks. In addition, it had an exhibit labeled "Silver Anniversary, 1927-1952" that featured an animated display 25 feet long by 8 feet high. The display had an electrically lighted scenic background with a highway containing over 90 moving miniature Divco trucks leaving the Divco plant and traveling across the country. Each scale model Divco on the display was painted with the colors and logo of a Divco customer.[32]

The Dividend Series and "Squared-Up" Models

The changing sales situation at Divco brought about the introduction of the first completely new Divco since the Model U in 1938 and the last completely new truck Divco ever introduced. In 1955, the venerable snub-nosed Divco received a stablemate—the Dividend Series, which was developed by Divco in response to a declining market for milk delivery trucks. That topic and more of the Dividend Series story are covered in Chapter 6. Here only a brief description of the Dividend Series is undertaken.

Divco knew that in order to maintain production at a profitable level, it would have to appeal to buyers beyond the milk truck business. The Dividend Series was designed for the store and wholesale multistop delivery market which included bakeries, wholesale florists, newspapers, dry cleaners and similar package and retail delivery operations. The Dividend Series was styled quite differently than its snub-nosed cousins. It had a Gross Vehicle Weight of 8,000 to 12,000 pounds, a "Super Six" (actually a Nash 252 cubic inch overhead valve six-cylinder) engine, and a cab-forward design with a wide, deep windshield that increased driver visibility.[33] Model designations for the initial Dividend Divcos were in the 40 and 50 series. The Model 40 had a 130 inch wheelbase, and the Model 50 had a 117 inch wheelbase.[34]

The Dividend Series stayed in production through the remainder of Divco's days in Detroit. Production of Dividend Series Divcos totaled 2,917 units from 1955 to 1967, which classifies the Dividend as neither a failure nor a tremendous success. The Dividend did broaden Divco's market and help keep total production fairly level in the 2,500 to 3,500 truck range during that period. A breakdown of Dividend Series Production (including buses based on the Dividend Series) by model year from

LEFT: *In 1955, Divco introduced the Dividend Series to appeal to the whole-sale delivery market. This factory picture shows what appears to be an early production model.*

(Courtesy, James Stegner)

BELOW: *Basic Dividend Series specifications are given in this page from a 1959 catalog.*

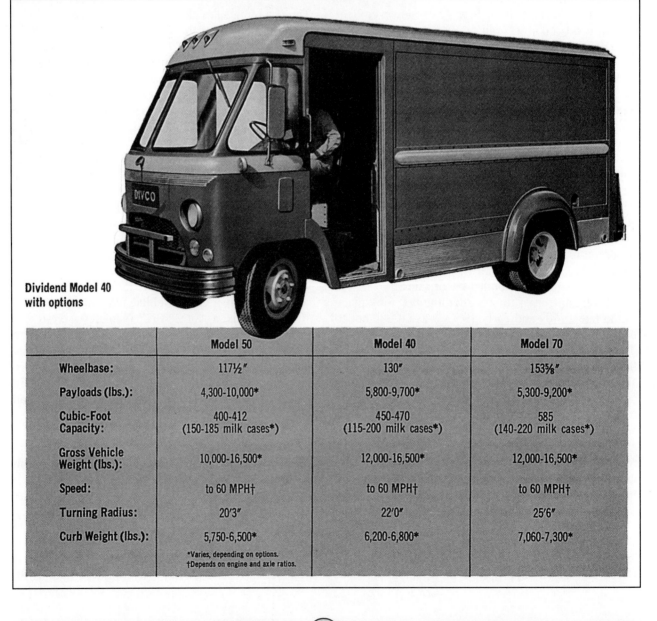

Dividend Model 40
with options

	Model 50	Model 40	Model 70
Wheelbase:	117½"	130"	153⅝"
Payloads (lbs.):	4,300-10,000*	5,800-9,700*	5,300-9,200*
Cubic-Foot Capacity:	400-412 (150-185 milk cases*)	450-470 (115-200 milk cases*)	585 (140-220 milk cases*)
Gross Vehicle Weight (lbs.):	10,000-16,500*	12,000-16,500*	12,000-16,500*
Speed:	to 60 MPH†	to 60 MPH†	to 60 MPH†
Turning Radius:	20'3"	22'0"	25'6"
Curb Weight (lbs.):	5,750-6,500*	6,200-6,800*	7,060-7,300*

*Varies, depending on options.
†Depends on engine and axle ratios.

company production records is given below. Figures in parentheses are Dividend Series as a percent of Divco production for the year.

Dividend Series Production (including buses based on the Dividend Series)		
MODEL YEAR	NUMBER PRODUCED	PERCENTAGE OF DIVCO'S TOTAL PRODUCTION
1955	82	(2.1%)
1956	131	(3.7%)
1957	216	(7.5%)
1958	306	(10.5%)
1959	636	(17.8%)
1960	533	(15.0%)
1961	223	(12.5%)
1962	178	(6.7%)
1963	141	(6.8%)
1964	192	(8.0%)
1965	111	(4.9%)
1966	102	(4.8%)
1967	66	(7.1%)

Dividend Series production was marginal for Divco; the mainstays of the line were still the snub-nosed models. The Dividend Series output exceeded 10 percent of production in only four model years (1958, 1959, 1960, and 1961). Although information on the costs of developing the Dividend Series is not available, the question must be raised: was the Dividend Series worth its costs? Divco needed to break into new markets, and the Dividend Series offered that opportunity, yet the low level of sales of this series must have been disappointing to Divco management.

RIGHT: *Divcos were tough trucks, but not tougher than a garden hose, according to this B.F. Goodrich ad from the May 1949 Better Homes & Gardens.*

Divco introduced another product innovation in 1955 in addition to the Dividend Series: the snub-nosed Divcos lost some of their familiar streamlined and rounded appearance when a new "squared-up" body appeared on the 115 inch wheelbase models. The "squared-up" body featured a clean-cut, straight roofline which increased headroom and added 1½ inches in interior width, thereby increasing cargo capacity with no significant change in outside dimensions. Maintenance and repair of the "squared-up" model was simplified with use of sectional panels which could be removed without disturbing any lining or insulation if body repair was necessary.[35]

Administration and Organization

When the name of the Divco-Twin Truck Company was changed to the Divco Corporation in 1944, there was virtually no change in the administration of the company. The name change was a reflection of the product being sold by the company rather than indicative of an executive reorganization. The executive line-up for The Divco Corporation in 1944 was exactly the same as it had been for the Divco-Twin Truck Company.

Dairies were at the heart of Divco's business. This 1958 photograph shows a Divco operated by Glenora Farms Dairy of Evanston, Illinois with Driver Bill Koseck.

(Courtesy, Bill Hyland)

1944 Divco Corporation Executives

Board of Directors	Officers
Frank R. Fageol, Chair	John Nicol, President
John Nicol	Ray A. Long, Vice President
Frank A. Willard	Nathan Fine, Treasurer
Ray A. Long	James Spencer, Secretary
Laurence M. Marks	
William B. Fageol	
Edward P. Taylor	

The Fageols, of course, were associated with Divco as a result of the combination with the Twin Coach delivery truck operation. John Nicol was a long-time Divco employee and executive who led the company through the organizational changes of the 1930s and the building of the Hoover Road plant.

In 1948, there was a minor change in the administration structure of Divco when J. M. Nicol II, son of the president, became a vice president and director. In 1949, Frank Fageol retired as Chair of the Board. That position was assumed by John Nicol, who turned the presidency of the company over to Ray Long. George E. Muma, who had been with Divco since the Divco-Detroit days when he was Service Manager, became a vice president. After the death of John Nicol on July 22, 1950, Frank Fageol again became Chair of the Board of Directors. George Muma now had the title of vice president for manufacturing and J. M. Nicol II (who had been head of the Detroit Divco Branch for a number of years) was vice president for sales.[36]

In 1953, J. M. Nicol II continued as a director but R. H. Sjoberg, a relative newcomer, having been with Divco only since 1952, became vice president of sales. A new position, vice president of service, was assumed by Frank R. Messing, Jr. who was associated with Divco since 1945. In 1954, George Muma became President, Ray Long remained as a director, and R. C. Robillard (who began in the accounting department in 1938) became Treasurer. Nathan Fine, who worked for Divco since 1932 and served as Treasurer since 1939, died in 1953. Henry Hedeen took over Muma's former position as vice president of manufacturing.

The ascendancy of George Muma to the presidency of Divco capped a 25-year career with the company. The *Detroit Free Press* described Muma as "quiet spoken, affable...a 'shirt-sleeves' executive used to grease and grime of the production line. When confronted with a tough problem that was stopping the line, he had been known to roll up his sleeves, grab a wrench, and help find a solution."[37] Henry Hedeen was another 25-year Divco veteran. As 1956 dawned, Divco was being run by seasoned Divco people. The team confronted a major challenge in 1956: Divco undertook a merger.

The Divco-Wayne Corporation (1956-1967)

As his train sped through the Indiana countryside one day in 1950, Newton Glekel caught a glimpse of the Wayne Works, a builder of bus bodies, in Richmond, Indiana. Glekel, a New York attorney and real estate entrepreneur, had been on his way to Indianapolis to buy a company. That deal fell through, but he remembered seeing a prospectus for the Wayne Works, which was for sale. Soon after a two-hour taxi ride from Indianapolis to Richmond, he owned the Wayne Works.[1] That event set the stage for the next significant decade in the history of Divco.

Newton Glekel and Harold Drimmer had become friends while in law school at Columbia University. After being admitted to the bar in 1938, they formed the law firm of Glekel and Drimmer. Most of their cases involved real estate and in 1944 they gave up their law practice and went into the real estate business. They traded actively in real estate and branched out into other businesses, including holding a controlling interest in the publishing firm of J.J. Little & Ives. Then in 1950, they acquired Wayne.[2] The deal gave Glekel and Drimmer and their respective families all the stock of Wayne.

Wayne, which was privately owned before the buyout,[3] traced its roots back to wagon building in 1837. The company began building bus bodies in Richmond, Indiana at the turn of the century. The principal manufacturing activities of Wayne took place in Richmond, Indiana, where it had 450,000 square feet of factory space. Wayne was one of the largest producers of school bus bodies in the U.S. and also sold "knocked-down" bus bodies for assembly at local and independently owned plants in Windsor, Ontario; Monterey and Mexico City, Mexico; Bogota, Colombia; and Caracas, Venezuela.

Wayne broadened its product line by acquiring the Meteor Motor Car Company of Piqua, Ohio, in

1953, and in 1956, buying the A.V. Miller Company in Bellefontaine, Ohio. Miller and Meteor were builders of hearses and ambulances.[4]

The Divco-Wayne Deal

On October 24, 1956, at corporate headquarters on Hoover Road, the Divco stockholders met and voted to buy Wayne Works, Inc. In the proxy statement sent to the stockholders asking for their approval of the deal, Divco noted the following reasons for purchasing Wayne:

The point-to-point and wholesale delivery vehicle business is highly competitive and is somewhat subject to cyclical fluctuations of a capital goods nature, since the users of such vehicles may repair existing vehicles and defer new purchases at times when they are not optimistic about the future. The addition of the Wayne line of school bus bodies, ambulances, and hearses will add diversification to Divco's business in fields which the Board of Directors believes to be less subject to such fluctuations.[5]

Glekel and Drimmer were the engineers of the Divco-Wayne merger. Their rationale was that bringing together Wayne (with its subsidiaries of Miller and Meteor) and Divco would create a combination of firms building custom-designed vehicles, each of which suited the needs of a specific market. Glekel wanted his firms to be as recession-proof as possible. He reasoned that by serving the school bus, funeral coach, and delivery truck markets, Divco-Wayne would gain a measure of immunity to economic declines because, in good times or bad, school children would be transported to school, people would

Table 5-1:
Divco and Wayne At Time of Merger
(Year Ended October 31, 1956)

(In thousands of dollars)

	1951	1952	1953	1954	1955
DIVCO					
Sales	$11,174	$8,746	$9,789	$9,121	$12,214
Net Earnings	$695	$387	$509	$385	$434
Earnings Per Share	$1.54	$.86	$1.13	$.86	$.96
WAYNE WORKS					
Sales	$8,153	$7,276	$6,597	$9,320	$13,111
Net Earnings (Loss)	$256	$552	$193	($244)	$396
Earnings Per Share (Loss)	$1.80	$3.90	$1.33	($1.71)	$2.78

Source: Notice of Special Meeting of Shareholders and Proxy Statement, Divco Corporation, proof of September 14, 1956, pp. 10-11.

become ill or die, and milk would be delivered to the front door.[6]

The companies combined in the Divco-Wayne merger were prominent in their respective industries. Wayne produced over 25% of the school buses in the U.S.; Miller and Meteor accounted for almost a third of the annual U.S. output of 3,000 ambulances and hearses, and about 75% of the nation's milk was delivered in Divcos.[7] Divco and Wayne were also closely matched in terms of sales in the early 1950s (see Table 5-1). Wayne, however, was not as profitable as Divco and even lost money in 1954.

Very little information is available on the dynamics of the negotiations between the Wayne interests and Divco that led to the 1956 merger. Access to board of directors minutes held by the Divco-Wayne successor company, Boise Cascade Corporation, was denied as a matter of general company policy. From media accounts, it is clear that Glekel had the objective of building Wayne through acquisition; the Miller and Meteor buyouts attest to the partial fulfillment of that objective. The *New York Times* reported that Glekel wanted to broaden Wayne and, therefore, "proceeded to merge the company with the Divco Corporation."[8]

The negotiations between Wayne and Divco took most of the month of August 1956. George Muma of Divco, in announcing the deal on August 27, 1956, was enthusiastic. The *Detroit Free Press* quoted Muma as saying, "This is a major step in a program of expansion and diversification."[9] Divco purchased all the assets, properties, business and good will of Wayne for the following consideration:[10]

A) A purchase price to be paid by Divco to Wayne as follows:
   (i) Payment of $50,000 in cash
   (ii) Issuance to Wayne of 200,000 shares of Divco common stock, par value of $1.00 per share; (thus increasing the Divco stock outstanding to 650,000 shares)
   (iii) Issuance by Divco of 20 negotiable promissory notes for $63,100 each with a total value of $1,262,000, maturing four months after the closing date of the sale. (These notes were secured with the stock of Wayne Works purchased by Divco. That is, Divco pledged the stock it held in Wayne Works as collateral against the notes.)

B) The assumption by Divco of the liabilities of Wayne.

Because Glekel and Drimmer (and their families) were the sole owners of Wayne Works, the transactions between Wayne and Divco gave them a significant holding of Divco-Wayne stock and put them in a position to control the firm. Richmond Industries, a holding company which owned 26% of Divco-Wayne stock after the merger, was co-owned by Glekel and Drimmer.[11]

The Divco-Wayne corporate organization chart at the time of the merger ended up as shown (above right) — we note in parenthesis whether the director or officer came from the Divco or Wayne side:[12] George Muma, in addition to holding the title of Executive Vice President of Divco-Wayne, had the title of President of the Divco Truck Division. The Wayne Works was headed by David Walker, Division Manager.[13]

Although the immediate post-merger corporate structure left Divco people in charge of the Divco operations, the center of power eventually gravitated toward the Wayne side of the business. Glekel and Drimmer maintained corporate executive offices in New York, while official Corporate Headquarters were in Richmond, Indiana. By 1962, the only director and officer left from the Divco era was

Divco-Wayne Corporate Organization Chart

DIRECTORS

Frank R. Fageol, Chair (Divco)
Harold Drimmer, Executive Committee Chair (Wayne)
Newton Glekel (Wayne)
George E. Muma (Divco)
F. W. Hall (Wayne)
Ray A. Long (Divco)
Edward P. Taylor (Divco)
John M. Nicol II (Divco)
Arthur Sheinberg (Wayne)

OFFICERS

Newton Glekel, President (Wayne)
George E. Muma, Executive Vice President (Divco)
Frank W. Hall, Executive Vice President (Wayne)
E. L. Walters, Treasurer (Wayne)
James H. Spencer, Secretary (Divco)

James Spencer. Frank Fageol retired in 1962 due to ill health.[14] After 27 years at Divco, George Muma retired in 1959 at age 65 and died in 1961.[15] In 1960, Holmes T. Collins, Divco Division Manager, was promoted to Corporate Manufacturing Vice President at Divco-Wayne and Max Downing, former Assistant Divco Division Manager, was made Operations Manager of the Divco Division.[16]

Divco-Wayne: A Profile

In Divco-Wayne, Newton Glekel and Harold Drimmer put together a conglomerate enterprise. Initially the company was in the custom and specialized vehicle industry. In 1958, though, steps were taken which broadened the activities of Divco-Wayne and eventually diminished the relative importance of the Divco Truck Division.

In 1958, Divco-Wayne entered the electronics industry with the purchase of the Electronics Division of the Gruen Watch Company for $1.5 million. At the time of the purchase, Glekel stated that the Electronics Division complemented the production of

Divco-Wayne vehicles because it could supply electronic housings to the Divco-Wayne divisions making trucks and buses.[17] In the *1958 Divco-Wayne Annual Report*, Glekel put a slightly different spin on the Gruen Electronics purchase; there he explained it as an opportunity to enter an industry supplying components to the national defense missile program.[18] However, the Electronics Division did not work out as hoped. It generated $3.8 million in sales, but, according to Glekel, its return on invested capital was substantially less than that made in the other divisions. At the time of the purchase, the Electronics Division ranked 55th in its field. A year later, it ranked 56th, so in 1959 Divco-Wayne disposed of it at no monetary loss to the company.[19]

During the 1960s, Divco-Wayne undertook a series of acquisitions and facilities consolidations to improve corporate efficiency and profits. In 1962, Divco-Wayne bought Vought Industries, Inc., a mobile home manufacturing division from Ling-Temco-Vought, Inc. of Dallas, Texas.[20] The new mobile home and travel-trailer division was supplemented by other acquisitions related to the mobile home industry in 1965 and 1966. These acquisitions included the purchase of Estevan Industries Ltd. of Canada, Nene Valley Coachworks Ltd. of England, and Kip Kampeerwagons of the Netherlands. The Mobile Home and Travel-Trailer Division, called Divco-Wayne Industries, was the world's leading producer of low-cost homes. Divco-Wayne Industries had 20 plants (14 in the U.S., 3 in Canada, 2 in England, and 1 in The Netherlands) and generated 62% of the company's sales by 1966.[21] In order to increase production efficiency, the Miller-Meteor funeral car and ambulance business was moved to Piqua, Ohio, from Bellefontaine.[22] It was expanded in 1965 with the acquisition of the Cotner/Bevington Coach Company of Blytheville, Arkansas. Cotner/Bevington produced a line of ambulances, professional cars, and limousines.[23]

In the 10 years following the Divco-Wayne merger, the Wayne Division expanded its product line beyond school buses. In 1966, Wayne was building school bus bodies for various chassis supplied by major truck manufacturers, inter- and intra-city buses, military transport vehicles, and kits for overseas assembly. Included in the Wayne product line was a "hi-mobility" educational laboratory on wheels that could move from school to school to provide specialized training. In 1966, Divco-Wayne confidently predicted that the demand for Wayne products would expand as school enrollments increased. Wayne was a growth division.[24]

One merger that did not materialize was with the Studebaker-Packard Corporation, which was diversified into a number of industries in addition to building Studebaker automobiles and trucks. Specific details are not available, but Newton Glekel was approached about selling Divco-Wayne to Studebaker-Packard at about the time the Gruen Electronics division was being liquidated in 1959. The motivation from the standpoint of Studebaker-Packard was that Divco-Wayne was highly profitable. Studebaker-Packard had $140 million of tax loss credits as a result of losses incurred in automotive operations in the 1950s prior to the introduction of the successful compact Lark automobile in 1959. Divco-Wayne profits could be charged against those tax loss credits.[25] Furthermore, the Divco-Wayne product line of buses and trucks would have complemented the Studebaker truck line, and the other Divco-Wayne operations would have been complementary to Studebaker-Packard's diversification strategy.[26] However, the negotiations between Studebaker-Packard and Divco-Wayne never became serious. Glekel believed merger with Studebaker-Packard would have involved a tremendous dilution of Divco-Wayne stock.[27]

The number of Divco trucks produced fluctuated within a narrow band between 1956 and 1966. Due to a strike in 1961 and early 1962, output in 1961 dropped to 1,783 units. In other years, Divco output ranged from 2,082 in 1963 to 3,796 in 1959. After 1960, when 3,572 Divcos were built, the company never again built over 3,000 trucks in a year. (See Appendix A, Divco Vital Statistics—Detroit, for production details.) During this period of time, a breakdown of the dollar sales and profits of the Divco Truck Division was not reported by Divco-Wayne. However, given that the rest of Divco-Wayne was growing rapidly, and Divco truck production was languishing, the Divco Truck Division was of decreasing importance to its parent firm. In fact, the Divco Division showed the least growth of all the Divco-Wayne divisions.[28]

Divco In Canada

Divco-Wayne had a wholly-owned Canadian affiliate called Welles Corporation Limited, in Windsor, Ontario. Corporate publications indicate that in the 55,000 square foot Welles plant, the company produced school bus bodies and multi-stop delivery trucks for the Canadian market. The plant was well equipped for assembly operations of that type.[29]

Welles assembled Wayne school bus bodies for the Canadian market from knock-down kits shipped from Richmond, Indiana.[30] Divco-Wayne viewed the purchase of Welles in 1963 as a natural complement to its operational patterns and as an opportunity to increase its share of the Canadian market.[31]

Very little in the way of records has survived on Divco's Canadian operations before 1956. From 1936 to 1941, *Moody's Manual of Investments* listed the Divco-Twin Truck Company of Canada as a wholly owned subsidiary of Divco-Twin. However, except for a footnote to its financial statements, no mention of that subsidiary is made in the corporate annual reports. The Divco-Twin annual report for 1941 reported that the Divco-Twin Truck Company of Canada, Limited was dissolved in 1941. There is no evidence that Divco built trucks in Canada before World War II—certainly no production facilities or assembly plants are mentioned in Divco-Twin publications or records.

On May 31, 1956, Divco Truck of Canada, Limited was formed. Its initial activities were to lease Divco trucks and handle the financial arrangements associated with leasing.[32] Although the Welles plant in Windsor, Ontario, was suited to assembly operations, it appears that Divcos sold in Canada continued to be shipped from Hoover Road. In fact, production records indicate that trucks for all of Canada—from Ontario to Vancouver and Quebec—continued to be built and shipped from Hoover Road even after the purchase of Welles in 1963.

Labor Relations

Except for minor work stoppages, Divco had relative labor peace until October 1961. Local 576 of the United Auto Workers-Congress of Industrial Organization (U.A.W.-C.I.O.) had represented Divco hourly factory workers at its principal manufacturing facility in Detroit since 1937. In 1948, a contract was signed with Local 114 of the International Union, United Plant Guards of America. Then on May 1, 1952, Local 889, U.A.W.-C.I.O. organized the office and engineering employees at Divco. At the time of the Divco-Wayne merger, Divco stated that it held frequent meetings with representatives of the Union and it regarded its relations with employees as satisfactory.[33]

Former employees of Divco and their family members are unanimous in commenting that, prior to the Divco-Wayne merger, Divco was an excellent place to work. Comments made in interviews includ-

ed several stating that working at Divco was like being part of a family. One person stated that the job at Divco was more interesting than later jobs he had at General Motors. Divco had annual picnics, Christmas parties, and nights at the Ice Capades for employees and their spouses, which helped build morale and worker loyalty. As a result, workers stated that they had pride in the plant and the units produced there.[34]

Pressures to control costs during the recessions of 1958 and 1960, combined with the drive for profits and a high return on shareholders' investment in a conglomerate, diversified firm such as Divco-Wayne caused a change in the labor relations environment in the early 1960s. During the late summer of 1961, labor relations were tense at Divco. There was a one-week wildcat strike in September, touched off by the disciplining of an employee. Later, Local 114 of the Plant Guards Union began to picket the Divco plant in a dispute over a decision by the company to hire detective agency guards rather than to employ its own people as guards. Then, on October 3, 1961, 350 members of United Autoworkers Local 576 went on strike against Divco following expiration of their contract on September 30, 1961.[35]

Kenneth Morris, retired Co-Director of Region 1 of the U.A.W. for the East End of Detroit (which included Divco) and U.A.W. representative for Divco-U.A.W. relations, stated in an interview that, over the years, the U.A.W. did not make significant demands on Divco because the company was neither wealthy nor strong. For example, Morris recalls going to New York to help negotiate a settlement to the 1961 strike. He said a major part of his time was spent serving as a mediator to resolve the plant guard dispute. The problem was that, even though the guards did not belong to the U.A.W., the U.A.W. members would not cross the plant guard picket line. Once the plant guard dispute was settled, arriving at terms on a contract for the U.A.W workers was easier.[36]

The U.A.W. strike lasted from October 3, 1961, to January 8, 1962. The new contract agreement included three annual productivity improvement factor increases of six cents an hour, fully paid hospitalization insurance, and improved pension and supplemental unemployment benefits plans.[37] Management stated that the three-year contract was noninflationary. Although the strike reduced the truck and parts inventories of Divco dealers to low levels, management believed that there was a minimal loss of orders because "the unique long-life characteristics of Divco trucks lead customers to defer replacement in the light of circumstances."[38]

Let's talk about price!

How Much Does A Milk Delivery Truck Really Cost?

You *won't* know the *real*, the *ultimate* cost of a truck until you've retired it. For whenever you figure cost you've got to include *upkeep* cost and *operating* cost, as well as the figure on the show room price tag.

HOW DO YOU FIGURE?

The best way to figure future costs is to look at the past. What do your books say about upkeep and operating and depreciation costs on the trucks you now own?

HAVE YOU OWNED A DIVCO?

If you own a Divco truck, chances are your records show very low upkeep costs for it because our experience has been that dairy after dairy operates its Divcos for more than ten years. Why? Because it's hard to wear a Divco out and Divcos do not become obsolete in appearance by frequent model changes. Ask to see proof of these statements. Your Divco dealer will be anxious to provide it and to demonstrate the cost-cutting features of the Divco truck and tell you of the many optional features available.

Drivers prefer Divco trucks because of saving in time and physical effort. Remember—your initial investment is only the beginning—the purchase of long lasting, time proven Divco Multi-stop trucks will save you dollars in the years of service to come.

DIVCO TRUCKS

 Over 80% of all Divcos ever built are still in licensed operation.

Divco always stressed that its trucks were economical and hard to wear out, but the claim that 80% of all Divcos made were still in use by the mid 1950s may have been exaggerated.

Divco—The Product

Although Divco accounted for a diminishing share of Divco-Wayne operations after 1956, the company continued product development, although not at the rate of the early 1950s. In the 1956-1967 period, Divco product development can best be described as "product refinement," because the basic product line of snub-nosed and Dividend Series trucks was continued.

In the late 1950s, Divco advertising stressed the durability and low-cost service provided by Divco trucks. In late 1950s advertising the company claimed, "Over 80% of all Divcos built are still in use." Actually, as of July 1, 1964, there were 41,351 Divco trucks officially registered in the United States, which accounted for only about 45% of Divco production from 1927 to 1964. Of the Divcos in service in 1964, 9,064 were built prior to 1951 and 17,220 were 10 years old or older.[39] There appears to be a contradiction between the company's advertising claims and the actual number of registrations. A large number of Divcos produced were not listed as registered. Exact reasons for this variance are unclear, but sales of trucks to large fleets and uncertainty of their registration status, trucks used in unregistered uses such as intra-plant, airports, and governments service, plus export sales may account for some of the differences.

A major Divco product innovation in the Divco-Wayne era was the introduction of the Divco Golden Missile four cylinder engine in late 1959. This gasoline engine was built by Continental and had overhead valves and 80 horsepower. The new four was available as optional equipment on all Divco Model Series 1, 104, 2, 204, 304 and on lighter Dividend Series multi-stop trucks.[40] After 1960, a number of engine options became available on Divcos, depending on the model. The engine options included

3-53N Diesel—101 HP
@ 2800 RPM, 2 cyl., 2 cycles

F-300, 6 cyl., OHV, 170 HP
@ 3600 RPM

Divco offered a complete line of four and six cylinder gasoline and diesel engines.

Continental, Ford, Hercules, and Nash overhead valve four and six-cylinder gasoline engines plus Detroit Diesel and Perkins diesel engines.

The last major product innovations coming out of the Detroit Divco operations were in 1963 and 1965. For the model year 1963, Divco introduced several major product improvements including the following:[41]

- Transistorized ignition as standard equipment.

- Alternator as standard equipment.

- Improved front suspension, including a new steering system with a U joint in the shaft to keep the column aligned.

- New wide-track front axle.

- A tighter, stronger body through use of a new welding technique. The body also featured greater resistance to corrosion because of a new method of applying the primer coat.

- Positive crankcase ventilation.

- Optional full-width rear doors.

For the 1965 model year, Divco made its last big new product and advertising "splash" in colorful double-page ads, it announced the new "Divco 6-Wides." The six case wide retail milk delivery truck increased milk case capacity by 20% from previous five case wide models. The improvement was made by making the rear fenders much narrower. To make its point on the " 6-Wide," Divco advertised "4 new Divco 6-Wides outwork 5 ordinary milk trucks." Divco claimed customers had a choice of nine engines, including two lightweight diesels, rated from 55 to 152 horsepower. The snub-nosed trucks were available in six body styles with payloads ranging from 2500 to 7500 pounds. The Dividend Series had three body sizes in 10ft., 12ft., and 14½ ft. models with payloads up to 9,200 pounds.[42]

One product that did not make it to market was a compact door-to-door delivery truck smaller than any existing Divco snub-nose or Dividend Series trucks. The proposal for a smaller Divco was initiated by the Michigan Bell Telephone Company, which held a meeting in 1959 with the chief engineers of American Motors, Chrysler, Divco, Ford, and General Motors to discuss a new telephone service vehicle. Representing Divco at the meeting was William R. (Ray) Chapman, Chief Engineer, who

DIVCO SNUB-NOSE REAR BODY STYLES

The solid back. Standard.

Solid back with windows.

Combination full opening doors.

Half width opening rear doors.

ABOVE: *These drawings from a 1962 Divco catalog show the different rear body styles and doors that were available.*

BELOW: *This drawing from a 1963 catalog features the 6-Wide models and shows the "squared-up" body design introduced in the mid-1950s.*

RETAIL
DELIVERY
TRUCKS

DIVCO
6-WIDE
SNUB-NOSE
MODEL
206

recalls that the vehicle makers were asked to submit a pilot vehicle of a closed van type. Chapman designed a small, unitized, van-type unit for Divco and in 1960 a prototype was built by the John Kehrig Body Company. The prototype sported Rambler hubcaps and wheels, but Chapman states American Motor components were never used in any Divco production models.[43]

The small Divco van prototype was tested at the former Packard Motor Car Company proving grounds, where it was demonstrated at a meeting of Divco dealers. Because the Michigan Bell Telephone contract by itself would not have justified the costs of tooling up for the smaller van, the dealers were asked for commitments to order the truck so that Divco could estimate the potential sales volume. The dealers did not make the necessary commitments and the vehicle never went into production. The prototype was destroyed after completion of the marketing studies.[44] In its 1960 annual report, Divco-Wayne stated that analysis of the sales of small compact

trucks introduced by foreign producers and U.S. automotive manufacturers did not justify full-scale production of a smaller Divco.[45]

During the 1960s, Divco product development included offering chassis on which fiberglass bodies were installed by the Field Body Company in El Monte, California. In a visit to Fields in 1967, Roy H. Sjoberg, Vice President of Divco sales and marketing, saw work being done on fiberglass bodies for installation on Divco chassis sold to Foremost Dairy. The chassis apparently came with the snub nose front clip up to and including the windshield, instrument panel and controls. Sjoberg noted that Field Body removed and did not use the front roof caps above the windshield. He recommended the roof caps be omitted on future orders which would save $30 per truck.[46]

Field Body installation of fiberglass bodies on Divco chassis was not just a "one-time" deal for Foremost Dairy; Divco worked with Field for several years and Sjoberg noted in a 1967 memo that he

In 1960, Divco built this small delivery van vehicle prototype. Dealers did not commit to a significant number of orders and the small van never went into production.

TOP: *Because Divcos were sold in relatively low volume, many Divco dealers (like Rihm Motor Sales in St. Paul, Minnesota) sold other truck makes.*

BOTTOM: *Tri-City Divco Sales in Rock Island, Illinois, owned by Ralph Bussard, sold Divcos from the end of World War II until Divco ended production in 1986. Tri-City Divco covered 42 counties in Illinois and Iowa. (Courtesy, Barbara Bussard)*

had visited the Field Body Company three years earlier. He also mentioned that he worked with Engs Motor Truck Sales, a large Divco dealer with three locations in California, to quote Divco chassis with either Divco steel bodies or Field fiberglass bodies for subsidiaries of the Carnation Milk Company.[47] According to Rampton Harvey, former General Manager of Engs, competitive pressures necessitated the offering of the Divco chassis for installation on the Field bodies. Several companies were making fiberglass bodies for installation on chassis built by other truck manufacturers. Harvey says that, while the largest customer was Foremost Dairy, the Divco/Field trucks became very popular throughout California.[48]

The "Six-Wides," attempts to build small vans for the telephone company, and sales of chassis for Field bodies were attempts to deal with the storm clouds that were gathering over Divco in Detroit in the 1960s. Output of Divcos in 1960 was 3,572. In 1962, even with recovery from the strike, output was only 2,883 trucks. The company explained the Divco situation to stockholders by saying, "Although industry sales have declined in those weight classes which account for the bulk of Divco's production, the Division has maintained its share of the market."[49] The statement on Divco's market share was only true in part. Most Divco trucks were sold in the 6,001 to 10,000 lb. and 10,001 to 14,000 lb. Gross Vehicle Weight (G.V.W.) classes. U.S. registrations in the 6,001 to 10,000 lb. G.V.W. class grew from 830,420 trucks in 1960 to 1,192,548 in 1964. Divco sales in that class declined from 2,072 in 1960 to 1,100 in 1964. However, most of the growth in that G.V.W. group was due to increased sales of larger pickups by the Big Three, which were not direct competition for Divco delivery trucks.[50]

The Divco claim is substantiated, though, by studying data for the 10,001 lb. to 14,000 lb. G.V.W. class which declined from 10,170 registrations in 1960 to 4,905 in 1964. Divco had an increase in registrations in that group from 817 in 1960 (8% of the market) to 1,014 in 1964 (20.7% of the market). In addition, Divco's market share of the multi-stop delivery truck market stabilized in the 5% to 8% range between 1961 and 1964 after declining steadily from its 36.3% market share in 1947.[51]

Selling Divcos

The strength of the Divco market position in its primary markets was attributed to the dealer network which assured that Divco owners and operators would receive prompt parts and maintenance service.[52] Divco advertising in the early 1960s listed where its trucks could be purchased and serviced. In February 1961, Divco had 100 dealers in the U.S., five in Canada, and two in Puerto Rico. That total of 107 dealers was an increase from 87 in 1953.[53] The dealers were the frontline in dealing with customers and making sure the production line stayed busy.

For 1965, Divco published some creative selling ideas for its dealers in a sales manual entitled "How To Sell a Divco." The manual quoted an address by Divco of Detroit Sales Manager Joe Holland to the 1964 Divco National Sales Meeting. Mr. Holland defined the concept of "Creative Selling" as creating in a prospect's mind a need or a desire for a product and then convincing the prospect your product is the best one to fill the need or desire. Following are some quotations from that address:

- *Creative Selling means getting to know your customer or prospect so well that you know his problems as well or better than he does. We have found that the solution to a customer's problems often was the addition of one or two new Divco trucks.*

- *...we asked our contact at London Dairy [in Port Huron, Michigan] to gaze out the window at an old—almost antique—truck which they were using for a spare. We recommended they purchase a new Divco to use for a spare. This would be an incentive for the routemen to bring their trucks in for service and repairs. London Dairy bought the idea...and the truck. Later, they informed us that the idea paid dividends almost from the start. The routemen did bring in their trucks at regular intervals and the trucks are lasting much longer. This is just another example of Creative Selling at work.*

- *Creative Selling makes use of psychology. Here's one example: At Detroit Divco we always keep a good stock of used trucks on hand. We put three or four year old competitive trucks up near the front gate and our own six and eight year old reconditioned Divcos are parked in the back. The comparison between the "enemy's" trucks and ours is very obvious. This makes it easier to point out how other make trucks wear out much faster than Divcos.*

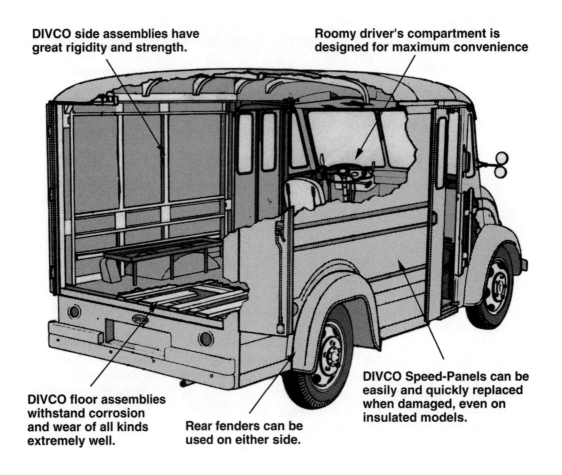

DIVCO side assemblies have great rigidity and strength.

Roomy driver's compartment is designed for maximum convenience

DIVCO floor assemblies withstand corrosion and wear of all kinds extremely well.

Rear fenders can be used on either side.

DIVCO Speed-Panels can be easily and quickly replaced when damaged, even on insulated models.

The Divco Sales Manual encouraged dealers and sales personnel to emphasize Divco's major construction features.

■ *Another offspring of our Creative Selling efforts has been the convincing of customers to trade faster. This can be extremely important to you. Think how much more profit you make when you sell a Divco every four years to a customer instead of every eight years. Also, when you take a four year old trade-in it costs much less to recondition than an eight year old truck. Thus you make a profit on the new truck you sell and on the trade-in. We try to instill in our customers, especially the many owner-drivers in our territory the desire for a new truck. Then we persuade them to trade while they still have sufficient equity in the truck that will provide an adequate down payment on a new truck. This approach works surprisingly well.*

■ *We take a new Divco truck out to the customer's or prospect's place of business. Whenever possible we park it alongside one of their older models. Then we almost literally take him by the hand from one feature to another and let him see for himself how the 1253 improvements in a 1965 Divco over a 1955 Divco will benefit him.*

■ *In summation, we always try to remember one rule. What's in it for the customer?*

The ideas of Mr. Holland and the push for all Divco dealers to engage in "Creative Selling" made marketing sense and, given the weakening market for Divcos in the mid-1960s, those marketing suggestions were a necessity. The reasons for Divco being in decline and the company's response to its challenges are the topic of the next chapter.

America's Favorite Milk Truck

In its *1958 Annual Report*, Divco-Wayne boasted "75% of the milk delivered in the U.S. is delivered in Divco Trucks."[1] There is no question Divco trucks delivered large quantities of milk to American homes. When Divco purchased Wayne Works, Inc. in 1956, the Divco Proxy Statement stated that approximately 88% of Divco truck sales were made to the dairy industry.[2] Divcos also were used for a variety of delivery tasks by bakeries, laundries and dry cleaners, parcel delivery firms, drug stores, florists, newspapers, magazines, diaper and linen services, food and beverage distributors, chemical houses, frozen food suppliers, and even airlines for servicing planes. In the end, though, it was the home milk delivery business that determined the fate of Divco.

In the 1930s, when Divco began to come into its own as "America's Favorite Milk Truck," no one could have foreseen that the seeds of the company's demise were being sown. It is one of the ironies of the Divco story that by the mid-1930s, and long before its peak years of production in the late 1940s, the factors that were to bring an end to the company were already taking form. By the end of World War II, changing market conditions in the dairy industry caused a number of complex factors to come together that were destined to cause problems for Divco as a builder of milk trucks.

In spite of Divco's attempts to broaden its markets, it was best known for being "America's Favorite Milk Truck."

Divco and the Home Delivery of Milk

When Divco-Detroit Corporation was formed in 1927 it was in response to the growing need for motorized vehicles in the milk home delivery market. Until after World War II, 80% of milk sold was retailed through home delivery. The lack of refrigeration (except for ice boxes) made daily home delivery of milk a necessity. In the nineteenth century, the milkman presided over a horse-drawn wagon laden with small tin cans of milk. Using a quart measure, the milkman poured the amount of milk the customer wanted into a pitcher. Later, the dozen or so small tin cans were replaced with two larger ones equipped with stirrers (to mix the unhomogenized milk) and faucets.[3] By the 1920s, the emergence of the motor truck as a replacement for the milk wagon and horse was under way (See Chapter 2). In the two decades between the World Wars milk wagons and, increasingly, milk trucks were familiar parts of the American landscape. Because Divco was best known for its milk trucks, its history was linked to fundamental trends in the consumption of dairy products. Figures 6-1, 6-2, and 6-3 show some of the trends that ultimately sealed the fate of Divco. A steady decline in the per capita consumption of milk and all dairy products after World War II and a steady increase in the price of milk established a trend that finally took its toll in the near disappearance of the home delivery of milk.[4]

World War II was an important turning point for the milk industry. For that reason, and due to the cessation of Divco truck production during the war from 1942 through most of 1944, much of the statistical analysis undertaken here is confined to the postwar era. Consistently reported production data on Divco are available only through September 1967 and registration data are available only through 1964. Therefore, complete statistical analysis beyond 1967 is not possible. Even 1967 data must be treated carefully because it deals with less than a full year of production. Therefore, the graphs are complete only through 1966, the last full year of Divco production in Detroit. Beginning with 1968, Divco output declined dramatically with the transfer of production to Delaware, Ohio. Whereas production in Detroit in 1965 and 1966 was about 2,000 trucks per year, in Delaware, it typically ranged from 100 to 150 trucks annually.

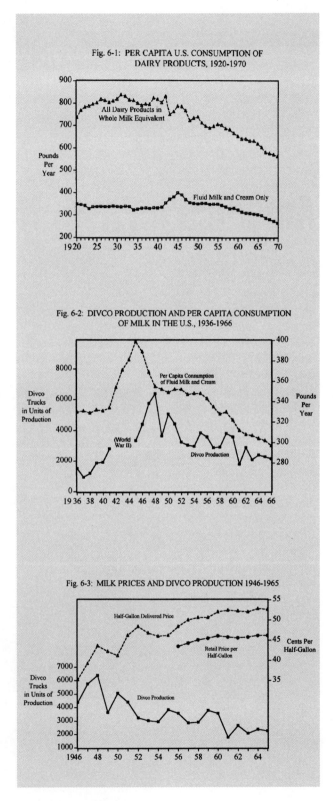

OPPOSITE AND PAGE 80: *Divco tried to reduce its dependency on the milk home-delivery market by making its trucks attractive to a wide variety of vocations as listed in these pages from the Divco Sales Manual.*

LISTING OF POTENTIAL DIVCO CUSTOMERS

A careful examination of this check-list of potential DIVCO truck customers may suggest to you many prospects whom you may never have considered before as possible customers. As you discover them, add other categories and vocations to this listing. Cross-check this list with the yellow pages of your local phone directory to obtain new sales leads and additional names for your mailing lists.

APPLIANCE & FURNITURE DELIVERIES

1. Appliance stores
2. Appliance maintenance services, i.e., washer, dryer, refrigeration, etc.
3. Carpet and rug installers
4. Carpet and rug, department and furniture stores
5. Furniture repair and reupholstery companies
6. Lamp and electrical fixtures stores
7. Sewing machine companies
8. Radio and television sales and maintenance shops

AIR LINES

1. Airport catering services
2. Air express pickup and delivery
3. Airport and airplane maintenance
4. Baggage handling and transfer

AUTOMOTIVE SUPPLY COMPANIES

1. Automotive repair—wholesale and retail service parts
2. Battery service and supply companies
3. Engine repair and rebuilding companies
4. Gasoline and oil companies—wholesale delivery
5. Radiator repair shops
6. Service station maintenance vehicles
7. Tire sales and service companies

ARMORED CAR MESSENGER SERVICE

1. Payroll, currency and securities delivery
2. Bonded messenger service

BAKING INDUSTRY

1. Bread deliveries—wholesale and retail
2. Pastry deliveries—wholesale and retail

BEVERAGE INDUSTRIES

1. Beer—wholesale and retail distributors
2. Breweries and distilleries
3. Liquor distributors—wholesale
4. Mineral water—retail deliveries
5. Soft drink bottlers
6. Soft drink distributors

CANDY & TOBACCO INDUSTRIES

1. Candy manufacturers
2. Candy and tobacco distributors—wholesale and retail
3. Confectioners

CATERERS

1. Sandwich shops
2. Caterer's service

COFFEE & SPICE DISTRIBUTORS

1. Wholesale and retail route deliveries

CONTRACTORS & SURVEYORS

1. General service vehicles
2. Maintenance vehicles

DAIRY INDUSTRY

1. Ice companies
2. Ice cream and related frozen dairy products, i.e., Dairy Queen, Dairy Freeze, etc.
3. Milk deliveries—wholesale and retail
4. Milk equipment processors
5. Producers and distributors of butter and cheese products—wholesale and retail

DELIVERY SERVICE COMPANIES

DEPARTMENT STORES

1. Branch store and retail deliveries

DRUG COMPANIES

1. Drug manufacturers
2. Drug deliveries—wholesale and retail
3. Drug store and pharmacy deliveries

ELECTRICAL CONTRACTOR & SUPPLY HOUSES

1. Installation and service vehicles
2. Wholesale delivery units

FOOD & FOOD SERVICES

1. Frozen foods—wholesale and retail deliveries
2. Frozen foods plan
3. Food locker plants

SALES MANUAL

POTENTIAL DIVCO OWNERS

LISTING OF POTENTIAL DIVCO CUSTOMERS (Cont'd)

FOOD & FOOD SERVICES (cont'd)
4. General groceries—retail deliveries
5. Meat deliveries—wholesale and retail
6. Produce deliveries—wholesale and retail
7. Supermarkets—retail deliveries
8. Wholesale food distributors

HOME MAINTENANCE SERVICES
1. Floor sanders and refinisher's vehicles
2. Painter's service trucks
3. Pest control service trucks
4. Plumber's service trucks
5. Carpenter's and heating specialist's service trucks
6. Sewer cleaner's service trucks
7. Wall paper hanger and remover's service trucks
8. Washer, dryer and refrigeration maintenance vehicles
9. Window shade, drapery and curtain installer's vehicles

INDUSTRIAL FIRMS
1. Catering and/or food service vehicles
2. General maintenance vehicles
3. Inter-intra-plant general utility vehicles
4. Plant mail vehicles
5. Short haul pickup and delivery

JANITORIAL SERVICES
1. Window cleaning service trucks
2. Floor cleaning and polishing service trucks

LANDSCAPERS & GARDENERS

LAUNDRY & DRYCLEANING INDUSTRY
1. Commercial linen and towel supply—wholesale and retail
2. Commercial uniform rental services
3. Diaper services
4. Dry cleaners—wholesale and retail
5. Fur storage service
6. Laundry pickup and delivery—wholesale and retail
7. Rug and curtain cleaners

MUNICIPAL, STATE, & GOVERNMENTAL AGENCIES
1. Water departments
2. Boards of education
3. General service vehicles; i.e., mail, messenger, etc.
4. Parks and recreation departments
5. Traffic signal maintenance vehicles
6. Public works departments (maint.)
7. Civil Defense ambulance units and service vehicles

NEWSPAPER, MAGAZINE, PRINTERS, PUBLISHERS, AND DISTRIBUTORS
1. General office supply houses
2. General printing houses
3. Newspaper and magazine deliveries—wholesale and retail
4. Printing paper supply houses

OFFICE MACHINE COMPANIES & DISTRIBUTORS
I. General delivery vehicles
2. Office machine repair, pickup and delivery vehicles

PARCEL DELIVERY SERVICES

PET SHOPS

POTATO CHIP MANUFACTURERS, DISTRIBUTORS & WHOLESALES

POULTRY AND EGG WHOLESALE & RETAIL DELIVERY

PLUMBING & HEATING
1. Independent plumbing and heating contractors
2. Wholesale and retail deliveries

PUBLIC UTILITY SERVICES
1. Service and repair trucks: gas, electric, telephone and telegraph, street lighting, street railway and bus lines
2. Mail and messenger service vehicles

REFRIGERATION SALES, SERVICE & MAINTENANCE

SOFT WATER SERVICES

STORAGE & TRANSFER COMPANIES

TELEVISION & RADIO STATIONS
1. Mobile TV and radio broadcasting and monitoring units
2. Transporters and maintenance vehicles

TRUCK RENTAL & LEASING SERVICES

VENDING MACHINE SERVICES

TRAVELING LIBRARIES & OFFICES

MOBILE SALES ROOMS

80

Borden's of Utica, New York delivered its milk in this fleet of Divcos. Fred Mazzi, chief mechanic, is on the left and Ed Merrifield, another Borden's of Utica employees, is on the right.

(Courtesy Oneida County Historical Society)

Per capita milk consumption peaked in the U.S. during World War II. In 1945 consumption was 399 pounds of fluid milk and cream per person. By 1966, it had declined about 25% to 297 pounds per person. That decline continued, and by 1985 (the last full year of Divco production), per capita consumption of fluid milk and cream was only 222 pounds. Consumption of all dairy products, which includes milk, cream, cheese, butter, and ice cream, (as measured in fluid milk equivalent), peaked in 1942 at 832 pounds per capita and decreased to 604 pounds by 1966.

Figures 6-1 and 6-2 show the sharp jump in milk consumption during World War II as well as the steady decrease in all dairy product and milk consumption after the war. Both civilian and military milk consumption increased during the war even though, at times, milk supplies were tight. Civilian consumption rose as a result of improved economic and employment conditions and rising purchasing power. The increased consumption of milk also was consistent with the advice of nutritionists who considered milk a prime wartime food because of the high percentage of daily food requirements it supplies.[5] In fact, concern arose during the war that fresh milk might have to be rationed to meet both civilian and military needs. In the end, however, milk rationing was avoided although cheese, butter and evaporated milk for civilian consumption were rationed.

Even though rationing of milk did not occur, there were significant changes during the war in the delivery of milk. Two major factors caused these changes:

first, there was a wartime need to conserve fuel and rubber at a point in time when there was excess milk delivery capacity. Milk trucks were not being fully utilized, because the load per route tended to be small. Second, consumer income fell during the Great Depression of the 1930s which hastened the trend of consumers buying milk from stores.[6]

As a result of the need to conserve trucks, fuel, rubber, and labor during World War II, the delivery of milk was converted to an every-other-day (EOD) system. When the refrigeration capabilities of households were limited, every-day delivery was a virtual necessity if families were to have fresh milk. The advent of mechanical refrigeration plus the desire of drivers to have a day off each week, led to six days per week delivery with each customer getting milk on alternate days. Later, delivery was limited to only five days per week.[7] Dairies embraced EOD because it reduced the relatively high cost of home delivery. The cost of retail delivery (including collection of accounts) was between four and five cents per quart in smaller cities and up to six cents per quart in Chicago and New York.[8] Four cents per quart was 28% of the 14.2 cents per quart average retail price of milk in 1942. Delivery costs of six cents per quart were 42% of the average retail price.[9]

Labor costs were increasing by the early 1940s. In 1929, the milk truck driver's average weekly earnings were equal to the farm price of 760 quarts of milk, by 1940 it was equal to the value of 1,320 quarts.[10] Increased relative wages combined with a reduction in the number of retail customers per mile caused a serious cost problem for dairies. The reduction in customers per mile and reduced loads was caused by the shift from home delivery to store purchases. Store purchases of milk were influenced by lower consumer income during the Depression and by an increase in the number of women working who found shopping at a grocery store on their way home from work convenient.[11] For example, store sales of milk in New York City rose from 30 percent of the total in 1930 to 50% in 1941.[12]

The war provided both an excuse and an opportunity for milk distributors to attempt to reduce delivery costs, and every-other-day service was a key element in the plan. After Pearl Harbor, EOD was adopted voluntarily by many milk dealers throughout the country. By May 1943, two-thirds of the milk delivered in the U.S. was on an EOD basis.[13] That month, the Office of Defense Transportation issued an order requiring EOD for home delivery. Deliveries were made every day, but only half of the route was served on a given day, and two days' supply of milk was delivered at one time. The net result was a reduction in route mileage and, consequently, a reduction in delivery trucks needed. A survey of Connecticut milk dealers revealed that going to EOD meant a

LEFT: *Miller Brothers Creamery Co. of Mount Clemens, Michigan, founded in the early 1920s, was a loyal Divco customer. Before Divcos, though, they used wagons. Shown here in a 1925 photo is Arthur Miller with his son, Ralph.*
(Courtesy, Macomb County Historical Society)

This crew of Miller Brothers drivers had the privilege of driving a new fleet of 1933 Model H Divcos.
(Courtesy, Macomb County Historical Society)

Through the years, Miller Brothers kept upgrading its Divco fleet. Here is Driver Del Reese with a 1948 Divco.
(Courtesy, Macomb County Historical Society)

40% reduction in the use of delivery equipment in addition to similar savings in labor, gasoline, tires, and oil.[14]

Following the war, every-other-day delivery evolved into three-day-a-week delivery. Drivers enjoyed the three-day-a-week plan because it assured them of having Sunday and certain holidays like Christmas off. Consumers liked the plan because they knew exactly which days each week they would get milk: half of the customers on a route would get milk on Monday, Wednesday, and Friday and the other half on Tuesday, Thursday, and Saturday. The elimination of Sunday deliveries meant 52 fewer delivery days each year with consequent savings in truck mileage. J. F. Malone, a representative of Borden's, reported at a Milk Industry Foundation convention in 1949 that a return to daily delivery from three-day-a-week would increase operating costs 2.5 cents per quart.[15]

In addition to hastening a reduction in the number of days milk was delivered, the war led to a change in the time of day for milk delivery. Dairies had assumed that milk had to be delivered before breakfast to keep customers happy. The driver, though, had to contend with collecting bills and selling which meant re-tracing the route a second time several days per week. To reduce mileage during the war, many milk dealers went to daylight delivery which meant the driver could deliver, collect, and sell all in the same trip.[16]

World War II, therefore, brought greater efficiency to the home delivery of milk and other dairy products. The advent of every-other-day and then three-day-a-week delivery reduced the mileage accumulated by milk trucks. As a result of trucks driving less mileage and making fewer trips, the load factors improved for milk delivery trucks. For example, in one Eastern market, a study of 1,051 milk routes showed that within one year of adopting EOD and daylight delivery, the quarts delivered per route per day increased from 303 to 359 (an 18% increase) and customers per route increased from 290 to 311 (a 7% increase).[17] Greater efficiency in delivery could only mean, in the end, a relative decline in the number of milk trucks needed with consequent long-term negative implications for Divco.

Divco may have had some concerns about the impact of changing milk delivery trends. The 1942 Divco-Twin Truck Company survey sent to all dairies in the United States had the objective of trying to forecast the demand for Divco-Twin type vehicles once wartime production restrictions were removed. Results of the survey were encouraging. "Replies to the questionnaire were very gratifying," wrote John Nicol, president of Divco-Twin. "Orders on hand and the results of the survey indicate that when we are permitted to manufacture trucks...our sales will be greatly increased over the last period of peacetime business."[18]

By the end of 1945, the effects of the nation's wartime shortage of motor vehicles were being felt by Divco, which had an impressive order backlog worth $13.5 million. Divco was so optimistic that the Board of Directors authorized $600,000 to double the capacity of the Hoover Road.[19] Figure 6-3 shows that the optimism at Divco was warranted in the immediate postwar period: in 1948, Divco production (6,385 trucks) reached a peak. By the end of the 1940s, though, the storm clouds began to gather.

"Carry Out" Milk

At the end of World War II, over 80% of the milk sold in America was still home delivered;[20] in 1963, 29.7% of milk was home delivered, and in 1985 (the last full year of Divco production), only 1.5% of milk was home delivered. By the 1990s, home deliveries of milk had dropped to one percent of all retail milk sales.[21] What happened and why did it happen? The trend to store sales of milk was not just a post-World War II phenomenon. The seeds of the retail store trend were sown a quarter of a century before the first Divco was produced. In the early 1900s, groceries and supermarkets carried milk as a convenience item to accommodate people who found they needed an extra quart after the milkman was gone.

The Depression of the 1930s hastened the rise of the retail store as an outlet for milk. The farm price and wholesale price of milk weakened early in the Depression. For example, the U.S. Department of Agriculture reported in the 1936 edition of *Agricultural Statistics* that the milk dealers' average buying price per hundredweight for 3.5% butterfat milk dropped from $2.81 in 1929 to $1.60 in 1933 before recovering somewhat to $2.05 in 1935. Even

with the decline in milk prices at the dealer level dairies were able to hold home delivered prices firm for a while. Eventually, though, the chain stores saw the increasing gap between retail and wholesale prices as an opportunity to obtain cheap supplies of milk and offer that milk to consumers at a reduced price on a "cash and carry" basis. As early as 1922, Harvey Hood II, of Boston's Hood Dairy complained at the Milk Dealers' Convention that supermarkets were selling milk and cream below cost. The Hood organization itself had opened a freestanding shop (i.e., one not adjacent to the milk plant) to sell fresh milk, cream, and buttermilk as early as 1899.[22] Stores often used milk as a loss leader item, and many consumers, because of their economic circumstances, took advantage of the typical one to two cents per quart price differential to help their budgets.[23]

In a 1941 article in the *Harvard Business Review*, Albert Freiberg argued home delivery of milk, far from being a necessity, was a luxury.[24] He noted that bread wagons disappeared when chain stores developed their own bakeries, distributed to their stores, and sold baked goods cheaper than the bread wagons. Similarly, home delivery of milk was considered a luxury because it was cheaper to sell fresh milk over the counter than to deliver it in quart bottles to the home.

The purpose of Freiberg's article was to argue that government resale price maintenance for milk was the true cause of higher milk prices, not the distribution system for which consumers, apparently, were willing to pay when they paid a premium for home delivery. The milk pricing system was complex. Basically, under the Agricultural Adjustment Act of 1933 and the Agricultural Marketing Agreement Acts of 1935 and 1937, a two-thirds majority of the farmers in an interstate region called a "milkshed" could establish the price paid by all milk dealers in the area. If the government relaxed these pricing regulations, Freiberg believed milk prices would come down.[25]

In arguing that consumers in 1941 were willing to pay extra for the luxury of home delivery of milk, Freiberg presented a scenario that helps explain the demise of home delivery. The changing patterns of home delivery during the Second World War, combined with home refrigeration capabilities. made home delivery of milk less necessary in the 1940s. As a result, home delivery became a convenience and luxury for which a diminishing proportion of consumers was willing to pay the additional cost.

Dairies engaged in the home delivery of milk were faced with a double marketing problem in the postwar period. One difficulty was that the dairy industry did not participate in the postwar economic boom, because milk and dairy product consumption declined on a per capita basis (see Figures 6-1 and 6-2). That decline occurred even though per capita disposable income (that is, the amount of after-tax income) more than doubled in the 1946 to 1966 period. Even after adjustments for inflation are considered, the purchasing power of after-tax income per person increased by almost 50%.[26]

Changes in milk consumption by American consumers and the emergence of grocery stores as major retailers of milk meant dairies were confronted with increased competition for home delivery. There was little doubt as to the objectives of food stores in the competitive battle over milk. At the 48th Annual Convention of the National Association of Retail Grocers (held in San Francisco from June 22 to 26, 1947), L. V. Eberhard, who owned a chain of grocery stores in Grand Rapids, Michigan, made the following statements:

Milk as a daily need is the main item in this [dairy] department and should be the important factor in luring Mrs. Consumer to your store — more times per week. The more you can get her to depend on you for her daily wants — the sooner she steps into your doorway — the better chance you have of selling her items from the grocery, meat, and produce departments. We should do all in our power to help move the milk business from home delivery to the retail stores.[27]

The major competitive advantage the grocery stores had was their pricing. Figure 6-3 shows the trend in the home-delivered and store-price of a half-gallon of milk. The only years for which comparative data are available on the delivered price and store price of a half-gallon of milk are 1956 through 1965 (see Figure 6-3). In 1956, the national average price of a home-delivered half-gallon was 48.4 cents while for a store-purchased half-gallon it was 43.5 cents, for an almost five cent or 11% differential. By 1965, the home-delivered price had increased to 52.6 cents, and the retail store price averaged 46.2 cents for an absolute difference of 6.4 cents or a nearly 14% differential.[28] In terms of both the cents per half-gallon and percentage spread, the price of home-delivered milk was increasing relative to store bought milk.

A statistical analysis was undertaken on the relationship of the delivered price of a half-gallon of milk and other variables and the production of Divcos from 1941 to 1966. The analysis shows that about 75% of the variation in the production of Divco trucks is statistically associated with the inflation-adjusted (real) rising price of home-delivered milk, along with two other variables including the participation rate of women in the work force and per capita consumption of milk and dairy products. (See Appendix G for more details on the statistical analysis.)

Although a home-delivered half-gallon of milk increased in price by 50% between 1946 and 1965, and all dairy products (on average) increased in price by 38%, other consumer prices rose by a larger amount. The Consumer Price Index for all items increased by 59% and for all food consumed at home, it increased by 64.4% in the same period. Therefore, milk and other dairy products became cheaper relative to other goods in general and other foods in particular. Given that dairy products became comparatively less expensive, economic theory would predict demand for them would increase. Yet meat, which increased in price by 87% had an 8.4% increase in per capita consumption in the 1946-1965 period. There was 43.3% price inflation for processed fruits and vegetables, but per capita consumption of canned vegetables increased 4.1% and frozen vegetables per capita consumption increased 590% from 1946-1965. Sugar and sweets increased in price by 63.4%, but per capita consumption of sugar increased about 29% in the 1946-1965 period.

What do these statistics mean for Divco? Essentially, they tell us Divco was a supplier to a declining industry—at least declining in its relative importance to the American consumer. Rising incomes meant fruits and vegetables, sugar and sweets, and meats commanded an increasing share of the consumer's food dollar. As Americans became more affluent, they consumed less milk and more of other food products per capita.

Milk dealers responded to the competitive threat to home delivery by increasing the variety of products sold from the milk truck and, ultimately, selling the trucks to the drivers. Many milk trucks became mini-grocery stores on wheels. The products that drivers began to sell from milk trucks included ice cream, chocolate milk, orangeade, and cottage cheese. Beginning in the mid-1930s, *The Milk Dealer* magazine had many articles discussing the marketing prospects for these various products.[29] Increasing the variety of products available through home delivery may have slowed the decline in home delivery, but it certainly did not halt it. As competition from the stores intensified, it became necessary for milk dealers to pay attention to the pricing of home delivered milk. As a result, by 1956, the use of quantity discounts for home-delivered milk had become widespread in 25 major urban milk markets. The single most important reason that dairies instituted quantity discounts was that the discounts were necessary to meet the competition of stores that had no delivery expense.[30]

The milk truck driver/salesperson also began to feel the heat generated by store competition. In order to keep the price of home-delivered milk competitive with store milk, drivers took steps to reduce milk prices. In 1954, drivers for six Detroit dairies (members of the Milk Drivers and Dairy Employees Local No. 155, American Federation of Labor) withdrew a request for a $12-a-week raise in return for an agreement by the dairies to cut milk prices an equivalent of $12 a week on each route. Under the plan, customers received a three cents per quart discount on purchases greater than 30 quarts per month and customers buying 89 or more quarts per month received the discount on their entire purchase.[31]

Another distribution innovation used in the 1960s was for dairies to sell or lease milk routes to the drivers. This attempt to counter declining home delivery volume and rising unit costs for delivered milk had a direct impact on the drivers.[32] Borden Farm Products Division of New York City leased its routes to supervisory personnel who were set up as sub-dealers. The routes were leased on a five year basis, which could be extended for successive five year terms. The sub-dealers had jurisdiction over an average of 20 routes each. In Detroit, Twin-Pines Dairy, with 550 retail routes and 35% of the city's home delivery business, began operating driver-owned routes in 1941. In 1959, the Sealtest (National Dairy Products) and the Borden operations in Detroit sold their routes to their drivers who were members of United Dairy Workers Local 83; 625 drivers were affected. Each driver invested $7,000 to $8,000 in the routes. The amount of the investment was based on accounts outstanding and value of the truck; payments were spread out to minimize hardship on the drivers. Another Detroit dairy, Ira Wilson, sold 151 routes to its drivers in 1960.[33]

And what happened to the leased routes over the next decade or so? By the early 1960s, only 30% of the milk sold was home-delivered. By 1970 (about the time the milk trucks purchased or leased in these deals were wearing out), home delivery was down to 15% of the market, and by 1980, it was only about 2%.[34] As home-delivered milk sales declined, not many of the drivers who had bought their routes in

the 1960s would have been able to afford the purchase of a new truck. No precise data are available, but we can assume that as trucks wore out and drivers aged, routes became consolidated, drivers retired along with their aging Divcos, and the market for "America's Favorite Milk Truck" shrank dramatically. From a production peak of 6,385 trucks in 1948, Divco production slipped to 3,839 in 1955, to 3,572 in 1960 and to 2,131 in 1966. After Divco moved to Delaware, production in the 1970s and early 1980s typically was about 150 units per year but in some years was fewer than 100.

Divco Responds to the Market

There are two dimensions to the Divco response to its changing market: efforts in the milk truck industry and an attempt to broaden the overall market for Divco products.

As the home delivery of milk began to decline, Divco adjusted by offering dairies larger trucks with more capacity. The move to every-other-day delivery and the suburbanization of America meant milk trucks had to travel longer distances with larger and heavier loads. In 1940, only 15% of Americans lived in suburbs in metropolitan areas. By 1950, suburbanites accounted for almost 25% of the population, and in 1960, over 30% of the U.S. population lived in the suburbs. The 1970 census reported that almost 40% of Americans were suburbanites while 30% lived in the central cities. By 1980 and 1990, the share of the population living in suburbia was about 45% and 47%, respectively.[35] Therefore, to survive in the competitive environment, Divco had to "suburbanize" its trucks to accommodate longer routes in suburban areas.

As early as 1939 Divco recognized the need for a truck larger than the 100¾ inch wheelbase Model UM. As a result, the 127½ inch wheelbase Model ULM was designed for combined wholesale-retail routes requiring a heavier and larger capacity truck. Whereas the Model UM carried 50 cases of milk, the first 1939 ULMs could handle 85. By 1948, Divco was advertising that the Model ULM-5 could carry 96 iced wood cases. In 1950, Divco further diversified its product line by bringing out the 115 inch wheelbase model.

The Series 1 trucks (Models 11, 12, 13, 14 and 15, variously equipped with four and six cylinder engines depending on customer orders) were considered "average duty" trucks by Divco; they were designed for the average multi-stop milk route of under 30 miles in length. Series 3, (Models 334 and 374) had 6-cylinder engines (either the 229.6, 75 horsepower or 252.6 cubic inch, 114 horsepower models). Considered heavy duty trucks, these models were for heavy city or suburban delivery, usually of routes under 50 miles. The "extra heavy duty" Divco was the Model 214 for "routes of most any length."[36]

Through the years, the Divco model line evolved to include larger trucks designed to meet the needs of longer suburban and country routes. As home delivery of milk declined, those dairies still offering the service looked for improved efficiency in their trucks. Therefore, in 1965 Divco further accommodated the need for larger trucks to serve longer routes by introducing its line of "Divco 6-Wides" which increased milk case capacity by 20% in the 200 and 300 series.

To secure and strengthen its position as the leading milk truck, Divco promoted its line of refrigerated models. For example, the *1953 Annual Report* stated that refrigerated trucks would have a beneficial effect on sales because the trend to refrigerated delivery was expected to continue in the future.[37] In another attempt to appeal to a wider segment of the dairy industry, Divco experimented with expanding the Dividend Series trucks to cover the wholesale milk delivery business. The "Val-U-Van" was introduced at the Dairy Industry Supply Association Exhibit in Chicago in the fall of 1960.[38] The "Val-U-Van" had a Dividend-style cab but with a separate large 16-foot refrigerated aluminum body capable of carrying 13,000 pounds of cargo. Divco hoped the Val-U-Van would provide customers who had large fleets of Divco vehicles with a companion Divco wholesale unit, thus saving maintenance costs by standardizing spare parts, tools, etc. The Val-U-Van was available with the customer's choice of gasoline, Perkins, or Detroit Diesel engines.[39]

When the "Val-U-Van" was introduced, Divco-Wayne said it was scheduled for field testing and "cautious market entry" during 1961.[40] Production records of the company do not reveal the quantity of production of this specific model. A prototype was built (a picture appeared in the January 1961 edition of *Commercial Car Journal*), but Ray Chapman, former chief engineer at Divco, said actual sales of the Val-U-Van are uncertain. However, it was an interesting concept aimed at the wholesale milk delivery market which was growing as more supermarkets became the center for retailing milk.

From Model ULMs to 6-Wides and refrigeration, Divco innovated its product line to respond to the challenges of a declining home-delivery market. But these innovations were not enough to keep Divco in business, even though the overall multi-stop truck business was growing. In 1947, there were 15,876 multi-stop trucks shipped from U.S. factories. By 1955, it was 23,853 and in 1966 it was 36,634.[41] Multi-stop delivery trucks encompassed a far broader market than just milk home delivery; included were everything from bakery and dry cleaner trucks to parcel delivery (such as United Parcel Service) and wholesale (store delivery) trucks. Divco's share of this market declined rather steadily for most of the period from 1947 to 1966, as shown in Figure 6-4. A more dramatic response was needed.

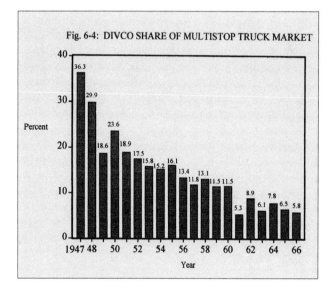

Fig. 6-4: DIVCO SHARE OF MULTISTOP TRUCK MARKET

Divco Responds to the General Multi-Stop Market

Early in its history, Divco recognized the importance of broadening its appeal beyond the milk-delivery market. In order to attract a wider range of customers, it published a large and impressive brochure in the late-1920s entitled, "Facts About House-to-House Sales," that was aimed directly at the home-delivered bakery business. This Divco brochure not only demonstrated the advantages of Divco Model B trucks but also attempted to expand the market by convincing bakeries they should engage in home delivery. Following is a quote from that brochure:

The most successful bakery organizations in the country realize that a direct contact with their customers assists in building up sales and creating consumer good will. This contact is obtained in a variety of ways, the most important of which is the delivery of bakery products to the home... In this way, a greater degree of independence is won from the grocery, delicatessen and other agencies of distribution that do little toward pushing the sale of a particular brand of bakery products.

The quotation suggests that even before the 1930s, Divco was aware and concerned about the growing trend for retail food distribution to move away from home delivery and toward grocery stores and supermarkets.

When the Model U was introduced in 1938, it was aimed at a wide market. The introductory brochure, "Divco-Twin Presents a Sensational New Model U," stated that the truck was designed for low-cost, door-to-door delivery for "Dairies, Bakeries, Laundries, Dry Cleaners, Department Stores, Parcel Delivery." Later in 1938, when the Model UL nine foot panel body truck was introduced, Divco published a brochure specifically aimed at "Laundries, Dry Cleaners, Department Stores, Parcel Delivery, Florists, and Wholesale Bakeries." The usual Divco features, including a low through-aisle and ability to idle seven hours on one gallon of gas, were enthusiastically described as meeting the needs of house-to-house delivery.

In spite of these efforts, only a very small percentage of Divco trucks were sold to non-dairy customers. In its *1941 Annual Report*, the Divco-Twin Truck Company listed 60 customers who had purchased 40 or more Divco-Twin trucks as of December 3, 1941; these 60 customers had a total of 10,376 Divcos in use. Two customers —Borden's (2,953 trucks) and National Dairy (1,551 trucks)— accounted for (43%) of those sales. Only 333 of the Divcos listed were owned by clearly identifiable non-dairy firms: 195 by Helms Bakery of Los Angeles and 138 by Spang Baking Company of Cleveland, Ohio. Sixty trucks were owned by Baker Truck Rental of Denver, Colorado, but their usage was uncertain. Therefore, only 3.2% of Divcos in use by major fleet buyers at the outbreak of World War II was for non-dairy purposes.

Divco management appears to have been keenly aware of the changing dynamics of the milk home-delivery market after World War II. Given the relatively small sales to non-dairy customers, a dispro-

portionate amount of space was devoted to these markets in the annual report to Stockholders for the 1946 to 1949 period. For example, in the *1946 Annual Report*, John Nicol stated:

"While in the past we have sold our product primarily to the milk industry, and secondly to the house-to-house bakery industry, we now find that practically all industries making house-to-house delivery are turning with great favor to our practical and patented type of vehicle."[42]

The 1946 through 1949 Divco annual reports display several pages of trucks sold to bakeries, breweries, newspapers, meat markets, coffee retailers, water-softening companies, and airlines.

Even though Divco continued to print brochures aimed at the non-dairy market, by the mid-1950s, it appeared as though the multi-stop delivery truck market was beginning to pass Divco by. Divco was able to boast in 1958 that 75% of the milk delivered in the U.S. was delivered in Divco trucks;[43] however, many of those trucks had been in service for years. As of July 1, 1959, there were 46,267 Divco trucks in use but only 13,019 (28%) were built in the previous five years. Ford, International, GMC and White, all principal competitors of Divco, had built between 36% and 44% of their trucks in use in the previous 5 years.[44] At the time of the merger of Divco and the Wayne Works, Divco stated that it "supplies approximately 50% of all vehicles sold for retail milk delivery and a much smaller percent of vehicles sold for retail delivery in other fields."[45] Clearly, Divco was still closely attached to and associated with the dairy industry, which accounted for 88% of its sales.[46]

Divco faced competition from five large producers of trucks in the multi-stop market.[47] Dodge, Ford, General Motors (GMC and Chevrolet), International, and White enjoyed market success in the 1950s, increasing their share of the multi-stop truck market as Divco's market share declined (see Figure 6-4). These firms engaged in aggressive marketing of their multi-stop vehicles, which included the Ford Parcel Delivery Van, International Metro, White PDQs, and Dodge Job-Rated Route Vans. In addition, Dodge, Ford, GMC/Chevrolet, and International all sold chassis on which delivery bodies were installed by manufacturers, such as Boyertown, Hoover-York, Montpelier, Dekalb, Hackney, Herman, Vanette, and others.

The Divco "milk-truck" image was difficult to change. Although it was serviceable, reliable, and adaptable to a variety of uses, the snub-nosed Divco

The Dividend Series was introduced to help Divco penetrate the wholesale delivery market, but this Dividend was sold by Tri-City Divco to a dairy.

(Courtesy, Barbara Bussard)

was still regarded as primarily a milk truck. To penetrate into the growing non-dairy multi-stop truck market Divco understood that a totally new truck had to be developed. The Dividend Series, introduced in 1955, was the Divco response to the changing conditions in the multi-stop truck market.

The Dividend Series Divcos were quite different from the snub-nosed models. Dividend Divcos were forward control trucks in the 8,000 to 16,500 pound Gross Vehicle Weight category. They were designed for such industries as bakeries, wholesale florists, dry cleaners, and similar wholesale and retail operations. The standard engine was the Divco Super Six, 252.6

cubic inch overhead-valve engine. The new models featured a wide, deep windshield giving the driver excellent vision—almost to street level—in front of the truck. In addition, new springing and double-acting shock absorbers provided a smooth ride.[48] Dividend Series Divcos initially were offered in 117- and 130-inch wheelbase models. (Specifications of representative Dividend models are shown in Appendix E.)

A study of advertising copy gives insights into the kinds of markets Divco targeted with the Dividend Series. A June 1960 ad in *Commercial Car Journal* (*CCJ*) quoted M. L. Adley, President of Adley Express Co. of New Haven, Connecticut, a common carrier, as saying, "We would recommend the DIVCO DIVIDEND to any common carrier for local freight pick-up and delivery." A November 1960 ad in *CCJ* showed a Dividend Series used as a walk-through mobile restaurant by an Ohio caterer. The same ad also showed a Dividend used for delivery of pocket-sized books by a book distributor. In late 1959, a Divco-Wayne Emergency Rescue vehicle based on the Dividend Series was introduced as a metropolitan city ambulance. The ambulance combined the interiors of the Miller-Meteor Division of Divco-Wayne with the Divco rugged multi-stop chassis. Among the purchasers of Divco ambulances was the City of New York Department of Hospitals, which purchased five.[49]

The Dividend Series line was expanded to include a number of interesting vehicles. A Divco "Lite-Weight" Dividend with aluminum body and steel-enclosed safety cab was offered in 1960. It had a 7,500 pound G.V.W. and was available with a standard

Dividend Series Divcos could be outfitted as Emergency Rescue Vehicles capable of holding four stretchers and a crew of twelve.

Among the Dividend Series models was the AlumiVan which saved up to 1000 pounds of weight. The cab was enclosed in steel and the cargo body was made of aluminum.

The protruding headlights and slightly different grill suggest this Dividend Series Divco is a prototype model. The picture, taken at the Divco plant on Hoover Road in 1955, is courtesy of Mrs. M. Schwandt whose husband, Marvin Schwandt, is shown at the far right of the picture.

The Divco Bantam Transit bus was designed for small group bus transportation. The Panoramic Series had many front and rear parts that were interchangeable. Note that the nameplate on this Dividend-based bus reads "Divco-Wayne."

Divco Golden Missile Four engine and optional Super Six. Another attempt at expanding the market for the Dividend Series was to build trucks for United Parcel Service (UPS). A UPS Divco Dividend Series truck appeared in a Divco-Wayne Corporation ad on pages 286 and 287 of the November 1960 issue of *Commercial Car Journal*. However, factory production records reveal only twelve Dividend Series trucks delivered to UPS in March 1959, and one truck sold to UPS in Chicago in May 1959.

Divco Buses

The merger with Wayne presented an opportunity for Divco to expand its product line into the bus market. In 1959, Divco introduced a line of buses based on the Dividend Series. The buses combined the engineering and design abilities of both Divco and Wayne. The Divco buses were named "Bantam Transit Buses" and were available in two series— Coachline and Panoramic — and could accommodate 12 to 26 passengers, depending on the model. The Divco Coachline models were conventional-looking, small buses with a squared-off body. The Panoramic model was streamlined and had an "is it coming or going?" appearance, because its Panoramic rear and front sections shared Dividend Series sheet metal and glass. Many of the front and rear components even had the same part numbers. The Dividend Series bus models 45, 55, and 75 also shared roof panel parts numbers with Dividend Series truck models 40, 50, and 70. However, the

roof panel for the Panoramic Model 76 was different. The side panels for bus model 45 were the same as the side panels for Dividend truck model 40, except the latter did not have the window openings.

The introduction of the Divco buses in 1959 was an evolutionary step for the firm. Divco began making bus bodies for mounting on chassis provided by other manufacturers in 1957. Most of the bodies built by Divco were 10-foot Coachline models, but at least one 12-foot Coachline body was mounted on a Dodge P400 chassis. The bus bodies were built for General Motors, Chevrolet, Dodge, and Ford chassis. When chassis modifications were necessary the work was done by Highway Equipment Sales Company of Warren, Michigan. According to the production records, the following buses were built and shipped from the Hoover Road Divco plant on chassis of other manufacturers between March 1957 and June 1959:

GMC	152 chassis	10 ft. body	7 buses
Chevrolet	3542 chassis	10 ft. body	2 buses
Dodge	P400 chassis	12 ft. body	1 bus
Dodge	P300 chassis	10 ft. body	11 buses
Ford	P-350 chassis	10 ft. body	6 buses

These production records indicate that the last of the buses built on other manufacturers' chassis was a 10 foot Coachline body on a Ford P-350 chassis shipped June 19, 1959. When Divco entered the market with its own Dividend-Series-based buses, it

ABOVE: *This Panoramic Series Divco bus is one of several sold to Youngstown Steel Corporation for plant-site transportation by Fogelman Truck Sales and Service of East Chicago, Indiana.*

Table 6-1:

Divco Buses: Models and Production 1959-1961

Bus Model	Body	Wheelbase	Seating Capacity[2]	Total Production
45	Custom[1]	130"	12 – 20	12
55	Custom[1]	117½"	9 – 16	17
75	Custom[1]	153⅝"	15 – 24	13
76	Panoramic	153⅝"	20 – 25	42

Total Divco Bus Production: 84

[1] Referred to in sales literature as "Coachline."

[2] Depending on seating arrangement selected.

Source: Divco Production Records, Divco Dividend Series Buses, Service Parts List, Divco Truck Division, Divco-Wayne Corporation, Detroit, Michigan, December 1961.

phased out the line of bodies for Ford, GM, and Dodge chassis.

The Dividend Series Divco buses were Divco products built at the Hoover Road plant, but a significant amount of the work on them was done off the assembly line. In an interview, Arnold Gentz, who worked on the assembly line at Divco from 1955 to 1963, gave some insights into the production of the Dividend Series buses. According to Gentz, seat installation and engine covers were done in an area of the plant referred to as "The Hole," which was a special repair area for finished trucks that had faults or problems needing attention before shipment.[50]

The Divco entry into the bus market was short lived. Production occurred only in 1959, 1960, and 1961. Table 6-1 shows the Divco bus offerings and production by model numbers. The service parts book for Divco Dividend Series Buses refers to Coachlines as "Custom" models; Divco bus literature, however, uses the Coachline and Panoramic designations. Early Divco bus-sales literature makes reference to a Model 46 Panoramic bus. However, there is no evidence that Divco produced that model and no listing for it appears in the Divco Dividend Series Bus Service Parts Manual.

The Divco Bantam buses targeted markets that included small-city transit lines, feeder lines in large or small cities, private schools, institutions, inter- and intra-plant transportation, and airport transportation. The first fleet of seven Divco Bantam buses was sold to Ann Arbor, Michigan. Other communities that used Divco buses included Norristown, Pennsylvania; Rockland, Maine; Birmingham, Alabama; Honolulu, Hawaii; and Richmond, Virginia.[51]

With production records showing only 84 Dividend Series buses built, the Divco bus-market experiment must be considered a failure. The buses were interesting products from an historical viewpoint, but, clearly, they did not bring sales success to Divco, which was in need of products that could be sold in significant volume to keep the assembly line running.

The Divco Response— Success or Failure?

The Divco response to a changing and declining milk home-delivery market involved changes and expansion of the line of snub-nosed trucks that began in the late 1930s and continued through the end of production. The response also involved the introduction of the Dividend Series to meet the needs of a wider segment of the multistop truck industry. Was the Divco response a success? Ultimately, of course,

Divcos were built at 22000 Hoover Road from 1939 through 1967. Here some new Divcos await shipment under the shadow of the Hoover Road plant water tower.

Divco ceased production. In that sense, the Divco response was a failure. A closer look is needed, though, at the Divco situation.

The introduction of the Dividend Series, in particular, probably prolonged Divco's life as a truck builder. After peaking in 1948, Divco production declined by over half, to 2959 in 1954. Through 1960, Divco output was close to or above 3,000 units each year. Those were not record levels, but for a time, the slide was halted. Production was 2,883 in 1962 and in the 2,000 to 2,500 range in 1963 to 1966 (see the Statistical Appendix for specifics on Divco production). Dividend Series production was a small fraction of total Divco production. However, in the late 1950s and early 1960s, when Dividend output accounted for 10% to 18% of Divco production, it may have been the margin that kept the truck division in business.

Nevertheless, the attempts to broaden the market for Divco trucks ultimately were unsuccessful and the company continued to be heavily dependent on the milk truck business. Clearly, the marketing and manufacturing people at Divco-Wayne Corporation saw what was coming in the milk home delivery market. The following is from the Divco-Wayne Corporation annual report for the fiscal year ended October 31, 1966:

> *To strengthen ourselves internally, we initiated negotiations during fiscal 1966 for the sale of our Divco Division... The Divco Division has shown little growth in recent years and has produced a low return on our investment...*
>
> *Although this division—manufacturers of more than 30 different truck models ranging from 6000 to 20,000 pounds—has been a leader in the design and manufacture of multi-stop trucks for many years, we have concluded that a disposition of this operation would release substantial funds for other areas of our expanding business, offering greater growth.*
>
> *During the past 30 years, about 75 percent of all milk sold at retail was delivered in Divco trucks. However, the demand for dairy trucks has been static in recent years due to consolidations within the industry and the rise of supermarket sales. As a result, this division has shown the least growth.*
>
> *Pending the outcome of the announced possible sale, management will continue to pursue every avenue to keep Divco's operations profitable in 1967.*[52]

The Divco Truck Division was sold to Transairco Inc. of Delaware, Ohio, in late 1967 and production was moved to Delaware, Ohio. The Dividend series was discontinued and the Divco product line was narrowed to the snub-nosed Models 200 and 300 after the sale. For a limited production truck manufacturer, the strategy of a limited product line was consistent with a "niche marketing" approach to selling Divco trucks. Because capacity was much lower in the new facility than at the Hoover Road plant, it was sensible to focus on the historically popular and easily identified snub-nosed Divcos. Although other multi-stop delivery markets (laundries and bakeries, for example) were serviced, the last 18 years of Divco production targeted the traditional milk home-delivery market. While a declining industry, it was sufficient to provide an outlet for limited production Divcos through the end of production in early 1986.

Divco on the Block

In December 1966, Divco-Wayne formally announced to the media that it was negotiating with three prospective buyers for its truck division. No final price had been established, as the final price would depend on what type of transaction could be worked out with an eventual buyer.[1] In August 1967, Divco-Wayne announced it was allocating $600,000 to cover the cost of the planned liquidation of the manufacturing operations of its truck division.[2]

Boise Cascade Corporation

Boise Cascade Corporation, a maker of factory-built homes, paper, and building materials located in Boise, Idaho, never really had anything to do with the production of Divco trucks. Boise Cascade appeared on the scene just as Divco-Wayne was attempting to sell Divco.

At about the same time that Divco-Wayne was considering divesting itself of the Divco Truck Division, the two top people at Divco-Wayne, Harold Drimmer, chair of the board, and Newton Glekel, president, decided to sell their stake in the company. Drimmer and Glekel owned Richmond Industries, Inc., a New York-based holding company which owned a controlling block of 296,388 shares, or 26% of Divco-Wayne stock. On June 19, 1967, R. V. Hansberger, president of Boise Cascade, Drimmer, and Glekel, made a joint announcement

that Boise Cascade was buying the 296,388 shares of Divco-Wayne common for 386,111 Boise Cascade common shares worth $11.9 million. The deal also included a plan by which Divco-Wayne would be merged into Boise Cascade. The remaining 841,157 Divco-Wayne common shares* were to be exchanged for 0.9123 shares each of Boise Cascade stock worth $35.7 million, making the merger deal worth $47.6 million.[3]

The Divco-Wayne directors rejected the initial Boise Cascade offer on August 16, 1967,[4] but after further negotiations, approved the deal on October 2, 1967. The terms of the final merger agreement were that Divco-Wayne shareholders of the 841,157 shares not owned by Drimmer and Glekel would receive one full share of Boise Cascade preferred for every share of Divco-Wayne common. At the then current market price for Boise Cascade preferred stock, the deal was worth $47.1 million to Divco-Wayne shareholders plus the value of the common stock in Boise Cascade obtained by Mr. Drimmer and Mr. Glekel.[5] In January 1968, stockholders of Divco-Wayne and Boise Cascade approved the merger and by February 1, Divco-Wayne ceased to exist as an independent firm.

During the 11 years in which Glekel and Drimmer were in charge at Divco-Wayne, the company became a conglomerate firm achieving growth through acquiring other companies. No longer did Divco trucks stand alone and receive all the corporate attention as had been the case prior to 1956. The Divco Truck Division was now merely a

---

*By 1967, the total number of shares of Divco-Wayne outstanding was 1,137,545 of which Glekel and Drimmer interests owned 296,388. At the time of the merger in 1956, total shares outstanding were 650,000, of which the Glekel and Drimmer interests owned 200,000. According to Divco-Wayne annual reports, the increase in the number of shares between 1956 and 1967 was due to the issuance of stock dividends in 1959, 1960, and 1962 and a four for three stock split in 1964.

financial asset that had to prove its worth by contributing its fair share to the corporate bottom line. Neither nostalgia nor product quality could save it when the division ceased to perform at the level of other Divco-Wayne assets. By 1967, Glekel and Drimmer were treating the Divco Truck Division as a very disposable financial asset, and Divco-Wayne's focus of attention was on Boise Cascade.

At the time of the sale, Divco-Wayne consisted of the Transportation Division (builder of school and transit buses, ambulances, and hearses), Divco-Wayne Sales Financial Corporation, (the credit subsidiary of Divco-Wayne), Divco-Wayne Industries (mobile homes and travel trailers), and Divco Division (delivery trucks). By the time the merger with Boise Cascade was completed, the Divco Division had been sold and was not part of the merger deal.

What did Boise Cascade want out of Divco-Wayne? The mobile-home business was the primary attraction because it complemented Boise Cascade's own factory-built home product line. In October 1968, Boise Cascade sold the Transportation Division and the Divco-Wayne Sales Financial Corporation for $15 million to Indian Head Inc., a diversified producer of metal products, auto parts, and textile specialties.[15] Boise Cascade did not want the Transportation Division, and we can conclude that Boise Cascade wanted nothing to do with the Divco Division either, which put pressure on Divco-Wayne to divest itself of the Divco Division and salvage whatever cash it could out of Divco. In the end, Boise Cascade never had to deal with Divco trucks, except to wind down the Service Parts Operation and to be a defendant in a lawsuit filed by Divco dealers.

The Deal Makers

Newton Glekel and Harold Drimmer were no longer associated with Divco-Wayne or Divco trucks after the merger. However, their subsequent careers were interesting and worth mentioning as an historical footnote.

In the spring of 1968, Glekel purchased a large block of stock in the A. S. Beck Shoe Corporation. Under Glekel, who became board chair of the firm, A. S. Beck Shoes acquired over twenty companies and changed the name to Beck Industries. The 1969-1970 recession was rough on Beck, and its stock dropped 90% in value.[6] Glekel resigned as a director and board chair in October 1970.[7] Beck stock, which had risen from $5⅛ to $40 when Glekel bought into the firm, fell to $1⅜ by the time he left.[8]

Glekel's activities in his post-Divco-Wayne days were not confined to Beck. In late 1968, he bought a 22% interest in Hygrade Food Products Corporation.[9] In

1968, he also became a director and chair of the acquisition committee of American Book-Stratford Press.[10] Another enterprise undertaken by Glekel was the founding of a newspaper called the *New York Daily Column*, which debuted on March 11, 1968. The paper was devoted to a cross-section of national columnists and political cartoonists. Co-founder of the paper was Jerry Finkelstein, a publisher who had been prominent in Democratic politics.[11] Glekel also bought a 24% interest in Fifth Avenue Coach Lines, Inc. from Gray Line Corporations in 1969.[12]

In 1970, Hygrade Foods did not perform up to expectations when sales and per share profits declined. As a result, Hygrade Stock, which went from $19½ to a high of $83 when Glekel bought it, fell to $19⅝ in 1970, down 75%. The *Wall Street Journal* noted that Glekel's reputation as a 'hot deal-maker' had been tarnished by the

weakness at Beck and Hygrade. Glekel was quoted as saying, "I accept that part of what's happened is my responsibility. But I must come back and I will."[13] However, as a corporate acquisition and deal-making genius, the days of prominence ended for the man who had been president of the company that made Divco trucks for ten years.

Little is known about Harold Drimmer after his days at Divco-Wayne. In 1972, he attempted to purchase one million preferred shares of the First Surety Corporation of Burbank, California, for one dollar per share. The sale was blocked when controlling shareholders obtained an order blocking issuance of the shares, and the California Commissioner of Corporations obtained another court order barring sale of First Surety preferred unless the stock was registered and qualified under California law, which the company stated it had no intention of doing.[14]

Divco Goes Postal

As early as the late 1930s, Divco had built bodies for other truck makers. In its September 1956 proxy statement Divco indicated a renewed interest in a program to build bodies to mount on the chassis of other manufacturers. In 1967, even as plans were being made to liquidate the truck division, Divco finally acted on its body-building hopes and contracted to produce 6,000 mail truck bodies for the Dodge Truck Division of Chrysler Corporation.[16] According to former Divco Chief Engineer William Ray Chapman, who designed the bodies for the postal van, the bodies were to be built at the Welles plant in Windsor, Ontario, because there was insufficient room at the Hoover Road factory.[17]

Glenn W. Way, owner of Transairco Inc. of Delaware, Ohio—the firm that ultimately bought Divco, (more on Mr. Way in the next chapter) believed that bidding on the mail truck bodies was almost whimsical on the part of Divco. He doubted that Divco thought it would actually get the contract because it had already begun the process of liquidation of the truck division. To everyone's surprise, Divco was awarded the contract. Way claimed Divco told Dodge it could not fulfill the contract but that Dodge, in turn, told Divco it had to—that under the conditions of a government contract, Divco-Wayne could be held accountable for damages for nonfulfillment.[18] The solution to the dilemma was for Divco-Wayne to sell the Divco truck operation to Highway Products Corporation. The deal was announced in August 1967 and finalized in November 1967.[19]

Highway Products had been founded in the early 1950s by Joseph T. Myers, who served as a director of Twin Coach located in Kent, Ohio. Twin Coach built buses from 1927 to the 1950s. Myers bought the bus rights, engineering drawings, tooling, factory, and equipment from Twin Coach and built buses under the name of Highway Products Twin Coach.* The first contract Highway Products had with its Twin Coach line was for Highway Post Office trucks built on Fageol truck frames. That contract involved

the firm with the Post Office, and led to contracts to build between 30,000 and 40,000 mail trucks on Jeep chassis.[20]

Highway Products wanted Divco for the purpose of building mail trucks and originally considered using Divcos as the basis for the trucks. This idea was quickly abandoned.

Though Highway Products had at first planned to build the mail trucks in Kent, ultimately it used the Divco plant to build the mail trucks on Dodge chassis. Joseph Thomas Myers II, son of the Highway Products founder, visited the plant on occasion as a teenager, but said it never was absolutely clear to him why the mail trucks were built in Detroit rather Kent. The only explanation he could think of was that Detroit was closer to the supply of chassis, which saved shipping costs. After the mail truck contract was completed the Divco plant was sold to Chrysler Corporation in February, 1969. Chrysler used the plant for office space and then sold it to industrial real estate investors in the 1980s.[21]

With the mail truck contract in hand, and after deciding not to use Divco chassis for mail trucks, Highway Products had no further use for Divco. The company sold Divco—minus the mail truck contract—to Transairco, Inc. under the leadership of Glenn Way of Delaware, Ohio, who started a whole new chapter in the Divco story. The official announcement was made in January 1968.[22]

---

* The subsequent history of Twin Coach buses is somewhat complex. In 1952, the transit bus rights were sold to the Flxible Company of Loudonville, Ohio, and the buses were built under the Flxible-Twin Coach name (source: J. Ralph Tshantz, Export Sales Manager, The Flxible Company, interview by Robert R. Ebert, Londonville, Ohio, October 29, 1965). Clearly, though, Highway Products retained some rights to manufacturing certain buses under the Highway Products Twin Coach name. In 1970, Highway Products offered a full line of Twin Coach "bare" shells in 24 and 28 foot lengths for customers desiring to build their own buses (source: James A. Wren and Genevieve J. Wren, Motor Trucks of America, Ann Arbor, University of Michigan Press, for the Motor Vehicle Manufacturers Association of the United States, Inc., 1979, p. 278). Subsequently, the Flxible-Twin Coach buses were named just Flxible. The Flxible company underwent several mergers and ownership changes including Rohr Corporation, Grumman Corporation, and General Automotive Corporation before filing for bankruptcy in 1996.

DIVCO

MILK
DELIVERY
TRUCKS

DIVCO TRUCK DIVISION
Divco-Wayne Corporation
22000 Hoover Road • Detroit 5, Mich.

The sale of Divco to Transairco marked the end of an era for Divco. No longer would the Divco line consist of both snub-nosed and Dividend Series trucks as shown in this picture from a Divco catalog. The last Dividend Series Divcos were produced in 1967. After the move of production to Delaware, Ohio, only snub-nosed Divcos were built.

Divco in Delaware

The story of how Divcos ended up being produced in Delaware, Ohio, a college town where Ohio Wesleyan University is located, is a complex and fascinating tale. Delaware was a new beginning for Divco—it was an operation like no previous Divco production effort. Though a mere shadow of the booming days of Hoover Road, the production of the Delaware Divcos was a serious business venture that lasted eighteen years. Involved at various points in time were big corporations, New York deal makers, small corporations, the

courts, and the determination of an industrial entrepreneur by the name of Glenn W. Way.

The Delaware Deal

At the time of the Divco purchase by Highway Products, Glenn W. Way's Transairco was busy producing Vanette truck bodies, Roustabout cranes, Sky-Workers (used for tree trimming, utility pole and wire service, etc.) and air conditioning in Delaware, Ohio.[1] Glenn Way had over a quarter of a century of experience in manufacturing and truck-body building and Frank Fageol had even approached him as early as 1953 or 1954 with an offer to sell Divco. Fageol, who had the largest block of Divco stock at the time, was getting up in years and wanted to sell his interest in the company. But Way was busy making fifty Vanette bodies per week in Delaware and had no interest in Divco.[2]

In 1967, though, Way was interested in Divco to supplement the Vanette operations. Highway Products needed cash and made a deal.[3] Way paid approximately $350,000 for the patents, rights, dies, Divco name, and parts.[4] Negotiations for the parts were directly with Divco-Wayne while rights to Divco truck production were negotiated with Highway

Glenn Way's Enterprises produced Skyworkers and Vanette delivery trucks. Pictured here is a unique experimental model that combined the major features of both the Skyworker and Vanette. (Courtesy, James Stegner)

Products. The sum of $350,000 was a bargain. Harry Hume, Chief Financial Officer for Glenn Way's operations, states the following:

> *The agreed upon price was very low, as they [Highway Products] were not in the least interested in manufacturing the [Divco] unit. The sum of approximately $350,000...was, in substance, the total money we disbursed for the entire package. ...Our major discussion re: the purchase of parts, dies, etc. was with Divco-Wayne. The dies, of course, represented a valuable part of the package.*[5]

The $350,000 sum appears low, but Divco-Wayne stood to gain tax benefits from the $600,000 it allocated to close the Divco operations and had sold the mail-truck body contract to Highway Products for an undisclosed sum. Records of the Divco Truck Company in Delaware show that the parts inventory was valued at $706,588 in 1970, $632,820 in 1971, and $670,921 in 1972. Given that Divco-Wayne wanted to sell the Divco Truck Division during 1967, and that it stood to gain tax benefits from doing so, and given the likely value of the inventory, the $350,000 that Way paid for it is a plausible sum—although it was clearly a bargain.

Way's purchase of Divco began an incredible odyssey by two semi-trailer trucks owned by Glenn Way's firms. Throughout 1968, these two trucks traversed the distance between Delaware, Ohio, and Detroit, Michigan, moving the inventory of parts and records of Divco.[6] It took 180 semi-truck loads to move the inventory.[7] Divcos were out of production for about a year while the move took place and operations were set up in Delaware. The official date Transairco assumed responsibility for Divco parts was November 1, 1968. The Divco Parts and Service Division of Divco-Wayne on Hoover Road closed on October 18, 1968, and operations began in Delaware on November 11, 1968. To facilitate the transfer, Transairco began producing some Divco parts in September 1968. During the late summer of 1968, some orders sent to Hoover Road were being filled with Transairco-made parts. Duane Kromis, Service Operations Manager at Hoover Road, became manager of the Divco Service Parts Operation at Transairco in Delaware. In addition to the parts operation, Transairco assumed responsibility for Divco warranties after November 1, 1968.[8]

Although Glenn Way purchased Divco rights in late 1967, the involvement of Divco-Wayne in the Divco truck story was not yet over. Some Divco dealers were not at all pleased with the events that occurred in late 1967.

The Dealers Go to Court

The events of the mid 1960s must have struck fear in the hearts of Divco dealers. The dealers stood between nervous customers who had outstanding orders for trucks and a supplier with an uncertain future. First Divco-Wayne revealed in its *1966 Annual Report* that the Divco Truck Division was not meeting profit objectives and was for sale. Then came the news of the proposed Boise Cascade merger, the sale of the Divco Truck Division to Highway Products, and the sale to Transairco.

The fears of Divco dealers were well founded. Prospective buyers of automobiles and trucks are reluctant to buy makes that might stop being built and become "orphans" without a supporting sales, parts, and service organization behind them. The problems of independent automobile producers in the 1950s and 1960s, including American Motors, Kaiser-Willys, and Studebaker-Packard, were made worse by speculation and rumors about their possible demise. Both American Motors and Studebaker-Packard acknowledged publicly that the orphan car argument had a negative influence on sales.[9]

In an apparent effort to calm the fears of Divco dealers that Divco would become an orphan vehicle, the company issued a letter to them on August 3, 1967, that said in part: "DIVCO TRUCK IS NOT AND WILL NOT BE GOING OUT OF BUSINESS! Divco trucks will be resuming and continuing production in the very near future."[10] Technically, the statement was accurate, but it was over a year before Divco was back in production. The delays in production caused several dealers to file suit against Boise Cascade (as successor by merger of Divco-Wayne), Transairco, and Highway Products. In time, the trial court directed a verdict in favor of Transairco and Highway Products and ruled that the plaintiff could look only to Divco-Wayne for damages.[11]

The dealers filing suit were Hoefferle Truck Sales, Inc. of Chicago, Illinois; August Schmidt Company of Milwaukee, Wisconsin; J.A. Fogelman Truck Sales and Service of East Chicago, Indiana; and Eastland Truck Sales, Inc. of Warren, Michigan. The suit was filed on October 28, 1970, and a jury trial commenced in February 1974 in the U.S. District Court for the Northern District of Illinois. After the jury awarded damages to the dealers, Boise Cascade appealed. The U.S. Circuit Court of Appeals rendered a decision on October 6, 1975. Details of the case are quite complex and can be found in the documents cited in endnote 10 to this chapter.

DIVCO-WAYNE CORPORATION   DIVCO TRUCK DIVISION

22000 HOOVER ROAD
DETROIT 5, MICHIGAN
JEFFERSON 6-5050

August 3, 1967

TO ALL DIVCO DEALERS AND
FIELD REPRESENTATIVES

There have been many rumors in the past few months as to what was going to happen to the Divco Truck Division. I have been authorized, and it gives me pleasure to announce that DIVCO TRUCK IS NOT AND WILL NOT BE GOING OUT OF BUSINESS!

Divco Truck will be resuming and continuing production in the very near future, and we will announce In a couple of weeks when production shipments will resume. In the meantime, we will continue to ship from our truck stock bank which is now nearly depleted.

Additional experienced automotive men are being brought into our Divco Truck picture, and we are formulating plans for additional products for our dealers and the vocations we are familiar with.

We will advise you the details within thirty days, and we are certain you will be pleased and also enthusiastic.

Very truly yours,

DIVCO TRUCK DIVISION

ROY H. SJOBERG
Sales Manager

RHS:aw

  MULTI-STOP DELIVERY TRUCKS • SCHOOL AND ADULT BUSES • AMBULANCES • FUNERAL COACHES

This letter of August 3, 1967 that announced Divco was not going out of business became a major piece of evidence in a lawsuit filed by several dealers.

The basic issues and the decision of the Appeals Court are described here.

Four major grievances claimed by the dealers[12]

1. DELAY
   The dealers incurred unnecessary operating expenses because Divco-Wayne failed to give a termination notice and falsely promised continued production.

2. TRUCK ORDERS
   The dealers lost profits on trucks ordered but not delivered.

3. WARRANTY
   Warranty claims by the dealers went unpaid.

4. PARTS
   Divco-Wayne refused to take back parts from the dealers.

Damages ascribed by the jury in each of the four grievances[15]

	EASTLAND	SCHMIDT	FOGELMAN
1. DELAY	$95,000	$44,000	$0
2. TRUCK ORDERS	76,000	34,000	13,500
3. WARRANTY	10,030	0	0
4. PARTS	5,000	0	1,600

Circuit Court of Appeals Judge William J. Bauer noted in his decision that the relationship between Divco and its dealers was set forth in a contract called the "Dealer Memorandum." The contract contained provisions enabling either party to terminate the dealership upon proper notification, thus obligating Divco to fill only those truck orders which it accepted, warranting new trucks sold by Divco to be free from defects, and providing for the return of usable parts upon termination of the agreement. Divco also maintained a policy of allowing each dealer to return a percentage of gross inventory of parts annually. The four dealers suing as plaintiffs in the case claimed the provisions of the "Dealer Memorandum" were violated when Divco-Wayne ended production in Detroit, when output of Divcos did not start by Transairco in Delaware until late 1968, and when it was late 1969 before production re-started with any efficiency.[13] Apparently, particularly damaging testimony was offered by Harold Streem, Executive Vice President of Divco-Wayne. The plaintiffs claimed that he admitted the statements made in the August 3, 1967 letter were untrue and were known to be untrue. Divco-Wayne had agreed to sell its manufacturing assets two days before the letter was published.[14] The jury trial resulted in awards being made to the dealers but the verdict was appealed.

One of the legal complexities in the case was that the District Court under Judge Thomas R. McMillen granted Boise Cascade's post-trial motion to set aside part and reduce part of the jury verdict. Eastland's award of $10,030 for warranty claims was reduced to $2,382, and the awards for trucks on order for Eastland and Schmidt were completely set aside. Hoefferle was not granted any damages.[16] In the Appeals Court decision, the awards made by the jury were upheld in part and set aside in part. The Appeals Court decision made the following statement with respect to profit damages for trucks on order: "Damages for the dealers' lost profits on truck orders accepted by Divco and which Divco therefore had an obligation to deliver were wholly proper. In addition, there was sufficient evidence to sustain the damages awarded for loss of after-market profits."[17]

The Appeals Court set aside the delay damages awarded to Eastland and Schmidt, reasoning that these damages were awarded for 1968 when the plaintiffs acknowledged they were aware the Divco truck facilities had been sold. The Appeals Court also agreed that the trial court's decision to reduce the award to Eastland for warranty claims from $10,030 to $2,382 was proper because the larger verdict was not supported by the evidence. All of Hoefferle's claims were refuted because, according to the Appeals Court, "the evidence, in short, created little more than a speculative inference of the extent of Hoefferle's injury...and the evidence was, as the trial court held, very much lacking with regard to the sufficiency of proof."[18]

Contained in the court's decision was other interesting information that came out of the case, including the dealers' net profits per truck in 1967.

Damage claims of the three dealers & reinstated jury awards[19]

EASTLAND CLAIM

Net profits for 53 trucks on order: $50,092
After-market profit loss:* $26,500
Total claimed loss: $76,592

JURY AWARD: $76,000

SCHMIDT CLAIM

Net profit for 28 trucks on order: $19,982
After-market profit loss:* $14,000
Total claimed loss: $33,982

JURY AWARD: $34,000

FOGELMAN CLAIM

Net profit for 9 trucks on order: $9,300
After-market profit loss:* $4,500
Total claimed loss: $13,800

JURY AWARD: $13,500

It was also revealed that each truck had a ten-year life expectancy with estimated after-market parts and service profits of $50 per year per truck.[20]

The lawsuit brought by the dealers gave insights into the delicate marketing and production problems confronting Divco as the transition was made from Detroit to Delaware. Once in Delaware, the destiny of Divco was in the hands of a firm quite different from the one that built trucks on Hoover Road.

Dealers net profits per Divco model (1967)

MODEL	PER TRUCK
200 C	$1100
206 C	$1100
206 D	$1100
300 D	$ 800

Glenn Way and Correct Manufacturing

The story of Glenn Way, his enterprises, and his involvement with Divco is the story of an entrepreneur, an individualist, and an industrialist. During his 87 years (1901-1988) he did things his own way and, in so doing, created a small industrial empire in Delaware, Ohio. In Appendix H, a detailed summary is given of the enterprises with which Glenn Way was associated over the years. Here, however, we pick up the story at the time of the purchase of Divco by the company owned by Way: Transairco, a diversified manufacturer of Vanette delivery truck bodies, air conditioning units, Sky-Worker utility truck bodies, and industrial heaters.

In 1967, even before he bought Divco, Glenn Way began to consider the problem of long-term management of Transairco, which he was running virtually single handedly. As a result, a couple of years following the purchase of Divco, Way decided to merge Transairco with companies owned by André J. Andreoli of Akron, Ohio (see Appendix H). By 1971, Way's and his family's ownership share in Transairco dropped to 26% and he resigned as president and from active management of the company that was building Divco trucks, although he remained a director of the firm. However, Way disagreed on how the finances of the firm were being handled, so he offered to buy back the Sky-Worker and Divco operations. On September 1, 1972 the Way family purchased back the operations in Delaware, Ohio where Divcos and Sky-Workers were being built[21]. The firm, now called Correct Manufacturing, with Glenn Way firmly in control of day-to-day management, produced Divcos and Sky-Workers until the end of production in 1986.

Although the history of Correct Manufacturing is complex, it is clear that Glenn Way's purchase of Divco in 1968 was based on sound business principles. He and his firm had produced Vanette bodies for a quarter of a century, so they were experienced in the truck-body business at the time of the Divco purchase. Divco complemented the Vanette line and made use of the facilities and skills already in use in Vanette production. In economic jargon: Glenn Way attempted to take advantage of "economies of scope." He expanded the scope of his operations with the vision of making a variety of products using common

The dealers claimed each truck sold yielded an annual $50 profit on parts and service for an estimated 10 year life expectancy.

Divco production in Delaware, Ohio was undertaken at this plant on London Road Extension. The plant was a cavernous facility with only a small percentage of the floor space used for Divco production.

production facilities. Economists have found that such operations can produce a variety of products at lower cost than if the products are produced in separate facilities.[22] As it turned out, Correct Manufacturing was more limited in its scope at the Delaware facility than Way had envisioned. For a brief time Vanettes continued in production but operations soon narrowed from a broad line of vehicle and air conditioning products to Divco and Sky-Workers.

It is clear from an interview with Glenn Way and publications of the Divco Truck Company Division (first of Transairco and then later of Correct Manufacturing) that Way knew the industry he was entering was in decline. In *The Divco News*, a corporate publication dated April 1970, the company observed that per capita consumption of milk and the number of persons delivering milk were declining, yet the publication was optimistic and noted that milk was still the most popular beverage in the country. In a 1976 interview, Way stated that the milk delivery business was on the decline and was not coming back. He explained that dairies were downsizing their truck fleets and not replacing old trucks as the home-delivery business declined.[23]

Although Divco was an established industry name, the purchase of Divco by Way must be viewed as the entry of a new firm into the multi-stop delivery truck industry. The Delaware operation was completely different from the Detroit factory. Whereas annual production at Hoover Road was measured in the thousands, in Delaware, estimated production never exceeded 300 trucks per year (see Appendix B). Essentially, Glenn Way entered the industry in

1967 as a specialized producer of delivery trucks aimed at very small niche markets. In a study of specialist motor vehicle producers, D. G. Rhys of the University of Cardiff, concluded that to remain competitive and profitable, specialist producers must remain small. An expansion of production, would require a complete change in the methods of production which would increase costs and require very large outputs to obtain economies of scale (that is, to reduce per unit costs to minimal levels).[24]

The overall size of the Delaware facilities (about 500,000 square feet) was over double that of Hoover Road. However, as initially operated, a large number of products were produced there. The Divco trucks built there had a very limited production basis and were virtually hand-built. Even with the parts storage and distribution operations, the total space devoted to Divco was a very small part of the factory. At the volume Divco generated, a limited production facility was sufficient. Expanding output to the Detroit level may have been feasible, given the size of the facilities, but it is doubtful that the declining market for Divco would have justified the capital investment such a move would have required.

Divco Production in Delaware

Initially, the Divco Truck Company offices in Ohio were in Ashland and the production facilities were in Delaware. On December 1, 1970, the Ashland office was closed and all operations were consolidated in Delaware.[25] In Delaware, Divco faced many of the problems typical of specialty producers, but a major difficulty was lining up consistent sources of components. In a 1980 letter, Way stated that Correct Manufacturing was making an increasing percentage of the truck in its own plant:

You can easily understand the reason for this: most everything in the automotive industry is based upon huge volume and we do not have huge volume, nor will we have with Divco. So a lot of the parts, which would normally be made of malleable iron or would be produced along with other components for production of higher quantity, is of such nature that the cost becomes absolutely outrageous and we then must make the material ourselves to bring the cost down.[26]

Divco production ceased during the move to Delaware, and establishing a sufficient and reliable supply of some components was a problem as plans were formulated to re-start production. In May 1969, in a letter to dealers, Way complained of shortages of some items and of difficulty in obtaining hubs, brake drums, and wheels ordered from Motor

Wheel Corporation of Lansing, Michigan. These shortages delayed the start up of production of Divcos in Delaware.[27]

Specialty producers must rely on other firms for major components such as engines and transmissions as well as for minor components. In the purchase of engines and transmissions from outside suppliers though, the specialty producer does have an interesting advantage. Divco was able to take advantage of major suppliers' economies of scale, because the Divco orders were supplemental to other orders. Therefore, the extra cost to suppliers of selling engines or transmissions to Divco was relatively low, so Divco procured the components at reasonable prices. This helped keep the production costs of the trucks relatively competitive.

During the period when Transairco operations were in transition and the Way family holdings declined to a 26% ownership share, there were management changes. In 1971, L. E. Craig, Jr. was made Vice President of Marketing, and K. E. Sharkey was made Vice President of Manufacturing for the Transairco manufacturing divisions. Both men held seats on the Executive Committee and Board of Directors.[28] Manufacturing Manager for the Divco

Inside the spacious Delaware plant, the Divcos were rolled along the makeshift assembly line by hand.

(Courtesy, William Aitchison)

Building Divcos on a limited-production basis in Delaware involved considerable amounts of hand work, as shown in this photo of the body-construction area.

Truck Company was John W. McNamee. George D. Foster was appointed Retail Sales Manager of the Divco Truck Company and Universal Sales, Inc. (Vanette bodies).[29]

George Foster had a tough time during his tenure as Sales Manager, because coordination between production and sales at Divco broke down. The 1972 model production run was ended on May 1, 1972, because Divco production exceeded shipments by 100 units; many of these units were on the storage lot in Delaware. On April 11, 1972, a letter was issued to dealers by McNamee and Foster telling them to get production orders in by April 21, 1972. After May 1, 1972, orders were filled from trucks in stock.[30] The letter of April 11, 1972, expressed an expectation of more efficient production in 1973. However, the Transairco management produced its last Divco Truck by May 1, 1972. The resumption of control of Correct Manufacturing by

the Way family on September 1, 1972, meant that Glenn Way was back in charge of Divco production.

Divcos were out of production from May 1972 through March 1973—an eleven month shutdown, which was the second lengthy shutdown since the end of 1967. Although there were sufficient trucks in inventory in early 1972 to maintain shipments, halting production must have been demoralizing to dealers who had endured the earlier shutdown. When a consistent production schedule is lacking, dealers fear customers will see the truck as an orphan, thus making it difficult to sell. On March 13, 1973, in a letter to Divco Dealers, Glenn Way announced that production start-up was scheduled for April 1973. He indicated, as well, that a new pricing policy was in effect:

As you know, we are in effect an entirely new organization and we are starting from scratch

1971 & 1973 base wholesale price lists for dealers (before Federal Taxes)

	1971 PRICES	1973 PRICES
Model 300 D *(115 inch wheelbase, 11,000 lb. G.V.W.)*	$4462	$5350
Model 306 F *(115 inch wheelbase, 15,000 lb. G.V.W.)*	$4850	$5810
Model 200 C *(127½ inch wheelbase, 15,000 lb. G.V.W.)* *120 to 140 milk case capacity*	$4775	$5720
Model 206 C *(127½ inch wheelbase, 15,000 lb. G.V.W.)* *140 to 190 milk case capacity*	$4908	$5882
Model 206 D *(127½ inch wheelbase, 18,000 lb. G.V.W.)* *140 to 190 milk case capacity*	$4987	$5980

Note: Divco retail prices are shown in Appendix D

Here, a Delaware Divco body nears completion.

With its snub-nose in place, a Delaware Divco is shown here almost ready for the body to be installed.

(Courtesy, William Aitchison)

so that whatever Transairco did is of no consequence so far as we are concerned...we discovered that even though they probably did not know it, Transairco were [sic] actually losing several hundred dollars on every unit [of Divcos] they produced.[31]

Way concluded that the price of Divcos had to be increased to cover costs; the wholesale price increase to dealers was almost exactly 20% over the base prices listed in the January 1971 Transairco price list.

During the period of transition at Transairco, the company had to decide whether to continue Vanette production. Initially, Transairco planned to bring out a new Vanette body in 1972 or 1973.[32] A prototype was completed, but with the management and ownership changes in 1972, the new Vanette never was put into production. Transairco offered the prototype Vanette to dealers for $6000 on March 1, 1975 and then for $4500 on July 10, 1975.[33]

Inside the Delaware Plant

For those accustomed to the mass production type of auto or truck assembly plant, a trip through the Delaware facilities was an educational experience: Divco in Delaware was definitely production on a limited scale. The accompanying pictures, taken by Bill Aitchison of Plain City, Ohio, near Delaware, and former Divco dealer, Jack Fogelman, show some of the steps in the production process at Delaware. Recollections of a December 17, 1976, tour of the Delaware plant by one of the authors include being surprised at the large amount of hand work done on the trucks. Correct Manufacturing did have stamping presses for the body panels; the stamping operations were limited, however. Jim Stegner and Bob Owens, former employees at Correct Manufacturing, said they would run a few parts and then change dies.

RETAIL DELIVERY TRUCKS

DIVCO
SNUB-NOSE

MODELS 306 AND 300

306 MODEL
- Wheelbase—115"
- Payloads—*6,000 to 8,500 lbs.
- Capacity—325 cu. ft. or 120 to 140 milk cases
- Gross Vehicle Weight—*15,000 lbs.
- Speed†—to 60 MPH
- Turning Radius—23'-0"
- Curb Weight—*5,770 to 5,930 lbs.
- Factory-Installed Insulation and Refrigeration Available

300 Model
- Wheelbase—115"
- Payloads—*5,000 to 6,000
- Capacity—256 cu. ft. or 100 to 120 milk cases
- Gross Vehicle Weight—*11,000 lbs.
- Speed†—60 MPH
- Turning Radius—23'0"
- Curb Weight—*5,000 to 5,500 lbs.
- Factory-Installed Insulation and Refrigeration Available

*Varies Depending on Chassis Options and Driver Controls
†Depends on Engines, Axle Ratios and Wheel Sizes

Model 300 and 306 Divcos were the smallest of the trucks made in Delaware. This page from a Correct Manufacturing Divco catalog gives basic statistics on the Models 300 and 306.

Final truck assembly was largely by hand.[34] Walter Kimball, General Plant Manager at the time of the 1976 tour reported on here, continually apologized for the messy plant. He had reason to be apologetic. The plant was cold, dark, and dirty with much clutter of parts, equipment, and trucks. In spite of the mess, though, the approximately 100 workers appeared motivated and busy. Kimball said the workers really took pride in their work; many parts made at Divco in Delaware had the worker's initials or name marked on them.[35] The Divco parts storage and shipping operation occupied more plant space than truck production at Delaware, and any part could be found easily and shipped out within twenty-four hours via United Parcel Service.[36]

The limited production nature of the Delaware operations meant that Divco did not need as many dealers as in the past. From over 100 dealers when production was underway at Hoover Road, the dealer network declined to 15 key dealers during the Delaware era. In addition to dealer orders, many trucks were sold to customers directly from the factory.[37]

Divco in Delaware— The Product

The Divcos offered from the Delaware plant (first under the Transairco name and later under the Correct Manufacturing name) were in the 300, 306, 200, and 206 model series. The 115 inch and 127½ inch wheelbase models constituted the basic line of snub-nosed delivery trucks built in Delaware; the 100¾ inch wheelbase models were discontinued with the move to Delaware. Elimination of the smaller Divcos from the product line reflected their decreasing popularity. As milk routes became more suburban and longer, larger trucks were needed. In 1960, the smaller trucks accounted for 35% of Divco output. By 1966, they represented only 13.8% of output.

The Delaware Divcos were familiar vehicles; anyone acquainted with Divcos would recognize them in an instant. Their outward appearance and many mechanical features made them similar if not identical to their Model 300, 306, 200, and 206 predecessors from Detroit. Both flat (squared-off) and rounded roof versions of the Delaware Divcos were made. Models 200 and 206 were available in the flat-roofed version. Catalogs show Model 306 with a flat-roofed version and Model 300 with a rounded roof. The accompanying photograph taken in July 1972 by

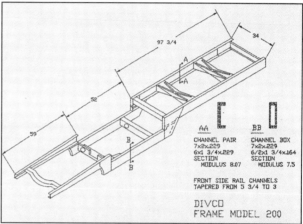

TOP: *Under Transairco management, Divco overproduced and ended 1972 production on May 1, 1972. This picture, taken in July 1972, shows both squared-off and rounded roofline Divcos in storage at the Delaware plant.*

(Courtesy, Barbara Bussard)

CENTER: *After production was moved to Delaware, Ohio, the drop-frame was constructed by welding frame sections together. The welded seams are evident in this AutoCad reproduction of a (damaged) company drawing.*

(AutoCad drawing by Jason Burgholder)

BOTTOM: *The welded frame used on production Divcos from Delaware is clearly visible in this picture of a truck on the assembly line.*

(Courtesy, William Aitchison)

MULTI-STOP WALK THROUGH CAB AND CHASSIS WITH SIT—STAND DRIVE

MODEL SWD

FOR PACKER BODIES UP TO 15 CUBIC YARDS

MODEL SWD	OPTIONS
• Gross Vehicle Weight—*15,000 lbs. to 18,000 lbs.	• Automatic transmission—3 speed (Ford MX)
• Wheel Base—127½" 139½" 151½"	• Power steering
• C.A. Dimension—60" 72" 84"	• 2 speed rear axle
• Curb Weight—*approximately 5600 lbs.	• Hand throttle on stickshift
• Speeds to 65 MPH	• Adjustable steering wheel
	• Right hand drive

*Varies depending on chassis options, driver controls and tire size.

Among the product innovations developed in Delaware was a chassis to accommodate packer (garbage truck) bodies.

One of the Divco garbage trucks was still in use in 1996 by Sipos Hauling Services of Bethlehem, Pennsylvania.

Ralph Bussard, owner of Tri-City Divco Sales in Rock Island, Illinois, shows a line of Divcos at the Delaware plant storage lot with both rounded and flat-roof lines.

A change that was not very visible on the Delaware Divcos (unless you crawled under the truck) was the construction of the famous drop-frame. The frame of the Divcos built in Detroit had pressed one-piece rails. The Delaware Divcos had frames made up of welded side rails with dimensions of 2"x5½"x3/16" for trucks with an 11,000 lb. G.V.W. rating, 2"x5¾"x3/16" for trucks with a 15,000 lb. G.V.W. rating, and 2"x8"x1/4" for trucks with an 18,000 lb. G.V.W. rating. The frames all had steel reinforcements in critical areas.[38]

Another difference between the Detroit and Divco trucks was the color of primer paint used. When shipped from Hoover Road, Divcos were painted in green primer. Divcos shipped from Delaware were painted in a red primer (customers had their trucks painted to custom specifications

after the trucks were delivered). Overall, though, standard Divco features were found on the Delaware trucks.

Two identical series of trucks were made in the Model 300 line, the 300 C and the 300 D. In a July 6, 1976 letter to Divco dealers, Walter Kimball explained the reason for different model designations on identical trucks:

These two trucks are identically the same [sic]. The reason they are listed separately is for purposes of Federal Excise Tax. If a truck is to be used for carrying loads in which the GVW never exceeds 10,000 lbs., it is not subject to the 10% tax. We rate the Model 300 C at 9,900 lbs. GVW and is therefore not subject to tax.

The Model 300 D is rated at 11,000 lbs. GVW and therefore subject to tax. The two trucks are identical—same axles, wheels, tires, springs, suspension, etc.

The Model 206L was the largest Divco snub-nose delivery truck ever built. This ad from the November 1976 issue of The Dairy Record *shows the longer profile of the 206L.*

Although the Delaware years were not marked by significant innovation or design changes, there were a few interesting, or at least novel, product developments. For example, in Delaware, Divco changed from using Styrofoam insulation to a urethane foam that was forced into the sides of refrigerated trucks with a gun.[39] Also, a few Divco garbage trucks were among the vehicles built in Delaware. The garbage trucks had a trash-compactor body fitted on the standard Divco chassis. Sales literature published by Transairco in 1971 stated the Model SWD for packer bodies up to 15 cubic yards was available in 15,000 lbs. G.V.W to 18,000 lbs. G.V.W. on 127½ inch, 139½ inch or 151½ inch wheelbases. One 1971 model was delivered by the William F. Deibert Divco dealership in Allentown, Pennsylvania, and in 1996, that truck was still in use by Sipos Hauling and Disposal Service in Bethlehem, Pennsylvania. Exactly how many garbage trucks were built is not clear from the production records that survive from Delaware.

On February 16, 1976, Walter Kimball sent a memo to Divco dealers announcing availability of a new, larger Divco. The new truck was designated a Model 206 L and was basically a 206 D with a 139½ inch wheelbase and a body two feet longer. The memo stated that the first 206 L was released for demonstration, but that it was sold by the first dealer who had it available. However, Kimball offered to work out a demonstrator schedule for the 206 L for interested dealers. The exact number of Model 206 Ls produced is not known because of lost production records. However, Smith's Dairy of Orrville, Ohio, continued to have a Model 206 L in service in early 1997. Its serial number is 206L-0055, which indicates that at least 55 of the longer trucks were built.

Correct Manufacturing consistently estimated that production of Divcos in Delaware averaged about 150 per year. That figure was mentioned by Walt Kimball and Glenn Way during the 1976 tour and was reaffirmed in a 1980 letter from Way as well as in

The Only Company Who Thinks Enough of The Dairy Industry to Build a Truck Especially for The Dairy Industry

If you haven't bought a DIVCO—you haven't bought a retail dairy truck.

DIVCO by Transairco is better than ever.

- Up to 2000 pounds lighter than most other body companies' modified chassis and body combinations.
- Nearly a half century of incomparable service with a perfectly engineered body and chassis by DIVCO
- Custom made to each dairy's needs
- A record of outstanding fuel economy, amazing trouble-free performance and capable of expressway speeds
- Excellent visibility with many requested and tested driver convenience features
- The most imitated dairy truck in the industry and yet never equaled in performance, design and quality construction
- Available for immediate delivery

First choice of the dairy industry from coast to coast

TRANSAIRCO, INC.

DIVCO

DIVCO Truck Co.—Delaware, Ohio 43015

This April 1971 ad, which appeared in Dairy & Ice Cream Field *and* American Dairy Review *attests to the importance of the dairy market for Divco in its Delaware days.*

interviews of four former employees of Correct Manufacturing.[40] Unfortunately, not all the records of Correct Manufacturing's Divco production survived in usable form. We did find notebooks giving production of Models 206 C from 1969 to 1978; 206 D from 1969 to 1981; 200 C from 1968 to 1982, and 300 D from 1968 to 1975. Several other notebooks that may have contained production records were found but had been submerged in puddles of water for some time, which rendered them totally illegible. Therefore, no exact records exist for output of Models 300C, 306 F, 300 D post-1975, or any models after 1982.

We know that there was significant production of some of the models for which records are missing. For example, although the production records for Model 306 F have not survived, the evidence suggests that at least 351 of these models were made in Delaware. The Christiansen Dairy Company of North Providence, Rhode Island, took delivery of a truck with serial number 306F0350 on July 6, 1984, and another Divco with number 306F351 on January 5, 1985.

In Appendix B, known and estimated production figures for Delaware are given. An estimated 2,100 Divcos were built in Delaware. If 1968 and 1986 are not counted (because of extremely low production in those years) and the 11 months without production from May 1972 to March 1973 are eliminated, then the average annual production works out to about 130 units. However, production was not consistent from year to year, and it appears output was greatest in the early years. Therefore, the production estimates by Glenn Way and former company personnel of 150 units per year in the late 1970s and early 1980s were probably optimistic. The only precise data we have found on the total number of Divco trucks built in Delaware is a remnant of a handwritten log which listed truck production sequentially by order number but without serial number from October 1980 to August 1982. The last truck entered in the log is order number 1733 built August 27, 1982. Divco built trucks for three years and five months after that date. If 2,100 trucks were built in Delaware, production there was 367 trucks in the period from August 1982 to February 1986. That figure is credible but might be on the high side.

DIVCO

SINCE 1923

Reliable, Always Dependable

GOLDEN ANNIVERSARY

We are mighty proud of our 50 year record of service to the dairies who deliver milk to homes and small commercial users and we extend a sincere wish that all our many friends in this good and honorable industry may enjoy a most happy, healthy and prosperous 1974, with a good Santa Claus twinkle for our special friend, "The Milkman".

DIVCO TRUCK DIVISION
CORRECT MANUFACTURING CORP.
P O Box 689, Delaware, Ohio 43015
Ph: 614/363-1951

The Divco Truck Division of Correct Manufacturing may have stretched the point a bit to celebrate the Divco Golden Anniversary in 1974 in this series of ads in The Dairy Record. (The first trucks to carry the Divco name were built in 1926.)

Over the years, the prices of the Divcos built in Delaware increased steadily along with general inflation. The retail price of 115 inch wheelbase models at the end of 1985 was $12,702[41]—233% of the base suggested retail price of $5,445 in 1970.[42] During that same 1970 to 1985 period, the Producers Price Index for motor vehicles, compiled by the Bureau of Labor Statistics, increased by 245.7%. So, Divco went up in price slightly less than the overall Producers Price Index.

Bankruptcy: Divco at an End

Divco never failed: it continued to make a profit for Correct Manufacturing in most years until the end of production. A combination of factors, including management continuity problems and serious product liability lawsuits on the Sky-Worker units produced by Correct Manufacturing and its predecessors, eventually contributed to the bankruptcy of Correct Manufacturing and termination of Divco production.

In the last decade of Divco production Glenn Way was an elderly man (he was born in 1901). Yet, he continued to exercise day-to-day control of operations at Correct Manufacturing. The Transairco deal in 1970 was, in part, a response to his concerns about management continuity. However, after Correct Manufacturing became a separate entity in 1972, Way again was in full control, and he endeavored to manage with a strong "hands-on" approach.

During the 1976 tour of the Delaware plant, Walt Kimball, Plant Manager, was asked what plans there were for management continuity. His response was the following:

Mr. Way completely runs the company. He works seven days a week, fourteen hours per day. He has people doing specific jobs but is fully in charge of manufacturing, buying, and sales. The matter of his age has been discussed with him. The family is not interested in the business. No continuity of management has been planned. Now he refuses to discuss the matter. He thinks he is going to live forever.[43]

Anecdotal evidence and recollections of family members and employees constitute the basis for understanding how Correct Manufacturing was managed in its last few years. Way's son, Alton Way, described his father as one of the most independent individuals he has known, and Glenn Way did not want anybody from the family involved in Correct Manufacturing's operations. He ran the company completely. As a result, when he was unable to run the business, there was nobody to take over.[44] In the early 1980s, (family members and former employees were uncertain whether it was in 1980 or 1981) Glenn Way suffered a stroke. Alton Way said that although his father recovered from the stroke, he was not capable of running the firm after that.[45]

Duane Beard, Accountant and Controller at Correct Manufacturing from 1972 to 1986, said he warned Glenn Way in 1984 that bankruptcy could result unless operations were modified. Beard felt they should put idle cash to work for them and control purchases of inventory, such as the steel. He wrote an extensive report to Way on controlling expenses, cash management and inventory. He doubts that Way ever read it.[46]

Complicating the situation at Correct Manufacturing in the 1980s was a series of product liability lawsuits. According to Stegner and Beard, a few of the lawsuits were a result of Divco front spindles breaking, which resulted in wheels falling off. The bulk of the lawsuits, though, were the result of people being injured while working with Sky-Workers.[47] Stegner believes that the problem with Sky-Worker lawsuits actually began in the late 1960s, which is consistent with concerns expressed by Glenn Way about Sky-Worker lawsuits during a 1976 interview. Way complained at that time about the far-reaching implications of product liability claims.[48] In the 1972 buyback of Correct Manufacturing from Transairco, Way tried to protect his interests. He attempted to write a clause into the agreement that would exempt Correct Manufacturing from liability for any products (including Sky-Workers) built by Transairco prior to September 1, 1972. In the final agreement, Transairco accepted responsibility for any and all liability for three years expiring December 21, 1975.[49]

Way stated in an October 8, 1979 letter that Correct Manufacturing had no liability for any products produced prior to September 1, 1972. According to Way, "At no time along the line did anyone purchase any liabilities from anyone else. It was specifically outlined when Correct took over these assets that we did so without any acceptance of liability in any way, shape, or form."[50]

Whatever perceptions Glenn Way had about product liability agreements and responsibilities, the courts had the view that Correct Manufacturing was liable in some cases. As a result, Correct Manufacturing ended up with several major judgments against it. By December, 1985, a total of $5,258,481 in product liability judgments from four lawsuits had been rendered against Correct Manufacturing. In addition, at that time there were 23 product liability suits still pending against the company.[51]

On January 10, 1986, Correct Manufacturing Corporation of Delaware, Ohio, filed for protection under chapter 7 of title 11 of the United States Code.[52] Correct was bankrupt and was seeking protection from creditors to enable it to be liquidated in an orderly manner. The bankruptcy petition was signed by Shawn M. Flahive, an attorney with Vorys, Sater, Seymour and Pease in Columbus, Ohio, and Glenn Way as President of Correct Manufacturing. The petition listed Correct Manufacturing assets of $3,306,183 and liabilities of $6,187,825. The liabilities included the $5,258,481 in product liability judgements.[53] Included in the assets of Correct was $1,897,695 in inventory (as of August 31, 1985) of parts and unfinished vehicles.[54] Without the product liability judgments and the threat of more to come, Correct Manufacturing would have been a solvent business firm.

The bankruptcy petition was a chapter 7 filing requesting the liquidation of the company. A Chapter 11 filing would have asked for reorganization and continued operation. Given the product liability judgments and management situation at Correct Manufacturing, it would have been difficult to reorganize the company. Liquidation was the only viable option. The court-appointed bankruptcy trustee for the estate of Correct Manufacturing was Larry Staats of Columbus, Ohio. In a letter dated February 8, 1996, Mr. Staats says:

The company filed bankruptcy because of the number of claims resulting from the failure of a part on its 'Sky-Worker' ('cherrypickers') equipment. There have been numerous adversary proceedings to collect accounts receivable, etc. There are many claims for personal injury and wrongful death.[55]

An auction was held to dispose of the assets of Correct Manufacturing. The auctioneer was Myron Bowling of Hamilton, Ohio. The auction raised almost two million dollars from the sale of parts and equipment.[56] Principal purchaser of a large number of Divco and Sky-Worker parts was Harry De Nune of Springfield, Ohio.[57] Mr. De Nune is owner of Dixie Distributing Company, a distributor for Harley Davidson Motorcycle parts and accessories and Divco parts.

The real estate property of Correct Manufacturing on London Road Extension in Delaware was not included in the auction. The property was held by Albetway Corporation, a Way family corporation named after Glenn Way's children, Alton and Betty. When the bankruptcy occurred, the property was turned over to Albetway because, technically, Correct did not own it. In 1994, Alton Way, on behalf of Albetway Corporation, sold the property east of the railroad tracks (where Divcos were built) to James Hinkle of Marvin Industries who, as of 1997, is using the plant to produce wood pallets and other products and as a trucking terminal. The newer buildings west of the tracks were sold to Horizon Industries, a foundry firm.[58] Larry Staats, as well as several former employees of Correct Manufacturing (Duane Beard, Robert Owen, Robert Sealey, and James Stegner), and Alton Way confirmed that very few Correct Manufacturing records survived the bankruptcy proceedings; most were destroyed. In fact, James Stegner recalls seeing barrels of records being burned prior to the auction.[59]

Divco parts could be bought for a period of about ten days after the bankruptcy filing but before the auction. A number of dealers and customers took advantage of that opportunity, and a significant quantity of parts were sold at the time.[60]

When Correct Manufacturing went bankrupt, a total of 23 "executory contracts" were listed in the proceedings. An executory contract is one where an order (for a Divco or a Sky-Worker) had been placed and a deposit paid. Holders of executory contracts usually have no standing in a bankruptcy proceeding. In some cases, it is difficult to ascertain from the listing whether the contract is for a Sky-Worker, a Divco, or parts. However, 10 of the executory contracts were with dairies, so we may conclude that these were contracts for Divco trucks.[61] No statement of the value of the contracts is given; therefore, it is not possible to determine whether each of the orders was for one or several Divco trucks.

Prior to the bankruptcy auction for Correct Manufacturing, Larry Staats, ordered the completion of three trucks that were in various stages of production. He determined that the three Divcos were worth more to the bankruptcy estate as completed vehicles. In late January or early February 1986, Robert Owens, supervisor of the fabricating department and an employee at Correct Manufacturing and its predecessor firms for 38 years, was called back to supervise the crew of workers that finished the three Divcos.[62] One day in late winter 1986, a new Divco was driven out one of the large overhead doors of the Divco section of the Correct Manufacturing plant on London Road Extension in Delaware, Ohio. Then, like a curtain on a stage at the end of a play, the large overhead door closed. The last Divco had been built.

DIVCO today

The demand for route delivery trucks has diminished, but it hasn't disappeared and countless Divco trucks are still at work today. Some, like those in the fleet of the Christiansen Dairy in East Providence, Rhode Island, are on the road daily, delivering Christiansen Dairy products. Others are kept in pristine condition to do promotional work for their owners.

But work isn't in the future for all of the shiny Divcos on the road. There is an increasing interest in restoring Divco route trucks just for the fun of it. Some restorers do it out of a need to preserve a piece of America's history. For others restoring a Divco brings back pleasant memories of the days when the friendly milk man came to their door and sometimes slipped a half pint of chocolate to the children of good customers. In some cases, the man polishing his newly restored Divco was the milkman. Whatever the reason, newly painted Divcos are showing up on American streets in increasing numbers and reminding generations of the good old days of America's Favorite Milk Truck.

Joe Mazzarella delivered milk in Divcos in the 1940s. After retiring he bought this 1950 model 13 and restored it to like-new condition.

While Borden's no longer uses Divcos to deliver milk, this restored snub nosed Divco still works for the company. The truck travels the country along with the other most recognized symbol of the dairy industry, Elsie the Cow, doing public relations for the company.

"Maxwell the Milk Truck" is a 1962 Divco that serves as transportation for Zorox the Clown in the Phoenix, Arizona area.

"Old Moo" is a beautifully restored 1967 Divco Model 300C owned by John Hess of Naples, Florida. "Old Moo" actually began life as an egg truck! Mr. Hess uses "Old Moo" as a daily driver. (Courtesy, John Hess)

Munroe Dairy continues to operate several Divcos on a daily basis and in its advertising promises to deliver very fresh milk via Divco! The Divco shown in the Munroe Dairy postcard is a 300 series 1974 truck. (Courtesy, Munroe Dairy)

This 1947 Divco Model UM was restored by David Roderick of South Dartmouth, Massachusetts. The New Bedford Creamery had been the family business. (Courtesy, David Roderick)

Smith Dairy of Orrville, Ohio had a dozen Divcos on the road every day including this rare this Model 206L in daily operation as of early 1997. The steel Divco side panels have been replaced with fibreglass due to rust-out. (Courtesy, Smith Dairy Products Company)

The Christiansen Dairy of North Providence, Rhode Island continued to operate a fleet of about a dozen Divcos on a daily basis in 1996. Among the Christiansen fleet are two very late model 306F Divcos. One truck was delivered in July, 1984 and the other in January, 1985. One of those 306Fs is shown here. The Christiansen Divcos are lovingly maintained and restored by the dairy's own mechanic, Ron Tassoni.

This 1965 Divco was originally a milk delivery truck, but has been converted to a 20 keg beer truck. In the early 1990s Heinemann Distributing Company was still carrying beer to events in the Port Clinton, Ohio, area and dispensing it through taps on the side.

John Straight of Mt. Pleasant, Michigan is shown getting ready to "deliver" some milk from his 1964 Divco. (Courtesy, John Straight)

Ted and Doug Merritt of Rocky Hill and Belle Meade, New Jersey own this beautifully restored 1929 Divco Model G which is an Antique Automobile Club of America Grand National winner. The Divco originally was sold to the Paulus Dairy of New Brunswick, New Jersey and was bought by the Merritt family in 1939. (Courtesy, Ted and Doug Merritt)

Jim Austin of Lebanon, New Hampshire owns this restored Divco Model A, one of the original 25 Divcos built as prototypes in 1926 -- 1927. (Courtesy of Jim Austin; Ozzie Sweet photo, used with permission.)

Divco—in Retrospect

To bring the story of Divco to a close, we must ask one final question. Were Divcos good trucks? Divco survived from 1926 to 1986 as an independent producer of multi-stop delivery trucks and in that time it built about 95,000 vehicles. Delivery trucks, along with bodies and buses based on them, were its only product (except during wartime production). An independent truck producer with essentially one product line could not survive for 60 years without producing a good product. A survivor firm is one that meets all the challenges of the market place, including the demands of customers, and Divco was a survivor.

Divco had plenty of competition in its early years. By World War II, though, Pak-Age-Car, Walker, Thorne, and others were only memories. Divco was a survivor because very early in its history, it established a reputation for reliability and durability. Several former and current owners and drivers of Divcos were interviewed and each of them attested to the durability of Divco trucks. For example, Wally Weingart of Willowbrook, Illinois, went to work for Capital Dairy in Chicago in 1927. The first milk trucks he drove were Divco Model B three-point control models. In his words, "They had a clumsy appearance, but they handled well and were very reliable."[1] Later, Weingart drove Model Gs which he calls "The prettiest little truck ever built." He said that, while driving the three-point Model Bs and side tiller Model Gs was not a problem, Model Hs were easier to drive because they had a steering wheel and that all the Divcos he drove were solid, reliable trucks.

Were Divcos perfect? No, they were not perfect. Frames rusted, wheel spindles broke, and there were occasional breakdowns in the field. At the end of the assembly line at Hoover Road was a place called "The Hole" for repairs of production faults, and very

few Divcos made it out of the plant without spending some time in "The Hole." But looked at another way, "The Hole" was indicative of Divco's commitment to quality: each truck was carefully inspected and all problems corrected before shipment to a customer.[2]

Carl Abell, whose family ran Elm Farm Dairy in Medina, Ohio, from 1934 to 1979, also attests to the quality of Divcos. The only trucks Elm Farm used were Model A Fords and Divcos. The Fords, according to Abell, did not hold up as well as the Divcos. The first Divco bought by Elm Farm was a 1929 Model B, purchased used. The last was a Delaware Divco purchased in the 1970s.[3]

Ten years after the last Divco was built, businesses engaged in home delivery still endeavor to keep their Divcos on the road. Christiansen Dairy of North Providence, Rhode Island, was running 12 Divcos on eight milk routes in 1997. Its first Divco was purchased in 1940, and Christiansen has used only Divcos since. Christiansen Dairy was among the last purchasers of Divcos from Correct Manufacturing in 1985. In an interview, John Christiansen stated, "Divcos are the best little trucks ever built."[4] Another dairy operating Divcos is Munroe Dairy in East Providence, Rhode Island. Robert Armstrong, President of Munroe Dairy says Divcos are "great trucks."[5] Munroe Dairy should know, because the company still uses three Divcos every day for home delivery of dairy products.

Bergmann's Laundry of Washington, D.C., used Divcos through the years. The laundry ran eight Divcos on home delivery routes until July 1996 when the trucks were sold. Richard Bergmann stated, "I have driven Divcos for many years, and they are one of the best trucks ever made for delivery."[6]

Two former drivers for Producers Dairy of Cleveland, Ohio, also attested to the durability of Divcos. Ted J. Theodore, who at the time was a

Divcos always made sure the milk was delivered—even in blizzards and floods, as shown in this November 1956 ad in The Milk Dealer.

school teacher, worked as a summer substitute for Producers Dairy from 1948 to 1960. From 1948 to 1953, he alternated between horse-drawn wagons and Divcos. For two weeks he was on a wagon, and for two weeks he drove a Divco. Theodore recalled that it took a while to get used to driving the Divco "sit/stand drive" controls. However, he said the Divcos were very maneuverable and reliable. In twelve years, he did not have a single mechanical breakdown in a Divco.[7]

Eugene "Sonny" Degyansky, a school teacher who worked for Producers Dairy as a summer and weekend substitute driver from 1955 to 1964, recalled the challenge of driving a Divco. The combination brake/clutch pedal was a particularly tricky device, he said, because it was difficult to release without jerking or stalling. His one criticism was that the Divcos tended to be top heavy, causing one he drove to fall on its side on icy pavement. He, too, attested to their durability and said he never had a mechanical failure in a Divco.[8]

Did Divco have to fail? In a sense, Divco did not fail. The company that built Divcos at the end, Correct Manufacturing, failed due to Sky-Worker product liability suits which caused bankruptcy and, ultimately, termination of Divco production. Divco was a strong product line to the end for Correct Manufacturing. Although Correct was still building Sky-Workers, their output dwindled to one every couple of weeks by 1985.[9]

Could Divco have survived? Divco could have survived under at least two scenarios:

1. Survival at Hoover Road would have required greater success with the Dividend Series. The Hoover Road plant was a proven profit-maker for Divco and later for Divco-Wayne. Divco had an excellent reputation as a builder of home delivery trucks, but the home delivery market was collapsing by the 1960s. The decline in the popularity of home milk delivery hurt the market for milk trucks and Divco lacked significant presence or repu-

tation outside that market. The result was a decline in Divco production. At the production levels of the mid-1960s (around 2000 trucks per year), Divco was at the margin of profitability. A major inroad into the wholesale multi-stop truck market to increase volume would have been necessary. In that market, Divco was up against well-established competition from Ford, General Motors, Dodge, and International Harvester. The larger companies had deep pockets, extensive advertising budgets, large dealer networks, and significant product development capabilities. Divco simply did not have the financial ability to succeed at Hoover Road when confronted with that type of competition. The other firms were entrenched in the wholesale multi-stop market before Divco became serious about that market with the Dividend Series.

2. Divco might have been able to survive at the Delaware, Ohio, plant as a niche producer of home delivery trucks on a very limited scale (150 trucks a year). Unfortunately, Correct Manufacturing lacked continuity of

Through one of these large overhead doors in the Delaware, Ohio, plant of Correct Manufacturing, the last Divco was driven one day in February 1986.

management and product liability lawsuits plagued the company. Without management continuity to assure that ongoing product development occurred, that the dealer force was strengthened, and that the customer base was expanded, the company was adrift. With better organized management and without the legal difficulties confronting Correct Manufacturing, Divco might have been able to survive into the 1990s. But, specialty motor vehicle producers, such as Divco, typically have a difficult and challenging time in the market, and long-term success cannot be assured.

Ironically, in some areas Divco may have been ahead of its time. The Bantam Buses based on the Dividend Series did not sell very well in the 1950s and 1960s. However, in the 1980s and 1990s, when many organizations including airports, senior centers, and child care centers have their own mini-buses, Divco might have been more successful with the Bantam Buses. Another advanced feature Divco worked on was a "non-skid braking system using pre-set pulsing action." In 1957, John Zeigler of Hamilton, Ohio, applied for and, in 1959, received Patent 2,906,376 for the non-skid braking system and assigned it to Divco-Wayne Corporation. The patented device could intermittently and rapidly apply and relieve braking force over 100 times per second. As far as is known, the non-skid braking device never was used on a production Divco; perhaps the idea was too radical and novel in 1957. In the mid-1970s, however, it might have received a more enthusiastic reception as truck builders and, later, auto producers embraced antilock braking systems.

In the end, the sun set on Divco—a truck that served its owners well for 60 years, a truck that had continuity of distinctive snub-nosed styling for nearly a half-century, a truck that endeared itself to several of generations of Americans who either delivered milk and other products or had milk and other products delivered to them. For 60 years, Divcos delivered milk, bread, laundry, flowers, and a multitude of other products. But Divcos delivered more— they delivered on their promise of reliability, durability, and longevity. Yes, Divcos were good trucks.

THE END

Divco Production and Financial Statistics (Detroit)

Company	Year[1]	Sales[2]	Net After Tax Earnings[2]	Per Share Earnings[2]	Dividends Paid[2]	Number of Common Stock Shares[2]	Dividends Paid Per Share Common Stock[2]	Common StockPrice/Share High/Low[2]	Truck Production[3]	Employment at Divco[2]
Divco-Detroit Corporation: 1927-1933; Financial data not available										
Continental-Divco	1933	NA	-$70,681	NA	NA	200,000	.00	NA	203	NA
	1934	NA	-9,916	NA	NA	200,000	.00	NA	1070	NA
	1935	$576,433	17,853	NA	NA	200,000	.00	NA	1661	NA
Divco-Twin	1936	1,292,907	109,226	NA	NA	220,000	.00	NA	1513	NA
	1937	1,552,239	110,185	$.25	$66,000	222,000	.15	$5.50/$2.50	937	200
	1938	1,572,060	70,414	.16	22,200	222,000	.05	4.375/2.375	1195	178
	1939	1,914,739	202,605	.46	89,000	222,000	.20	8.25/3.50	1863	250
	1940	2,517,217	347,281	.77	168,750	225,000	.375	9.875/5.75	1922	250
	1941	4,049,884	477,795	1.06	225,000	225,000	.50	8.00/3.75	2799 (est.)	250
	1942	1,840,424	122,185	.27	56,250	225,000	.125	5.125/3.125		225
	1943	3,145,456	154,034	.34	56,250	225,000	.125	7.00/3.75		263
Divco Corp.	1944	1,433,404	135,438	.30	56,250	225,000	.125	14.50/5.375		240
	1945	3,566,369	383,778	.85	112,500	225,000	.25	34.25/11.25	3339	358
	1946	7,223,597	954,138	2.12[5]	393,750	450,000[5]	.875[5]	28.375/15.25[5]	4392	468
	1947	10,856,078	1,415,258	3.14	472,500	450,000	1.05	19.50/15.25	5756	642
	1948	13,428,463	1,710,348	3.80	990,000	450,000	2.20	20.50/13.875	6385	416
	1949	7,950,450	739,786	1.64	720,000	450,000	1.60	17.00/9.875	3632	428
	1950	9,853,285	1,047,736	2.33	720,000	450,000	1.60	15.25/12.25	5069	472
	1951	11,174,308	695,079	1.54	630,000	450,000	1.40	16.875/12.00	4414	518
	1952	8,749,958	387,342	.86	315,000	450,000	.70	12.125/8.00	3237	452
	1953	9,789,339	509,115	1.13	315,000	450,000	.70	12.00/7.75	3038	529
	1954	9,121,298	385,144	.85	270,000	450,000	.60	11.75/8.75	2959	529
	1955	12,214,391	434,463	.96	270,000	450,000	.60	11.75/9.50	3839	636
Divco-Wayne Corp.[4]	1956	13,297,856	443,879	.98	270,000	450,000	.60	13.375/9.00	3570	636
	1957	28,154,015	1,140,695	1.75	422,500	650,000	.65	13.25/9.625	2871	NA[7]
	1958	26,460,770	1,122,218	3.78	520,000	650,000	.80	26.875/9.875	2919	NA[7]
	1959	35,956,561	1,672,535	2.37	704,290[6]	650,000	.30[6]	29.25/21.375	3796	NA[7]
	1960	32,833,376	1,146,928	1.26	906,268[6]	764,032	1.20[6]	28.50/15.125	3572	NA[7]
	1961	28,757,885	826,990	1.78	462,285	768,618	.80	21.00/15.625	1783	NA[7]
	1962	57,007,205	1,837,788	4.51	407,384[6]	835,575	.50[6]	21.875/12.25	2883	NA[7]
	1963	70,953,608	2,226,907	4.11	540,626	831,456	.80	30.50/19.00	2082	NA[7]
	1964	82,005,874	2,856,903	3.41	836,553	1,121,608	.90	30.50/20.25	2394	NA[7]
	1965	100,803,115	3,542,337	2.73	1,293,950	1,129,300	1.20	37.875/23.125	2276	NA[7]
	1966	109,332,542	3,875,685	2.84	1,360,470	1,137,545	1.20	44.125/20.125	2131	NA[7]
	1967[8]								926	NA

[1] Divco operated on a November 1 - October 31st fiscal year in the 1936-1966 period.

[2] Financial and employment data taken from *Moody's Manual of Investments* and annual reports of Divco-Twin Truck Company, Divco Corporation, and Divco-Wayne Corporation for several years.

[3] Production figures from Divco corporate records on a calendar year basis.

[4] Divco-Wayne data includes all corporate activities including school bus and other bus bodies, mobile homes, etc. A separate breakdown for Divco was not available.

[5] Common stock split 2 for 1 on February 20, 1946. Per share earnings, dividends paid per share, and price per share reflect the after-split status.

[6] Stock dividends having a dollar value of $1,714,375 in 1959, $932,289 in 1960 and $259,031 were paid. The per share value of the stock dividends was 10 percent in 1959, 5 percent in 1960, and 2 percent in 1961.

[7] Employment data following 1956 reflects combined Divco-Wayne operations. Totals ranged from 1200 in 1957 to 1961, to 3000 in 1962 when Vought industries was purchased, to 2800 in 1963-1964, 4200 in 1965, and 4300 in 1966. No separate breakdown of employment at Divco is available. Given production levels after 1957, an approximation of employment at Divco would be in the 400 to 500 person range.

[8] No annual report or detailed financial breakdown were published for 1967 due to the merger with Boise-Cascade.

Divco Production (Delaware)

Production Year	Confirmed Production[1]	Estimated Additional Production	Estimated Total Production[2]
1968	11	0	11
1969	243	25	268
1970	257	25	282
1971	232	20	252
1972	210	20	230
1973	20	5	25
1974	75	10	85
1975	60	8	68
1976	36	70	106
1977	30	70	100
1978	37	70	107
1979	27	70	97
1980	28	70	98
1981	17	73	90
1982	2	73	75
1983	1	73	74
1984	NA	70	70
1985	NA	60	60
1986	3	0	3
TOTAL:	1289	812	2101

[1] From surviving production records.

[2] Based on interviews with former employees of Correct Manufacturing, Glenn W. Way, President, and Walter Kimball, Production Manager.

Divco Production by Model

Model	Year Produced	Number Produced
Early Trucks		
A	1926	25
B	1927-32	908
C	1928-29	158
G	1929-31	1468
H	1931-33	702
K	1932-34	47
M	1932-34	203
Q	1934-35	103
R	1934-35	497
S	1935-37	2657
Snub-Nosed Models		
UB	1939	27
UBM	1940-41	173
UL	1938	30
ULM-1	1939	50
ULM-2	1940	100
ULM-3	1941	2
ULM-4	1941-47	2501
ULM-4B	1947-49	377
ULM-5	1947-48	655
ULM-5B	1947-48	345
ULM-6	1948-50	1020
ULM-6B	1948-50	380
UM-1	1938	965
UM-2	1938-39	1686
UM-3 & -4	1939-41	1919
UM-5	1941-42	3129
UM-6	1944-47	6201
UM-7	1947	4000
UM-8	1947-49	5788
UM-8B	1947	325
UM-8E	1948-49	310
UM-9	1949-50	2404
UM-9B	1949-50	240
UM-9E	1949-50	421
UM-9E6	1949-50	534
11	1950-61	7343
12	1950-60	534
13	1950-61	222
14	1950-51	1833

Model	Year Produced	Number Produced
Snub-Nosed Models cont'd		
15	1950-61	3046
21	1950-54	1477
22	1950-55	414
24	1953-55	11
31	1950-52	476
32	1950-52	99
33	1951-55	1621
34	1951-55	256
35	1951	1
36	1952-55	378
37	1952-55	1337
114	1956-61	402
124	1956-61	240
134	1956-61	684
154	1956-61	2021
214	1955-61	1715
224	1956-61	111
244	1957	1
334	1955-61	3714
344	1955-61	252
364	1955-61	824
374	1955-61	4802
100A	1962-63	8
100B	1961-67	1176
100BX	1962-67	359
100C	1961-65	188
100CX	1961-67	945
10A	1961	1
10B	1961-67	401
10C	1963-65	6
200A	1961-66	88
200B	1961-67	1156
200C (Detroit)	1961-67	1355
200C (Delaware)*	1968-86	159
200C	TOTAL:	1514
206C (Detroit)	1964-67	488
206C (Delaware)*	1969-86	182
206C	TOTAL:	670
206D (Detroit)	1965-67	451
206D (Delaware)*	1968-86	685
206D	TOTAL:	1621
300A	1961-64	24
300B	1961-67	804

MODEL	YEAR PRODUCED	NUMBER PRODUCED		MODEL	YEAR PRODUCED	NUMBER PRODUCED
Snub-Nosed Models cont'd				**Buses**		
300C (Detroit)	1961-67	2344		45BUS	1959-61	12
300C (Delaware)	1968-86	**		55BUS	1959-61	17
300D (Detroit)	1961-66	1059		75BUS	1959-61	13
300D (Delaware)*	1968-86	440		76BUS	1959-61	42
300D	TOTAL:	1499				
206L (Delaware)*	1976	55				
300E	1961-67	1000				
300L	1964-65	2				
306E	1965-67	198				
306F (Detroit)	1965-67	446				
306F (Delaware)*	1969-86	351				
306F	TOTAL:	797				
Dividend Series						
41	1956-61	374				
42	1955-61	700				
43	1960	1				
44	1959	26				
51	1957-61	113				
52	1956-61	437				
53	1960	1				
54	1959-61	28				
57	1959-61	120				
58	1960-61	11				
71	1959-61	55				
72	1959-61	88				
73	1959	5				
74	1959	5				
40A	1961-66	41				
40B	1961-66	23				
40C	1961-67	79				
40D	1961-67	59				
40E	1961-67	166				
50A	1961-64	33				
50B	1962-67	46				
50C	1961-67	38				
50D	1961-65	53				
50E	1961-67	37				
50F	1961-67	106				
70A	1962-64	6				
70B	1961-66	40				
70C	1961-67	35				
70D	1961-67	107				

* Delaware production figures are estimates for some models and years due to incomplete production records being available and apparent breaks in serial number sequencing for some models.

** Model 300 C was built in Delaware but production figures are unavailable

Sources: Divco Production Records. *Branham Automobile Reference Book,* 1926-1987 editions, Chicago: Branham Printing Co.

Divco Prices

Year	Base Model	Price* (Base Model)	Expensive Model	Price* (Expensive Model)
1926	A	$2,195.00	NA	NA
1927	B	$2,195.00	NA	NA
1928	B	$2,095.00	NA	NA
1929	G	$1,595.00	C	$2,095.00
1930	G	$1,595.00	B	$2,095.00
1931	B	$1,300.00	H	$1,525.00
1932	B	$1,100.00	K	$1,595.00
1933	H	$1,295.00	K	$1,595.00
1934	R	$1,425.00	K	$1,495.00
1935	R	$1,425.00	Q	$1,475.00
1936	S	$1,140.00	NA	NA
1937	S3	$1,170.00	S4	$1,250.00
1938	UM-1	$1,250.00	UL	$1,350.00
1939	UM-2	$1,250.00	ULM-1	$1,350.00
1940	UM-3	$1,250.00	ULM-2	$1,350.00
1941	UM-4	$1,250.00	ULM-3	$2,295.00
1942	UM-5	$1,300.00	ULM-4	$1,575.00
1943—	*N O P R O D U C T I O N*	—		
1944	UM-6	$1,628.55	NA	NA
1945	UM-6	$1,628.55	ULM-4	$1,954.05
1946	UM-6	$1,603.49	ULM-4	$1,988.54
1947	UM-6	$1,628.55	ULM-4	$2,231.25
1948	UM-8B	$2,030.00	ULM-6	$2,550.00
1949	UM-8B	$2,030.00	ULM-6	$2,550.00
1950	UM-9B	$2,030.00	ULM-6	$2,550.00
1951	12	$2,140.00	21	$2,688.00
1952	12	$2,200.00	21	$2,835.00
1953	12	$2,295.00	21	$2,950.00
1954	12	$2,295.00	21	$2,950.00
1955	12	$2,450.00	214	$3,150.00
1956	12	$2,575.00	214	$3,415.00
1956	52Div	$3,428.00	41Div	$4,096.00
1957	12	$2,740.00	214	$3,635.00
1957	52Div	$3,605.00	41Div	$4,315.00
1958	12	$2,740.00	214	$3,635.00
1958	52Div	$3,538.00	41Div	$4,315.00
1959	12	$2,822.00	214	$3,762.00
1959	52Div	$3,538.00	41Div	$4,269.00
1960	12	$3007.68	214	$4,122.40
1960	52Div	$3582.58	41Div	$4,683.52
1961	10A	$3,205.53	200C	$4,517.79
1961	50A-Div	$3,627.76	70D-Div	$5,137.84

YEAR	BASE MODEL	PRICE* (Base Model)	EXPENSIVE MODEL	PRICE* (Expensive Model)
1962	10B	$3,328.30	200C	$4,614.02
1962	50A-Div	$3,804.79	70D-Div	$4,663.26
1963	10B	$3,455.78	200C	$4,712.30
1963	50A-Div	$3,990.47	70D-Div	$4,813.42
1964	10B	$2,588.13	206C	$4,812.67
1964	50A-Div	$4,185.20	70D-Div	$4,968.41
1965	10B	$3,726.00	206D	$4,915.00
1965	50C-Div	$4,390.00	70D-Div	$5,129.00
1966	100BX	$3,962.00	206D	$5,025.00
1966	50C-Div	$4,521.00	70D-Div	$5,288.00
1967	100BX	$3,962.00	206D	$5,025.00
1967	50C-Div	$4,521.00	70D-Div	$5,288.00
1968	300D	$5,459.75	206D	$6,148.75
1969	300D	$5,459.75	206D	$6,148.75
1970	300D	$5,445.00	206D	$6,085.00
1971	300D	$5,445.00	206D	$6,085.00
1972	300D	$5,445.00	206D	$6,085.00
1973	300C	$6,430.00	206D	$7,070.00
1974	300C	$6,745.00	206D	$7,326.00
1975	300C	$7,233.00	206D	$8,587.00
1976	300C	$7,810.00	206L	$10,341.00
1977	300C	$8,018.00	206L	$10,549.00
1978	300C	$8,101.00	206L	$10,549.00
1979	300C	$8,018.00	206L	$10,549.00
1980	300C	$8,950.00	206L	$11,772.00
1981	300C	$10,735.00	206L	$13,981.00
1982	300C	$11,252.00	206L	$14,652.00
1983	300C	$12,702.00	206L	$15,216.00
1984	300C	$12,702.00	206L	$15,216.00
1985	300C	$12,702.00	206L	$15,216.00

*Prices are for the lowest priced and highest priced Divco models in each year. From 1956 to 1967, a second line for each year is included for the Dividend Series. Prices shown are inclusive of federal taxes. These prices are representative only and do not include optional equipment. "Div" designation after model number indicates Dividend Series.

Prices for 1960, 1962, 1963, 1964, 1980, 1982, and 1983 models listed are estimated by authors from available data.

Sources: *Branham Automobile Reference Book*, 1933-1986 editions, Chicago: Branham Printing Co.; and Divco price records and dealer correspondence.

Divco Specifications: Representative Models

Introduction

In its 60 years of production, Divco produced many models of trucks with varying specifications and offering many options. It would be difficult to summarize those specifications in a comprehensive way. We chose, instead, to provide some representative specifications for several models of Divcos in tables E1 through E7. These specifications are not intended to be a complete list of all trucks, models, and options available from Divco through the years. Rather, they are presented to give the reader a general introduction to the variety of trucks and buses produced by Divco from 1926 to 1986. In the tables that follow, where blank spaces appear, the data were either not available or we were not able to determine the specifications from standard Divco specifications sheets.

Table E1: Representative Specifications: Early Divco Models Through 1937

	MODEL A —	MODEL B 1927-1932	MODEL C 1928-1929	MODEL G 1929-1931
RATED LOAD CAPACITY	3,000 lbs.	2,000-3,000 lbs.	2,000 lbs.	2,000-3,000 lbs.
TOTAL WEIGHT	—	3,500-4,000 lbs.	—	3.250 lbs.
CHASSIS WEIGHT	2,400 lbs.	2,450-2,500 lbs.	2,560-2,710 lbs.	2,470-2,710 lbs.
WHEELBASE	—	86"	—	94"
ENGINE				
Make	Continental	Continental	Continental	Continental
Design	L-Head	L-Head	L-Head	L-Head
Number of Cylinders	4	4	4	4
Displacement (cubic inches)	152.1	152.1	152.1	152.1
Horsepower (A.M.A. rating)	18.23	18.23	18.23	18.23
Governed Engine Speed	1470 rpm	1470 rpm	1470 rpm	1470 rpm
Governed Road Speed	—	18 mph	—	—
Bore x Stroke	3⅜x4¼	3⅜x4¼	3⅜x4¼	3⅜x4¼
Oil Capacity	4 qts.	4 qts.	4 qts.	4 qts.
Gas Capacity	—	10 gals.	—	11 gals.
Water Capacity	—	—	—	12 qts.
TRANSMISSION	—	3 Speed	—	3 Speed
AXLE RATIO	—	7.28	—	—
TIRES				
Front	—	30x5	—	30x5
Rear	—	30x5	—	30x5
CONTROL		Three Point		Dual Drive

Table E1: Representative Specifications: Early Divco Models Through 1937 cont'd...

	MODEL H 1931-1933	MODEL K 1932-1934	MODEL M 1932-1934	MODEL Q 1934-1935
RATED LOAD CAPACITY	2,00-3,000 lbs.	3,000 lbs.	3,000 lbs.	3,000-4,850 lbs.
TOTAL WEIGHT	4000 lbs.	—	—	
CHASSIS WEIGHT	2,885-3,118 lbs.	3,440-4,530 lbs.	3.340-4,430 lbs.	3,290 lbs.
WHEELBASE	96"	—	—	109"
ENGINE				
Make	Continental	—	—	Continental
Design	L-Head	—	—	L-Head
Number of Cylinders	4	6	6/4	4 (W-10)
Displacement (cubic inches)	152.1	—	—	—
Horsepower (A.M.A. rating)	18.23	27.34	27.34/18.23	24.02
Governed Engine Speed	1470 rpm	—	—	—
Governed Road Speed	18 mph	—	—	35 mph
Bore x Stroke	3⅜x4¼	—	—	3⅞x4¼
Oil Capacity	4 qts.	—	—	5 qts.
Gas Capacity	12 gals.	—	—	16 gals.
Water Capacity	10.5 qts.	—	—	15.5 qts.
TRANSMISSION	3 Speed	—	—	3 Speed
AXLE RATIO	7.28	—	—	6.6
TIRES				
front	5.50x20	—	—	32x6
rear	32x6	—	—	32x6
CONTROL	Single Point	Single Point	Single Point	Single Point

	MODEL R 1934-1935	DIVCO MODEL S 1936	DIVCO-TWIN MODEL S 1937-1938
RATED LOAD CAPACITY	3,000-4,575 lbs.	2,000 lbs.	—
TOTAL WEIGHT	—	3,875 lbs.	—
CHASSIS WEIGHT	3,140 lbs.	2,740 lbs.	—
WHEELBASE	109"	113.5"	—
ENGINE			
Make	Continental	Continental	—
Design	L-Head	L-Head	—
Number of Cylinders	4 (C-400)	4 (C-400)	4 (F-4162)
Displacement (cubic inches)	143	143	162
Horsepower (A.M.A. rating)	18.22	18.23	18.91
Governed Road Speed	25 mph	25 mph	35 mph
Bore x Stroke	3⅜x4	3⅜x4	3⁷⁄₁₆x4⅜
Oil Capacity	4 qts.	4 qts.	—
Gas Capacity	16 gals.	14 gals.	14 gals.
Water Capacity	14 qts.	12 qts.	—
TRANSMISSION	3 Speed	4 Speed	4 Speed
AXLE RATIO	7.2	7.2	7.2
TIRES			
front	32x6	6.00x20	6.00x20
rear	32x6	6.50x20	6.00x20
CONTROL	Single Point	Single Point	Single Point

Specifications are representative of these models. Other combinations are possible.

Table E2: Representative Specifications: Divco Model U Through 1947

	MODEL U 1938	**MODEL U** (option) 1938	**MODEL ULM** (prewar) 1941
RATED LOAD CAPACITY	2,000 lbs.	2,000 lbs.	—
TOTAL WEIGHT	3,950 lbs.	—	—
CHASSIS WEIGHT	2,925 lbs.	—	—
WHEELBASE	100¾"	100¾"	127½"
ENGINE			
Make	Continental	Continental	Continental
Design	L-Head	L-Head	L-Head
Number of Cylinders	4	4	6
Displacement (cubic inches)	140	162	218
Horsepower (A.M.A. rating)	16.26	18.91	25.40
Governed Engine Speed	2200 rpm	2590 rpm	—
Governed Road Speed	25 mph	35 mph	—
Bore x Stroke	3 3/16x4 3/8	3 7/16x4 3/8	3¼x4 3/8
Oil Capacity	4 qts.	4 qts.	—
Gas Capacity	12½ gals.	12½ gals.	20 gals.
Water Capacity	14 qts.	12 qts.	16 qts.
TRANSMISSION	4 Speed	4 Speed	4 Speed
AXLE RATIO	7.2	6.375	6.6
TIRES			
front	7.00x16	7.00x16	6.00x20
rear	7.50 x16	7.50 x16	6.00x20

	MODEL ULM 1945	**MODEL UM** 1947	**MODEL ULM-6** 1947
RATED LOAD CAPACITY	12,000 lbs.	9,000 lbs.	12,000 lbs.
TOTAL WEIGHT	5,240 lbs.	4,220 lbs.	5,240 lbs.
CHASSIS WEIGHT	3,365 lbs.	2,925 lbs.	3,365 lbs.
WHEELBASE	127½	100¾	127½
MILK CASE CAPACITY	100	50	112
ENGINE			
Make	Continental	Continental	Hercules
Design	L-Head	L-Head	L-Head
Number of Cylinders	6	4	6
Displacement (cubic inches)	226	162	229.6
Horsepower (A.M.A. rating)	26.63		28.35
Horsepower (brake)	62	18.91	75
Governed Engine Speed	2700 rpm	—	2700 rpm
Governed Road Speed	40 mph	32/35 mph	40 mph
Bore x Stroke	3 5/16x4 3/8	—	3 7/16x4 1/8
Oil Capacity	—	4 qts.	—
Gas Capacity	20 gals.	14 gals.	14 gals.
Water Capacity	14 qts.	12 qts.	—
TRANSMISSION	4 Speed	4 Speed	4 Speed
AXLE RATIO	6.6	6.6-7.2	—
TIRES			
front	6.00x20	7.00x16	6.50x20
rear	6.50x20	7.50x16	6.50x20 dual

Table E3: Specifications: Selected "Traditional" Snub Nosed Divco Models (Detroit Built)

	MODEL 11	MODEL 12	MODEL 13	MODEL 15
RATED CAPACITY (Gross Vehicle Weight)	7,500 lbs.	6,000 lbs.	*6,500-7,300 lbs.	*6,500-9,000 lbs.
TOTAL WEIGHT, CHASSIS AND BODY (Empty Truck with Water, Gas, Spare Tire, and Rim, Ready for Road)	4,430 lbs.	4,323 lbs.	*4,315-4,422 lbs.	4,408-4,515 lbs.
CHASSIS WEIGHT	2,925 lbs.	2,865 lbs.	*2,880-2,940 lbs.	*2,935-2,995 lbs.
WHEELBASE	100¾"	100¾"	100¾"	100¾"
MAXIMUM MILK CASE CAPACITY (Qts.) Square Bottles	57	—	52	57
ENGINE:				
Design	Divco L-Head	Divco L-Head	Divco L-Head	Divco L-Head
Number of Cylinders	4	4	4	6
Compression Ratio	6.1:1	6.1:1	6.1:1	6.1:1
Displacement Cubic Inches	162.4	162.4	162.4	229.7
Horsepower A.M.A. Rating	18.91	18.91	18.91	28.35
Horsepower Brake	47 @ 2640rpm	47 @ 2640rpm	47 @ 2640rpm	75 @ 2700rpm
Crankshaft (Fully counterbalanced on Models 41, 42, 51, 52, 244, & 364)	1045 Steel replaceable bearings	1045 Steel replaceable bearings	1045 Steel replaceable bearings	Tocco Hardened steel backed bearings
Governed Engine Speed	2640 rpm	2640 rpm	2640 rpm	2700 rpm
Governed Road Speed	36 mph	—	43 mph	44 mph
CAPACITY:				
Oil	3½ qts.	3½ qts.	3½ qts.	5 qts.
Gas	17 gals.	17 gals.	17 gals.	17 gals.
Water	11 qts.	11 qts.	11 qts.	12½ qts.
TRANSMISSION	4-Speed Spur Type	3-Speed Synchromesh	4-Speed Spur Type	4-Speed Spur Type
TURNING RADIUS:				
Right	17 ft. 8 in	17 ft. 8 in	17 ft. 8 in	17 ft. 8 in
Left	18 ft. 6 in.	18 ft. 6 in.	18 ft. 6 in.	18 ft. 6 in.
FRONT AXLE: Reverse Elliott with Heavy High Carbon Drop Forged I Beam Center	Capacity 4,500 lbs.	Capacity 4,500 lbs.	Capacity 4,500 lbs.	Capacity 4,500 lbs.
REAR AXLE: (Full Floating Type)				
Capacity	8,500 lbs	8,500 lbs	8,500 lbs	8,500 lbs
Ratio	5.57 / 6.16 / 4.88	5.57 / 6.16 / 4.88	5.57 / 6.16 / 4.88	5.57 / 6.16 / 4.88
SPRINGS: Semi-Elliptic Type: # of leaves in ( )				
Diversified Delivery: Front	—	36" x 2¼" (8)	36" x 2¼" (8)	36" x 2¼" (8)
Rear	—	46¾" x 2¼" (10)	46¾" x 2¼" (10)	46¾" x 2¼" (10)
Milk and Heavy Duty: Front	36" x 2¼" (9)	—	36" x 2¼" (9)	36" x 2¼" (9)
Rear	46¾" x 2¼" (16)	—	46¾" x 2¼" (16)	46¾" x 2¼" (16)
Number: Main-Spacer-Helper Leaves	10-2-4	10-2-4	10-2-4	10-2-4
TIRES:				
Diversified Delivery: Front	—	7.00-16 6 ply	7.00-16 6 ply	7.00-16 6 ply
Rear	—	7.00-16 6 ply	7.00-16 6 ply	7.00-16 6 ply
Milk and Heavy Duty: Front	7.00-16 6 ply	—	*7.50-16 8 ply	*7.50-16 8 ply
Rear	7.50-16 8 ply	—	*7.50-16 8 ply	*7.50-16 8 ply

* Varies depending on equipment: Model 15 achieves 9,000 lbs. G.V.W. by adding 750-16 8 ply front tires and 8.25-16 rear tires.

NOTE: All case capacities listed in catalog are U.S. Quart Square Glass Bottles, case size 12⅛" x 15".

Table E3: Specifications: Selected "Traditional" Snub Nosed Divco Models (Detroit Built) cont'd...

	MODELS 21, 22, 24	MODELS 31, 32, 33, 34, 36, 37	MODELS 100AX, 100BX, 100CX	MODELS 10 A, B, C 100 A, B, C
RATED CAPACITY (Gross Vehicle Weight)	7,500-12,000 lbs	—	7,500-12,000 lbs	—
TOTAL WEIGHT, CHASSIS AND BODY (Empty Truck with Water, Gas, Spare Tire, and Rim, Ready for Road)	4,900-5,059	4,538-5,798	—	—
CHASSIS WEIGHT	3,127-3,200 lbs.	3,160-3,315 lbs.	—	—
WHEELBASE	127½"	115"	115"	100¾"
MAXIMUM MILK CASE CAPACITY (Qts.) Square Bottles	115	100	—	—
ENGINE:				
Design	Continental/ Hercules L-Head	Continental/ Hercules L-Head	See Footnote	Continental L-Head
Number of Cylinders	4 or 6	4 or 6	4 or 6**	4
Displacement Cubic Inches	*	*	*	162.4
Horsepower A.M.A. Rating	*	*	*	18.91
Horsepower Brake	*	*	*	55
Governed Road Speed	*	43-47 mph	*	*
CAPACITY:				
Oil	—	—	—	—
Gas	17 gals.	17 gals.	17 gals.	17/21.5 gals.
Water	—	12.5 qts.	11-12.5 qts.	11 qts.
TRANSMISSION	3 or 4-Speed	3 or 4-Speed	3 or 4-Speed/Auto	3 or 4-Speed/Auto
REAR AXLE (Ratio Full Floating Type)	6.6	5.14 or 6.6	5.29 / 6.2 / 6.8	4.86 / 5.14 / 5.83 / 6.17
TIRES:				
Diversified Delivery: Front	7.00-16	7.00-16	7.00-16	7.00-16
Rear	7.50-16	7.50-16	7.50-16	7.50-16
Milk and Heavy Duty: Front	6.50-20	6.50-20	7.00-17	—
Rear	6.50-20 Dual (R)	7.50-20	7.00-17	—

*Varies depending on equipment
**The following engine options were available: Continental (gas); Ford (gas); Detroit (diesel); Perkins (deisel)

Table E4: Specifications: Selected "Squared-Up" Snub Nosed Divco Models (Detroit Built)

	MODEL 114	MODEL 124	MODEL 134	MODEL 154
RATED CAPACITY (Gross Vehicle Weight)	7,500-9,000 lbs.	6,000 lbs.	*6,500-9,000 lbs.	*6,500-9,000 lbs.
TOTAL WEIGHT, CHASSIS AND BODY (Empty Truck with Water, Gas, Spare Tire, and Rim, Ready for Road)	4,811 lbs.	4,704 lbs.	*4,696-4,803	*4,789-4,896
CHASSIS WEIGHT	2,390 lbs.	2,880 lbs.	*2,900-2,950	*2,704-2,948 lbs.
WHEELBASE	100¾"	100¾"	100¾"	100¾"
MAXIMUM MILK CASE CAPACITY (Qts.) Square Bottles	75	—	75	75
ENGINE:				
Design	Divco L-Head	Divco L-Head	Divco L-Head	Divco L-Head
Number of Cylinders	4 (Super 4)	4 (Super 4)	4 (Super 4)	6
Compression Ratio	6.25:1	6.25:1	6.25:1	6.56:1
Displacement Cubic Inches	162.4	162.4	162.4	229.7
Horsepower A.M.A. Rating	18.91	18.91	18.91	28.35
Horsepower Brake	55 @ 2000rpm	55 @ 2000rpm	55 @ 2000rpm	75 @ 2700rpm
Crankshaft (Fully counterbalanced on Models 41, 42, 51, 52, 244, & 364)	1045 Steel replaceable bearings	1045 Steel Moraine	1045 Steel Moraine	Tocco Hardened steel backed
Governed Engine Speed	2900 rpm	2900 rpm	2900 rpm	2700 rpm
Governed Road Speed	—	—	—	—
CAPACITY:				
Oil	3½ qts.	3½ qts.	3½ qts.	5 qts.
Gas	17 gals.	17 gals.	17 gals.	17 gals.
Water	11 qts.	11 qts.	11 qts.	12½ qts.
TRANSMISSION	4-Speed Spur Type	3-Speed Synchromesh	4-Speed Spur Type	4-Speed Spur Type
TURNING RADIUS:				
Right	17 ft. 8 in	17 ft. 8 in	17 ft. 8 in	17 ft. 8 in
Left	18 ft. 6 in.	18 ft. 6 in.	18 ft. 6 in.	18 ft. 6 in.
FRONT AXLE: (Reverse Elliott with Heavy High Carbon Drop Forged I Beam Center)	Capacity 4,500 lbs.	Capacity 4,500 lbs.	Capacity 4,500 lbs.	Capacity 4,500 lbs.
REAR AXLE: (Full Floating Type)				
Capacity	8,500 lbs	8,500 lbs	8,500 lbs	8,500 lbs
Ratio	5.57 / 6.16 / 4.88	5.57 / 6.16 / 4.88	5.57 / 6.16 / 4.88	5.57 / 6.16 / 4.88
SPRINGS: Semi-Elliptic Type: # of leaves in ( )				
Diversified Delivery: Front	—	36" x 2¼" (8)	36" x 2¼" (8)	36" x 2¼" (8)
Rear	—	46¾" x 2¼" (10)	46¾" x 2¼" (10)	46¾" x 2¼" (10)
Milk and Heavy Duty: Front	36" x 2¼" (10)	—	36" x 2¼" (10)	36" x 2¼" (10)
Rear	46¾" x 2¼" (20)	—	46¾" x 2¼" (20)	46¾" x 2¼" (20)
Number: Main-Spacer-Helper Leaves	11-2-7	11-2-7	11-2-7	11-2-7
TIRES:				
Diversified Delivery: Front	7.00-16 6 ply	7.00-16 6 ply	7.00-16 6 ply	7.00-16 6 ply
Rear	7.00-16 6 ply	7.00-16 6 ply	7.00-16 6 ply	7.00-16 6 ply
Milk and Heavy Duty: Front	7.50-16 8 ply	—	*750-16 8 ply	*750-16 8 ply
Rear	7.50-16 8 ply	—	*750-16 8 ply	*750-16 8 ply

* Varies depending on equipment: Model 114, 134, 154 become 9,000 lbs. G.V.W. by adding heavy duty springs, 7.50-16 8 ply front tires and 8.25-16 10 ply rear tires. Model 214 requires heavy duty springs and Super 6 engine for 13,500 lbs. G.V.W.

NOTE: All case capacities listed in catalog are U.S. Quart Square Glass Bottles, case size 12⅛" x 15".

Table E4: Specifications: Selected "Squared-Up" Snub Nosed Divco Models (Detroit Built) cont'd...

	MODEL 214	MODEL 224	MODEL 334
RATED CAPACITY	12,000-13,500 lbs.	8,000 lbs.	10,800 lbs.
(Gross Vehicle Weight)			
TOTAL WEIGHT, CHASSIS			
AND BODY, (Empty Truck with Water, Gas,	6,042 lbs.	5,295 lbs.	5,465 lbs.
Spare Tire, and Rim, Ready for Road)			
CHASSIS WEIGHT	3,662 lbs.	3,200 lbs.	3,315 lbs.
WHEELBASE	127½"	127½"	115"
MAXIMUM MILK CASE CAPACITY	116		100
(Qts.) Square bottle cases			
ENGINE:			
Design	Divco L-Head	Divco L-Head	Divco L-Head
Number of Cylinders	6	6	6
Compression Ratio	6.56:1	6.56:1	6.56:1
Displacement Cubic Inches	229.7	229.7	229.7
Horsepower A.M.A. Rating	28.35	28.35	28.35
Horsepower Brake	75 @ 2700 RPM	75 @ 2700 RPM	75 @ 2700 RPM
Crankshaft (Fully counterbalanced on	Tocco Hardened, steel	Tocco Hardened, steel	Tocco Hardened, steel
Models 41, 42, 51, 52, 244, & 364)	backed bearings	backed bearings	backed bearings
Governed Engine Speed	2700 rpm	2700 rpm	2700 rpm
Governed Road Speed			
CAPACITY:			
Oil	5 qts.	5 qts.	5 qts.
Gas	17 gals.	17 gals.	17 gals.
Water	12½ qts.	12½ qts.	12½ qts.
TRANSMISSION	4-Speed Spur Type	3-Speed Synchromesh	4-Speed Spur Type
TURNING RADIUS:			
Right	23 ft. 4 in.	19 ft. 2 in.	21 ft. 3½ in
Left	24 ft. 3 in	20 ft. 7¾ in	23 ft. 8 in.
FRONT AXLE: (Reverse Elliott with Heavy	Capacity	Capacity	Capacity
High Carbon Drop Forged I Beam Center)	4,500 lbs	4,500 lbs	4,500 lbs
REAR AXLE:(Full Floating Type)			
Capacity	11,000 lbs.	8,500 lbs.	11,000 lbs.
Ratio	5.14 / 6.6 / 7.2	5.14 / 6.6	5.14 / 6.6 / 7.2
SPRINGS: Semi-Elliptic Type: # of leaves in ( )			
Diversified Delivery: Front	—	36" x 2¼" (9)	—
Rear	—	46¾" x 2¼" (11)	—
Milk and Heavy Duty: Front	36" x 2¼" (11)	—	36" x 2¼" (10)
Rear	46¾" x 2¼" (21)	—	46¾" x 2¼" (20)
Number: Main-Spacer-Helper Leaves	12-2-7	11-0-0	11-2-7
TIRES:			
Diversified Delivery: Front	6.50-20 6 ply	7.00-16 6 ply	—
Rear	6.50-20 8 ply (Duals)	7.50-16 8 ply	—
Milk and Heavy Duty: Front	*7.50-20 8 ply	—	*6.50-20 8 ply
Rear	**7.00-20 8 ply (Duals)	—	**7.50-20 10 ply

* Varies depending on equipment: Model 214 requires heavy duty springs and Super 6 engine for 13,500 lbs. G.V.W.

** Models 214 and 334 available with both 17" and 20" dual wheel equipment.

NOTE: All case capacities listed in catalog are U.S. Quart Square Glass Bottles, case size 12⅛" x 15".

Table E4: Specifications: Selected "Squared-Up" Snub Nosed Divco Models (Detroit Built) cont'd...

	MODEL 344	MODEL 364	MODEL 374
RATED CAPACITY (Gross Vehicle Weight)	7,500 lbs.	6,500-8,000 lbs.	9500 lbs.
TOTAL WEIGHT, CHASSIS AND BODY (Empty Truck with Water, Gas, Spare Tire, and Rim, Ready for Road)	4,938 lbs.	4,850 lbs.	5,013 lbs.
CHASSIS WEIGHT	3,175 lbs.	3,112 lbs.	3,232 lbs.
WHEELBASE	115"	115"	115"
MAXIMUM MILK CASE CAPACITY (Qts.) Square bottle cases	—	—	80
ENGINE:			
Design	Divco L-Head	Divco L-Head	Divco L-Head
Number of Cylinders	6	4 (Super 4)	6
Compression Ratio	6.56 to 1	6.56 to 1	6.56 to 1
Displacement Cubic Inches	229.7*	162.4	229.6*
Horsepower A.M.A. Rating	28.35	18.91	28.35
Horsepower Brake	75 @ 2700 rpm	55 @ 2900 rpm	65
Crankshaft (Fully counterbalanced on Models 41, 42, 51, 52, 244, & 364)	Tocco Hardened steel backed bearings	1045 steel Moraine Bearings	Tocco Hardened steel backed bearings
Governed Engine Speed	2700 rpm	2900 rpm	2700 rpm
Governed Road Speed	—	—	43-50 mph
CAPACITY:			
Oil	5 qts.	3½ qts.	5 qts.
Gas	17 gals.	17 gals.	17 gals.
Water	12½ qts.	12½ qts.	12 ½qts.
TRANSMISSION	3-Speed Synchromeshe	3-Speed Synchromesh	3 or 4-Speed
TURNING RADIUS:			
Right	19 ft. 2 in.	19 ft. 2 in.	—
Left	20 ft. 7¾ inn	20 ft. 7¾ in	—
FRONT AXLE:(Reverse Elliott with Heavy High Carbon Drop Forged I Beam Center)	Capacity 4,500 lbs	Capacity 4,500 lbs	— 4,500 lbs
REAR AXLE:(Full Floating Type)			
Capacity	8,500 lbs.	8,500 lbs.	11,000 lbs.
Ratio	5.57 / 6.16 / 4.88	5.57 / 6.16 / 4.88	5.14 / 5.57 / 6.66
SPRINGS: Semi-Elliptic Type: # of leaves in ( )			
Diversified Delivery: Front	36" x 2¼" (9)	36" x 2¼" (8)	—
Rear	46¾" x 2¼" (10)	46¾" x 2¼" (10)	—
Milk and Heavy Duty: Front	—	—	—
Rear	—	—	—
Number: Main-Spacer-Helper Leaves	10-0-0	10-0-0	11-2-7
TIRES:			
Diversified Delivery: Front	7.00-16 6 ply	7.00-16 6 ply	7.50- 16
Rear	7.50-16 8 ply	7.00-16 6 ply	8.25-16
Milk and Heavy Duty: Front	**	7.50-16 8 ply	—
Rear	**	8.25-16 10 ply	—

* Divco used both 229.6 and 229.7 cid to refer to this engine. The manufacturer, Hercules, refers to this as a 230 cid engine.

** Models 214 and 344 available with both 17" and 20" Dual wheel equipment.

NOTE: All case capacities listed in catalog are U.S. Quart Square Glass Bottles, case size 12⅛" x 15"

Table E5: Specifications: Selected Snub Nosed Divco Models (Delaware Built)

	DTC-300-D	DTC-306-F	DTC-200-C
WHEELBASE	115"	115"	127½"
G.V.W.	11,000 lbs.	15,000 lbs.	15,000 lbs.
ENGINE	F-240	F-300	F-300
TRANSMISSION	T-18 4-speed/Automatic	T-18 4-speed/automatic	T-18 4-speed/automatic
CONTROLS	Sit / Sit-Stand	Sit / Sit-Stand	Sit / Sit-Stand
SPRINGS:			
Front	9 Lf.	10 Lf.	10 Lf.
Rear	21 Lf.	23 Lf.	23 Lf.
TIRES:			
Front	7.50-20 10 ply *8.25-17 10 ply	7.50-17 10 ply	7.50-20 8 ply
Rear	S/7.50-20 10 ply *S/8.25-17 10ply	D/7.50-17 10 ply	D/7.50-20 8 ply
AXLE TYPE**	C	C	C
BRAKES			
Front	12⅛ x 2¼	12⅛ x 2¼	12⅛ x 2¼
Rear	15 x 4	14⅛ x 3½	15 x 4
SIDE DOORS	Folding	Folding	Folding
CLUTCH DIAMETER	11"	12"	12"

	DTC-206-C	DTC-206-D
WHEELBASE	127½"	127½"
G.V.W.	15,000 lbs.	18,000 lbs.
ENGINE	F-300	F-300
TRANSMISSION	T-18 4-speed/automatic	T-18 4-speed/automatic
CONTROLS	Sit / Sit-Stand	Sit / Sit-Stand
SPRINGS:		
Front	10 Lf.	11 Lf.
Rear	23 Lf.	25 Lf.
TIRES:		
Front	7.50-20 10 ply	7.50-20 12 ply
Rear	D/7.50-20 10 ply	D/7.50-20 12 ply
AXLE TYPE**	C	D
BRAKES		
Front	12⅛ x 2¼	12⅛ x 2¼
Rear	15 x 4	15 x 4
SIDE DOORS	Folding	Folding
CLUTCH DIAMETER	12"	12"

* Extra Cost Option

** Rear axle - Timken - Only Ratios Available in C and D were 5.29 to 1 and 6.2 to 1. Optional available front axle (extra cost) 6,000 lbs. - Budd wheels front and rear.

Table E6: Specifications: Selected Dividend Series Divco Models

	MODEL 52	MODEL 42	MODEL 51	MODEL 41
RATED CAPACITY (Gross Vehicle Weight)	*7,000-14,000 lbs.	*7,000-14,000 lbs.	16,500 lbs.	16,500 lbs.
TOTAL WEIGHT, CHASSIS AND BODY (Empty Truck with Water, Gas, Spare Tire, and Rim, Ready for Road)	*5,400 lbs.	*5,800 lbs.	6,073 lbs.	6,429 lbs
CHASSIS WEIGHT	3,281 lbs.	3,370 lbs.	4,277 lbs.	4,307 lbs.
WHEELBASE	117½"	130"	117½"	130"
ENGINE:				
Design	Valve in Head	Valve in Head	Valve in Head	Valve in Head
Number of Cylinders	Super 6	Super 6	Super 6	Super 6
Compression Ratio	7½ to 1	7½ to 1	7½ to 1	7½ to 1
Displacement Cubic Inches	252.6	252.6	252.6	252.6
Horsepower A.M.A. Rating	29.4	29.4	29.4	29.4
Horsepower Brake	114 @ 3500 RPM	114 @ 3500 RPM	114 @ 3500 RPM	114 @ 3500 RPM
Crankshaft (Fully counterbalanced on Models 41, 42, 51, 52, 224, &364)	Special Carbon Steel Surfaces Tocco Hardened	Special Carbon Steel Surfaces Tocco Hardened	Special Carbon Steel Surfaces Tocco Hardened	Special Carbon Steel Surfaces Tocco Hardened
Governed Engine Speed	3500 RPM	3500 RPM	3500 RPM	3500 RPM
Governed Road Speed	57.0 MPH	57.0 MPH	52.0 MPH	52.0 MPH
CAPACITY:				
Oil	6 qts.	6 qts.	6 qts.	6 qts.
Gas	17 gals.	17 gals.	17 gals.	17 gals.
Water	17 qts.	17 qts.	17 qts.	17 qts.
TRANSMISSION	4-Speed Synchromesh	4-Speed Synchromesh	4-Speed Synchromesh	4-Speed Synchromesh
TURNING RADIUS:				
Right	19 ft. 11 in.	21 ft. 11 in	19 ft. 11 in.	21 ft. 11 in.
Left	20 ft. 11½ in.	22 ft. 11½ in.	22 ft. 11½ in.	22 ft. 11½ in.
FRONT AXLE:(Reverse Elliott with Heavy High Carbon Drop Forged I Beam Center)	4500 lbs.	4500 lbs.	4500 lbs.	4500 lbs.
REAR AXLE:				
Full Floating Type				
Ratio	5.57	5.57	7.2	7.2
SPRINGS: Semi-Elliptic Type: # of leaves in ( )				
Milk and Heavy Duty: Front	36" x 2¼"	36" x 2¼"	36" x 2¼" H.D.	36" x 2¼" H.D.
Rear	51¾" x 2¼"	51¾" x 2¼"	51¾" x 2¼" H.D.	51¾" x 2¼" H.D.
TIRES:				
Front	7.50-16 8 ply	7.50-16 8 ply	7.00-20 10 ply	7.00-20 10 ply
Rear	7.50-16 8 ply	7.50-16 8 ply	7.50-20 10 ply	7.50-20 10 ply

* Varies depending on equipment.

Table E7: Specifications: Dividend Series Bus Models

	MODEL 45	MODEL 55	MODEL 75	MODEL 76
SERIES (Body)	Custom	Custom	Custom	Panoramic
WHEELBASE	130"	117½"	153⅜"	153⅜"
ENGINE:				
Design	Valve in Head	Valve in Head	Valve in Head	Valve in Head
Number of Cylinders	Super 6	Super 6	Super 6	Super 6
Compression Ratio	7½ to 1	7½ to 1	7½ to 1	7½ to 1
Displacement Cubic Inches	252.6	252.6	252.6	252.6
Horsepower A.M.A. Rating	29.4	29.4	29.4	29.4
Horsepower Brake	114 @ 3500 RPM	114 @ 3500 RPM	114 @ 3500 RPM	114 @ 3500 RPM
Crankshaft	Special Carbon Steel Surfaces Tocco Hardened	Special Carbon Steel Surfaces Tocco Hardened	Special Carbon Steel Surfaces Tocco Hardened	Special Carbon Steel Surfaces Tocco Hardened
Governed Engine Speed	3500 RPM	3500 RPM	3500 RPM	3500 RPM
Governed Road Speed	57.0 MPH	57.0 MPH	52.0 MPH	52.0 MPH
TURNING RADIUS:				
Right	23 ft. 9½ in.	19 ft. 11 in.	25 ft. 4 in.	25 ft. 4 in.
Left	25 ft. 5 in.	20 ft. 11½ in.	24 ft. 10 in.	24 ft. 10 in.
TRANSMISSION	4 Speed Synchromesh	4 Speed Synchromesh	4 Speed Synchromesh	4 Speed Synchromesh
SPRINGS: Semi-Elliptic Type: # of leaves in ( )				
Front	36⅛" x 2¼" (11)	36⅛" x 2¼" (11)	36⅛" x 2¼" (11)	36⅛" x 2¼" (11)
Rear	51¾" x 2¼" (16)	51¾" x 2¼" (16)	51¾" x 2¼" (16)	51¾" x 2¼" (16)
TIRES:				
Front	7.50-16 8 ply	7.50-16 8 ply	7.50-16 8 ply	7.50-17 8 ply
7.50-17 8 ply				
Rear	8.25-16 10 ply	7.50-16 8 ply	7.50-17 8 ply	7.50-17 8 ply
7.50-17 8ply				
SEATING CAPACITY	12 to 20	9 to 16	15 to 24	20 to 25
(Depending on Seating Arrangement)				

Patents Held by Divco

PATENT	TITLE	ASSIGNORS	FIRM	DATE
DES89574	DELIVERY VEHICLE BODY	Nicol, John	CD	4/4/33
DES109521	DELIVERY VEHICLE	Nicol, John	DT	10/9/37
1544816	SELF-PROPELLED DELIVERY WAGON	Cummings, William L.	DT	7/7/25
1596001	FOOT PEDAL	Cummings, William L.	DT	8/17/26
1619775	RE: 17610 TO WALKER & DIVCO: DELIVERY VEHICLE	Whitney, Eddy R.	DD	3/4/30
1692535	STEERING MECHANISM - MTRVEH	Bacon, George M.	DD	11/20/28
1737489	CONTROL MECHANISM - MTRVEH	Bacon, George M.	DD	11/26/29
1768225	DOUBLE CONCENTRIC GEARING	Whitney, Eddy R.	DD	6/24/30
1777966	DELIVERY TRUCK	Fageol, William B.	TW	11/7/30
1812887	STEERING MECH - DEL TRUCKS	Maurer, Edwin R. & D.M. Ferguson	DD	7/7/31
1815772	MOTOR VEHICLE ATTACHMENT (SHIFT LEVER/ACCEL)	Gray, Joseph H. and E. Eichenberg	DD	7/21/31
1831360	TRUCK BODY CONSTRUCTION	Maurer, Edwin R. & D.M. Ferguson	DD	11/10/31
1831405	MOTOR DRIVEN DELIVERY VEHICLE	Bacon, George M.	DD	11/10/31
1874327	INTERNAL COMBUSTION ENG.	Maurer, Edwin R. & D.M. Ferguson	CD	8/30/32
1874526	BRAKE OPERATING MECHANISM	Herman, K. R. & D.M. Ferguson	CD	8/30/32
1899205	DELIVERY VEHICLE	Maurer, Edwin and D.M. Ferguson	CD	2/28/33
1903529	DROP CENTER DELIVERY VEH.	Maurer, Edwin R. & D.M. Ferguson	CD	4/11/33

FIRM TO WHICH PATENT WAS ASSIGNED:

CD: Continental-Divco Company
DC: Divco Corporation
DD: Divco-Detroit Corporation
DT: Divco-Twin Company
TW: Twin Coach Company
DW: Divco-Wayne Corporation

PATENT	TITLE	ASSIGNORS	FIRM	DATE
1911872	MOTOR DELIVERY VEHICLE	Bacon, George M.	CD	5/30/33
1925893	MILK DELIVERY MOTOR VEHICLE	Bacon, George M.	CD	9/5/33
1942181	MECHANISM FOR CONTROL-DELIVERY VEHICLE	Maurer, Edwin R. & D.M. Ferguson	CD	1/2/34
1957645	DELIVERY VEHICLE	Herman, Kenneth R.	CD	3/8/34
1972224	MOTOR DELIVERY VEHICLE	Herman, Kenneth R.	CD	9/4/34
1990748	MOTOR DRIVEN VEHICLE	Oberkircher, E.C. & C.G. Kaelin	CD	1/12/35
2003431	MOTOR VEHICLE CONTROL	Fageol, William B.	TW	6/4/35
2018443	LOW BED DELIVERY TRUCK	Fageol, William B.	TW	10/22/35
2097391	VEHICLE DRIVE AND CONTROL MECHANISM	Fageol, William	DT	10/26/37
2203599	SITTING DRIVE DELIVER VEHICLE	Nicol, John	DT	6/4/40
2234121	SEALING STRIP AND JOINT	Hedeen, Henry V.	DT	3/4/41
2240412	VEHICLE DOOR LOCK CONSTR.	Nyquist, George M.	DT	4/29/41
2242138	VEHICLE SEATING AND CONTROL	Muma, George E.	DT	5/13/41
2257852	COMB. TRANSMISSION AND THROTTLE CONTROL.	Nicol, John	DT	10/7/41
2280157	STAND DRIVE VEHICLE	Mead, Lynn D.	DT	4/21/42
2298773	VEHICLE	Nicol, John	DT	10/13/42
2301636	VEHICLE BODY BUILDING JIG	Nicol, John	DT	11/10/42
2307850	METHOD-DRAW WATER REFRIGERATION	Muma, G.E. & L.A. Demore	DT	1/12/43
2314730	VEHICLE CONTROL MECHANISM	Nicol, John	DT	3/23/43
2334193	VEH SEAT ADJUSTMENT/LOCK	Hedeen, Henry V. and C.	DT	11/16/43
2340339	VEHICLE CONTROL MECHANISM	Nicol, John	DT	2/1/44
2448043	FUEL FEEDING APPARATUS FOR I..C. ENGINE	Nash, Carl B.	DC	8/31/48
2574483	CONVERTIBLE TRUCK FLOOR	Jack, Robert K.	DC	11/13/51
2906376	NON-SKID BRAKING MECHANISM	Ziegler, John M.	DW	9/29/59

A Statistical Analysis of the Demand for Divco Trucks[1]

Can the hypothesis suggested in Chapter 6, that the decline in demand for Divco trucks was associated with economic trends and variables, be verified through formal statistical analysis? That is the question studied in this appendix. The economic variables studied as possible determinants of the decline in Divco's fortunes include increases in the price of home-delivered milk, decreased per capita consumption of milk, and an increased labor force participation rate for women.

The principal use of Divco trucks was for the home delivery of milk. The statistical analysis that follows concludes that the increase in the inflation-adjusted price of milk and decrease in the per capita consumption of fluid milk and cream in the 1941 to 1966 period are closely associated with the decline in demand for Divcos.

Ordinary least squares regression analysis was the statistical technique used to determine the variables associated with the demand for Divco trucks. A large number of variables were tested as possible determinants of demand for Divcos. In addition, a statistical analysis of the per capita demand for milk was undertaken using some of the variables noted in Table G1. The latter analysis did not yield conclusive results because of problems of multicollinearity where the independent variables were related to each other, causing unreliable regression coefficients, low t-statistics, and reversal of signs.[2]

Table G1: List of Variables Used in Statistical Analysis

- Annual per capita consumption of each of the following in the U.S. in pounds (independent variables)
  1. Fluid milk and cream (also tested separately as a dependent variable)
  2. Meat
  3. Canned fruit
  4. Canned fruit juice
  5. Frozen fruit juice
  6. Sugar, cane, and beet
  7. Coffee
  8. Canned vegetables
  9. Frozen vegetables
  10. Cheese

- Participation rate of women in the labor force in percent (independent variable)

- Number of grocery stores (independent variable)

- Real price of a half gallon of milk home delivered, which is derived from the nominal price of a half gallon of milk home delivered and the Consumer Price Index for dairy items (1967=100) (independent variable)

- Production of Divco trucks on an annual basis (dependent variable)

NOTE: Milk consumption is measured in pounds, participation rate in percent, and real price in cents.

[1] Nicole R. Price contributed substantively to this statistical analysis.

[2] Data used for statistical analysis in this appendix are taken from the following: data on food prices, consumption, milk and other dairy product consumption, prices related to the dairy industry, and the participation rate of women in the labor force from *Historical Statistics of the United States, Colonial Times to 1970*, Part 1, Washington D.C.: U.S. Department of Commerce, 1976; *Milk Facts*, U.S. Milk Industry Foundation, Washington, D.C.: 1993; and *Agricultural Statistics*, U.S. Department of Agriculture, Washington D.C.: U.S. Government Printing Office, annual editions, 1936-1993; data on number of grocery stores from *Historical Statistics of the United States, Colonial Times to 1970*, Part II; data on production from "Calendar Year Truck and Buses Production by Makes," "New Truck Registrations by Make and G.V.W.," *Automotive Industries* magazine, selected issues, 1937-1970, and production records of the Divco Corporation.

Through correlation analysis and experimentation with model specification,[3] it was demonstrated that production of Divcos was most closely related to the real (inflation adjusted) half-gallon delivered price of milk;[4] the participation rate of women in the labor force lagged one year; and the decrease in per capita milk consumption lagged three years. The lags were included to reflect the time it took available information and market adjustments to influence the demand and production schedule for Divcos.

An estimate of the equation for production using the 23 observations during the period 1941-1966 is provided. The year 1941 is the starting year because it represents the beginning of the period for which all data are available. The ending year is 1966 because it was the last full year of Divco output on a mass-production basis. (Using data from the Delaware years would distort the results because of the extremely low volume of Delaware production.) The model adjusts for the years of World War II when there was no Divco production. The equation estimate is as follows:

Production of Divcos in a given year = 12031.55 + 21.99 (Milk consumption of three years earlier)
- 94.15 (Participation rate of women in the labor force one year earlier)
- 223.17 (Real, inflation adjusted, half gallon delivered price of milk)

A summary of the regression coefficients, t-statistics, and correlation coefficients for the independent variables with the dependent variable for the period 1941-1966 appears in Table G2. The t-statistics for milk consumption lagged three years, and the real price for a half-gallon of delivered milk are significant at the 95% confidence level, meaning that there is 95% confidence that the estimates are correct and were not obtained by chance alone. The t-statistic for women in the labor force is significant at a confidence level of approximately 85%. The relatively low t-statistic on the participation rate of women in the labor force lagged one year may be caused by multicollinearity.

The test Durbin-Watson statistic of 2.407 is inconclusive regarding the existence of autocorrelation. The critical Durbin-Watson statistic is 2.34; since an estimate of the autocorrelation coefficient may be incorrect with a small sample,[5] corrections were not made for autocorrelation.

The adjusted R^2 for the equation is 0.745 indicating that 74.5% of the variation in Divco production is associated with the independent variables in the regression equation. With an adjusted R2 of 0.745, it may be concluded that the decline in per capita milk consumption, the increase in the labor force participation rate of women, and increases in the real half-gallon delivered price of

Table G2: Regression Statistics: Demand for Divco Trucks, 1941-1966

INDEPENDENT VARIABLES	REGRESSION COEFFICIENT	T-STATISTIC	CORRELATION COEFFICIENT WITH PRODUCTION
Milk consumption (3 year lag)	21.99	2.42	.842
Women in the labor force (1 year lag)	-94.15	-1.55	-.602
Real half gallon delivered price	-223.17	-2.34	-.714
Constant term	12031.55		

Dependent variable = Production of Divco trucks on an annual basis, 1941 to 1966

Adjusted R^2 = .745

[3] The correlation coefficients and t-statistics change substantially with small changes in the sample size observed, which indicates that the model is somewhat unstable.

[4] The following formula was used to calculate the real half gallon delivered price of milk: Real price of a half gallon = (Nominal price/Consumer price index for dairy items)*100. The price index base year is 1967=100.

[5] It may be best to ignore autocorrelation with a small sample because it is difficult to get a good estimate of the autocorrelation coefficient. (Brown. William S., *Introduction to Econometrics*. St. Paul, MN: West, 1991. p. 178). A small sample is defined as one with less than thirty observations. (Anderson, David, Dennis J. Sweeney, and Thomas A. Williams. *Statistics for Business and Economics*. fifth ed. St. Paul, MN: West, 1993. p. 342).

milk contributed to the decline of Divco truck output (data for these variables are found in Table G3). However, about 25% of the variation in Divco demand remains unexplained by these variables. Therefore, some variables as yet unidentified have been omitted from the equation. For example, the number of grocery stores in the United States, which has a correlation coefficient of -0.697 with Divco production for the period of 1946-1961, was omitted due to the limited range of available data. We suggest that the increased number of grocery stores made shopping for milk more convenient. However, because the number of grocery stores has correlation coefficients of 0.856, 0.815, and 0.839 with per capita milk consumption lagged three years, women in the labor force lagged one year, and the real price of a half gallon of delivered milk respectively, inclusion of this variable would raise the problems of multicollinearity as and an inadequate data sample.

Another variable we omitted from the analysis, which is discussed in Chapter 6, is the length of time trucks would be used. A longer truck life would mean lower demand for new trucks. Unfortunately, accurate time series data on Divco truck life is unavailable. Also excluded as a possible variable is the increase in home refrigeration capabilities, which meant people could store milk longer, which, in turn, reduced the number of times per week milk had to be delivered to the house. Also, improved home refrigeration capabilities meant a substantial amount of milk could be purchased in one trip to the supermarket.

Overall, in spite of the limitations of statistical analysis, we can conclude that variables suggested by economic theory are associated with three-fourths of the demand for Divco trucks. The rising price of home delivered milk caused consumers to substitute store bought milk, thereby decreasing the demand for home delivery and Divcos. Decreased per capita consumption of milk, accompanied by substitution of other food products also reduced the demand for home delivery of milk and Divcos. Although the statistical results are less robust for the association between an increasing labor force participation rate for women and the decline in demand for Divcos, the results are intuitively sensible. As more women went to work outside of the home, it became more convenient for them to shop at supermarkets for all of their grocery needs including milk, thereby contributing to the decline of Divco.

Table G3: Divco Regression Analysis Data

Year	Divco Production in Units	U.S. Per Capita Consumption of Fluid Milk and Cream in Pounds	Real Price of 1/2 Gallon of Milk Home Delivered in Cents/Gal.	Percent of Women in Labor Force
1941	2799	334	61.82	28.5
1942	NA	354	60.85	30.9
1943	NA	371	58.60	35.7
1944	NA	381	59.43	36.3
1945	3339	399	59.32	35.8
1946	4392	389	54.24	30.8
1947	5756	369	53.55	31.8
1948	6385	355	54.16	32.7
1949	3632	352	57.49	33.2
1950	5069	349	56.75	33.9
1951	4414	352	57.04	34.7
1952	3237	352	57.35	34.8
1953	3038	347	56.45	34.5
1954	2959	348	57.29	34.6
1955	3839	348	57.61	35.7
1956	3570	343	58.81	36.9
1957	2871	335	59.03	36.9
1958	2919	328	58.91	37.1
1959	3796	330	58.50	37.2
1960	3572	322	58.82	37.8
1961	1783	312	58.35	38.1
1962	2883	308	58.52	38.0
1963	2082	307	58.49	38.3
1964	2394	304	58.86	38.7
1965	2276	302	58.44	39.3
1966	2131	297	57.93	40.3

Glenn Way—Entrepreneur

Glenn W. Way was an entrepreneur, an individualist, and an industrialist. During his 87 years (1901-1988), he created many jobs, did things his own way, and built thousands of Vanettes, Sky-Workers, cranes, air conditioning units, and Divcos. His many business interests were complex, and we attempt only a brief summary here. The primary source of the information presented below about the history of Way's enterprises is a letter dictated by Glenn Way in 1979.[1]

■ Hughes-Keenan Company of Mansfield, Ohio, founded in 1904, was a manufacturer of machinery and equipment bought by Way in 1940. At the time, Way was working for Gerstenslager Company of Wooster, Ohio, a truck body manufacturer.

■ Burkett Closed Body Company of Dayton, Ohio, purchased by Way in 1942. Burkett supplied bodies to International Harvester.

■ Correct Manufacturing Company was organized in Delaware in 1942 as a partnership between Way and his first wife, Zuilla (who died in 1958). Correct Manufacturing produced heavy equipment and components, including during World War II, a front-loading shovel apparatus for bulldozers. Correct Manufacturing became a corporation in 1947. Hughes-Keenan, Burkett Closed Body Company, and Correct Manufacturing were consolidated into one corporation known as Hughes-Keenan Corporation in 1947. Operations of all three companies were consolidated in Delaware, Ohio, by 1949. Principal products of the companies included; Hughes-Keenan:Roustabout Cranes. Burkett Closed Body: sleeper cab, milk truck, and panel truck bodies for International Harvester. Correct Manufacturing: Vanette truck bodies.

■ Hughes-Keenan was merged into United States Air Conditioning Corporation (US Airco) in 1957 and was listed on the American Stock Exchange. US Airco, at the time, was in Philadelphia. Operations were moved to a new building in Delaware in 1958. US Airco was the succeeding corporation and Hughes-Keenan ceased to exist. Products of US Airco continued to be truck bodies (Burkett Closed Body products and Vanettes), Roustabout Cranes, and air conditioning.

■ The Sky-Worker division of EMHART Manufacturing Company of Hartford Connecticut was purchased in 1960 and production moved to Delaware.

■ Rybolt Heater Company of Ashland, Ohio was controlled with half of its stock purchased in 1965. The remainder of its stock was purchased in 1966.

■ Curtis Air Conditioning Company of St. Louis, Missouri, was purchased in 1965.

■ Aldrich Company of Wyoming, Illinois, was purchased in 1966.

■ The United States Air Conditioning Corporation name was changed to Transairco, Inc. in 1966 with no other major change in the corporate structure.

■ Divco was purchased in late 1967 and moved to Delaware, Ohio, in 1968. Also purchased in 1967 was Aqua-Heat of New Jersey.

■ Glenn Way, at age 66 in 1967, began to consider the long-term management of the company. Negotiations were entered into, and in April 1970, two corporations owned by André J. Andreoli of Akron, Ohio, were merged into Transairco. The Andreoli interests owned luxury hotels, cable TV, a racetrack, and shopping malls.

■ In 1970, Transairco merged with Associated Equities Inc. and Associated Dayton Equities Inc. The Way family interest dropped to 26%.

■ After internal management difficulties and disagreements in 1971, Glenn Way resigned as President, but remained as a director of Transairco. In May, 1971, all manufacturing divisions of Transairco were merged into a manufacturing entity entitled Hughes-Keenan Manufacturing Company. After disagreements on how the finances of Transairco were being handled, Glenn Way offered to buy back the Correct Manufacturing operations.

■ On September 1, 1972, the Way family relinquished to Transairco all of their stock and received in return all of the stock of Correct Manufacturing. In 1973, a corporation called Albetway (for Alton Way and Betty Frye, the children of Glenn Way) was organized by a Way family trust to purchase the real estate in Delaware, Ohio, from Transairco. The new firm was called Correct Manufacturing, was owned by the Way family, and produced the Sky-Workers and Divcos until the end of production in early 1986.

[1] Way, Glenn W., letter to Devine, Millimet, Stahl and Branch (attorneys), Manchester, New Hampshire, October 8, 1979.

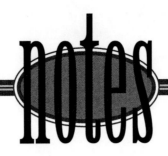

CHAPTER 1. Divco: The Early Years

1. Moran, Mary Ann, The Lackawana Historical Society, Scranton, Pennsylvania, letter from August 28, 1996.

2. Muma, G.E., "Divco Corporation and its Predecessors," Detroit: Divco Corporation, September, 1956, p. 1.

3. See Muma, p. 2 and La Marre, Tom, "Detroit Electric," *Automobile Quarterly*, vol. 27, no. 2, pp. 161-170.

4. Parker, George W., "Alas, The Horse!" *Detroit Free Press*, October 16, 1955, p. 2B.

5. Muma, p. 2.

6. "Industry Busy With New Cars," *New York Times*, May 29, 1927, XX, p. 13, col. 7.

7. "The Death of Carl H. L. Flintermann," *Detroit Saturday Night*, January 24, 1931, p. 3.

8. "Three-Control Truck New Detroit Product," *Automotive Industries*, vol. 56, no. 21, May 28, 1927, p. 817.

9. Muma, p. 3.

10. "New Delivery Truck Has Three-Point Control," *Automotive Industries*, vol. 56, no. 23, June 25, 1927, p. 973.

11. *Automotive Industries*, June 25, 1927, p. 973.

12. Muma, p. 4.

13. Parker, p. 2B.

14. Muma, p. 4.

15. Stigler, George J., "The Economies of Scales," *Journal of Law and Economics*, vol. 1, October, 1958, pp. 54-71.

16. Shepherd, William J., "What Does the Survivor Technique Show about Economies of Scale?" *Southern Economic Journal*, vol. 34, July, 1967, pp. 113-22.

17. "Free Aisle Feature of New Divco Truck," *Automobile Topics*, January 17, 1931, p. 878.

18. "Divco-Detroit Acquires Step-N-Drive Company," *Automotive Topics*, September 20, 1930, p. 515.

19. "Many Big Dairy Companies Lower Costs With Ford Trucks and Cut Overhead," *Ford Dealer News*, April 15, 1931, pp. 18-19.

20. *Automobile Topics*, September 20, 1930, p. 515.

21. "Divco Consolidates Manufacturing Units," *Automobile Topics*, January 3, 1931, p. 664.

22. See, for example, ad entitled "Bigger Profits For You," *Ford Dealer News*, April 15, 1931, p. 53.

23. "Herman Chief Engineer," *Automobile Topics*, August 24, 1929, p. 198.

24. *Automobile Topics*, January 17, 1931, p. 878.

25. Muma, pp. 4-5.

26. National Automobile Chamber of Commerce, New York, letter to Ward Motor Vehicle Company, Mt. Vernon, New York, May 4, 1932.

27. *Moody's Manual of Investments*, 1933, pp. 458-459.

28. *Moody's Manual of Investments*, 1933, p. 459 and 1935, p. 492. For more information on the Continental automobile and history of Continental Motors, see: Gross, Ken, "1933 Continental Beacon," *Special-Interest Autos*, Jan.-Feb., 1977, pp. 23-65, and Naul, G. Marshall and Norleye, Jan P., "A Brief History of the Continental Engine Company," *Special Interest Autos*, Jan.-Feb., 1977, pp. 28-33.

29. *Moody's Manual of Investments*, 1930, p. 34; 1933, p. 459.

30. "Staff Is Selected by Continental-Divco," *Automobile Topics*, May 28, 1932, p. 179.

31. Almanac Issue, 1938, *Automotive News*, September 10, 1938, p. 57 and "Nicol Heads Divco Corp.," *Automobile Topics*, September 27, 1930, p. 595.

32. *Continental Motors Corporation, Annual Report for Fiscal Year Ending October 31, 1932*, Detroit, Michigan, January 6, 1933.

33. *Automobile Topics*, May 28, 1932, p. 179.

34. *Historical Statistics of the United States, Colonial Times to 1957*, Washington, D.C.: U.S. Department of Commerce, 1960, pp. 125-126.

35. Nicol, John, Vice President and General Manager, Continental-Divco Company, Detroit, Michigan, letter to M. J. Duryea, Longmeadow, Mass., December 12, 1935.

36. *Moody's Manual of Investments*, 1935, p. 492; 1937, p. 3145.

37. *1931 Annual Report of the President of Continental Motors Corporation for the Year Ending October 31, 1930*, Detroit, January 2, 1931.

38. *Continental Motors Corporation, Annual Report for the Fiscal Year ended October 31, 1935*, Detroit, December 31, 1935.

39. *Continental Motors Corporation, Annual Report for the Fiscal Year ended October 31, 1934*, Detroit, December 31, 1934.

CHAPTER 2. Divco Derails Dobin and Takes on the Competition

1. Lefebure, Regis, "Scientific Feeding, Stable Labor Control, Reduce Horse Route Costs," *The Milk Dealer*, January 1936, pp. 40-41.

2. "Multi-Stop Units Dub Dobbin a Dud," *The Commercial Car Journal*, vol. 43, no. 2, April 1932, pp. 18-21.

3. "Door-to-Door Units Promote the Trend to Direct Selling," *The Commercial Car Journal*, vol. 45, no. 2, April 1933, pp. 18-20.

4. Daly, Matt T., Vice President, Borden's Farm Products Division New York, "A Horse and A Milk Wagon," *The Select Circle*, August 1946.

5. Daly, p. 3.

6. Miller, Julie, Corporate Affairs Office, Borden Inc., Columbus, Ohio, letter from, August 3, 1995, citing statement by Walter C. Sanders, Assistant Sales Manager, Borden's Farm Products of New York in March 1962.

7. Lewin, Barry, "The Last Horse," *The Milk Dealer*, January, 1964, pp. 38 and 76, and "End of the Road for Bessie," *Business Week*, July 27, 1963, p. 28.

8. "White Starts Production on its New Light Delivery," *Automotive News*, November 12, 1938, p. 24.

9. "White Truck in the Black," *Fortune*, vol. 23, February 1941. p. 126.

10. "Metro Expands Its Line of Extra Capacity Bodies," *Automotive News*, November 11, 1938, p. 8.

11. "International Announces All-New Lineup of Multi-stop Trucks," *The Milk Dealer*, March 1965, p. 62.

12. Wren, James A. and Wren, Genevieve J., *Motor Trucks of America*, Ann Arbor, Michigan: University of Michigan Press (for the Motor Vehicle Manufacturers Association of the United States, Inc.) 1979, pp. 85 and 117.

13. Newell & Spencer, Patent Attorneys, New York, letter to Ward Motor Vehicle Company, Mount Vernon, New York, July 29, 1929.

14. See, for example, Newell & Spencer, Patent Attorneys, New York, letter to Ward Motor Vehicle Company, Mt. Vernon, N.Y., September 4, 1929.

15. See, for example, letter to the Ward Motor Vehicle Company from Newell & Spencer, Patent Attorneys, New York, September 5, 1929.

16. Brown, Jackson, Boettcher & Diener, Chicago, letter to Newell & Spencer, Patent Attorneys, New York, September 5, 1929.

17. Nicol, John, Vice President and General Manager, Divco-Detroit Corporation, Detroit, letter to Ward Motor Vehicle Company, Mt. Vernon, New York, October 15, 1929.

18. Nicol, John, Vice President and General Manger, Divco-Detroit Corporation, letter to Newell & Spencer, Patent Attorneys, New York, October 9, 1929; and Newell & Spencer, Patent Attorneys, New York, letter to Ward Motor Vehicle Company, Mt. Vernon, New York, October 24, 1929.

19. Ward Motor Vehicle Company, Mt. Vernon, New York, letter to Newell & Spencer, Patent Attorneys, New York, October 28, 1929.

20. "Walker Vehicle Shows New Dynamotive Model," *Automotive News*, November 12, 1938, p. 24.

21. Thorne, Niblack "Bill," "The Thorne Gas-Electric Truck," *The Bulb Horn*, vol. 56, no. 2, April-June 1995, p. 22.

22. Thorne, *The Bulb Horn*, April/June 1995, pp. 22-23.

23. "Pak-Age-Car—Without Chassis or Foot Pedals," *Autobody*, May, 1927.

24. "Stutz Motor Car Company of America, Inc.," *Moody's Manual of Investments*, 1936, p. 2071 and 1939, p. 1346.

25. "Auburn Automobile Company," *Moody's Manual of Investments*, 1940, p. 1405

26. "Diamond T Motor Car Co.,"*Moody's Manual of Investments*, 1943, p. 540.

27. Georgano, G. N., ed., G. Marshall Naul, consulting ed., *The Complete Encyclopedia of Commercial Vehicles*, Osceola, Wisconsin: Motorbooks, International, 1979, p. 482.

28. *The Complete Encyclopedia of Commercial Vehicles*, p. 632.

29. National Automobile Chamber of Commerce, Detroit, Michigan, letter to Ward Motor Vehicle Company, Mt. Vernon, New York, June 26, 1933.

30. "Twin Coach Co.," *Moody's Manual of Investments*, 1937, p. 1336.

31. "Continental Motors Corp.," *Moody's Manual of Investments*, 1936, p. 475, and "Divco-Twin Truck Co.," *Moody's Manual of Investments*, 1937, p. 3145.

CHAPTER 3. Divco-Twin and the Model U, 1936-1944

1. "Divco Development Spans Half A Century," *Divco News*, vol. 1, no. 1, published by The Divco Truck Co., Delaware, Ohio, April 1970, p. 1.

2. Georgano, G. N., ed., and Naul, G. Marshall, U.S. Consulting Editor, *The Complete Encyclopedia of Commercial Vehicles*, pp. 226, 227, and 631-632.

3. Wren, James A. and Wren, Genevieve J., *Motor Trucks of America*. Ann Arbor, Michigan: The University of Michigan Press (for Motor Vehicle Manufacturers Association of the United States, Inc.), 1979, p. 125.

4. "Stock Exchange Notes," *New York Times*, February 26, 1936, p. 36, col. 2.

5. "Truck Companies United," *New York Times*, April 18, 1936, p. 23, col. 8.

6. *Moody's Manual of Investments*, 1937, p. 1336.

7. *Continental Motors Corporation, Annual Report, 1936*, Detroit, Michigan, December 23, 1936.

8. "Divco-Twin Truck Company," *Moody's Manual of Investments*, 1937, p. 3145.

9. "Continental-Divco and Twin Coach Divco Merge," *Automobile Topics*, vol. 121, no. 12, April 20, 1936, p. 450.

10. "New Listings on Curb," *New York Times*, May 27, 1937, p. 28, col. 2.

11. Muma, G.E., President, Divco Corporation, "Divco Corporation and Its Predecessors," September 1956, p. 6.

12. *Moody's Manual of Investments*, 1937, p. 3145, and 1938, p. 235.

13. *Who's Who In Commerce and Industry*, 3rd International Edition, vol. III, 1940-1941, p. 561.

14. "Mead Joins Divco-Detroit," *Automobile Topics*, August 10, 1931, p. 888.

15. "Divco Has New Model," *Automobile Industries*, November 13, 1937, p. 701.

16. *Divco-Twin Truck Company, Annual Report, 1938*, Detroit, December 30, 1938, p. 1.

17. "Divco-Twin Presents a Sensational New Model U," *Detroit: Divco-Twin Truck Company*, September 1939 (sales literature).

18. *Detroit: Divco-Twin Truck Company*, September, 1939 (sales literature).

19. "New Divco Model Idles Seven Hours on Gallon," *Automotive Daily News*, November 27, 1937, p. 18.

20. Divco and Divco-Twin registration and production data are taken from selected issues of *Automotive Industries Magazine* and *Automotive News* from the 1936-1970 period.

21. *Divco-Twin Truck Company, Annual Report, 1938*.

22. *Divco-Twin Truck Company, Annual Report, 1937*, Detroit, December 30, 1937, p. 1.

23. Willis, James F., Primack, Martin L., *An Economic History of the United States*, 2nd ed., Englewood Cliffs, NJ: Prentice-Hall, Inc., 1989, p. 370, and Tindall, George Brown and Shi, David E., *America, A Narrative History*, 4th ed., vol. 2, New York: W.W. Norton, 1996, p. 1150.

24. "Repays $325,000 RFC Loan," *New York Times*, March 12, 1940, p. 33, col. 6.

25. *Divco-Twin Truck Company, Annual Report, 1940*, Detroit: December 31, 1940, p. 2.

26. *Divco Corporation, Annual Report to Stockholders, 1946*, Detroit, January 24, 1947, p. 12.

27. *Divco Corporation, Annual Report to Stockholders, 1947*, Detroit, January 15, 1948, p. 12.

28. *Divco-Twin Truck Company, Annual Report to Stockholders, 1939*, Detroit, December 30, 1939.

29. *Divco-Twin Truck Company, Annual Report, 1938*, Detroit, December 30, 1938, p. 1.

30. *Divco-Twin Truck Company, Annual Report, 1938*, p. 1.

31. *Divco-Twin Truck Company, Annual Report, 1940*, Detroit. December 31, 1940, p. 6.

32. *Divco-Twin Truck Company, Annual Report, 1939*, p. 15.

33. *Divco-Twin Truck Company, Annual Report, 1940*, p. 2.

34. Montville, John B. Mack, *A Legend of the Highway,*Tucson, Arizona: Aztex Corp., 1981, p. 102.

35. National Automobile Chamber of Commerce, New York, letter to Ward Motor Vehicle Company, Mt. Vernon, N.Y., September 29, 1931.

36. Langley, Bogle, and Middleton, Attorneys and Counselors, Detroit,letter to Ward Motor Vehicle Company, Mt. Vernon, New York, November 28, 1931.

37. Wagner, James K., *Ford Trucks Since 1905*, Glen Ellyn, Illinois: Crestline Publishing Company, 1978, pp. 87-88.

38. National Automobile Chamber of Commerce, New York, letter to Ward Motor Vehicle Company, Mt. Vernon, New York, May 4, 1932.

39. National Automobile Chamber of Commerce, New York, letter to Ward Motor Vehicle Company, Mt. Vernon, New York, October 10, 1932.

40. National Automobile Chamber of Commerce, New York, letter to Ward Motor Vehicle Company, Mt. Vernon, New York, October 14, 1932.

41. Langley, Bogle, and Middleton, Attorneys and Counselors, Detroit, Michigan, letter to Ward Motor Vehicle Company, Mt. Vernon, New York, October 30, 1933.

42. National Automobile Chamber of Commerce, New York, letter to Ward Motor Vehicle Company, Mt. Vernon, New York, October 6, 1932.

43. "Patent Suit Withdrawn," *Automobile Topics*, November 6, 1937, p. 71.

44. See, for example, National Automobile Chamber of Commerce, Detroit, Michigan, letter to Ward Motor Vehicle Company, Mt. Vernon, New York, November 24, 1933.

45. "Divco Wins Patent Rights," *Commercial Car Journal*, vol. 56, no. 3, November 1938, p. 120.

46. "Grants Patent License," *Automobile Topics*, March 6, 1939, p. 177.

47. "Divco Patents Upheld," *Commercial Car Journal*, vol. 57, no. 2, April 1937, p. 80.

48. Vinson, Taylor, "When War Came: How Government Regulated the Production of Civilian Passenger Cars," *Automotive History Review*, no. 28, Winter 1993-94, pp. 4-5.

49. *Divco-Twin Truck Company, Annual Report to Stockholders, 1941*, Detroit, January 7, 1942, p. 2.

50. *Divco-Twin Truck Company, Annual Report to Stockholders, 1942*, Detroit, January 7, 1943, p. 2.

51. *Divco-Twin Truck Company, Annual Report, 1942*, p. 2.

52. *Divco-Twin Truck Company, Annual Report, 1942*, p. 2.

53. *Divco-Twin Truck Company, Annual Report, 1942*, p. 2.

54. *Divco-Twin Truck Company, Annual Report to Stockholders, 1943*, Detroit, January 3, 1944, p. 2.

55. *Divco-Twin Truck Company, Annual Report, 1944*, p. 2.

56. *Divco Corporation, Annual Report to Stockholders, 1944*, Detroit, January 3, 1945, p. 2.

57. "Truck Company Changes Name," *New York Times*, January 20, 1944, p. 26, col. 17.

CHAPTER 4. Divco Comes of Age
(The Divco Corporation: 1944-1956)

1. *Divco Corporation, Annual Report to Stockholders, 1944*, Detroit, January 3, 1945.

2. *Divco Corporation, Annual Report, 1944*.

3. *Divco Corporation, Annual Report to Stockholders, 1945*, Detroit, January 28, 1946.

4. *Divco Corporation, Annual Report to Stockholders, 1946*, Detroit, January 24, 1947 pp. 1-2, 6, 12.

5. *Divco Corporation, Annual Report, 1947*, pp. 1-2, 7.

6. *Divco Corporation, Annual Report, 1947*, pp. 1-2.

7. *Divco Corporation, Annual Report, 1946*, pp. 1-2.

8. *Divco Corporation, Annual Report, 1947*, p. 6.

9. *Divco Corporation, Annual Report, 1947*, p. 3.

10. Bain, Joe S., *Barriers to New Competition*, Cambridge: Harvard University Press, 1956, p. 306.

11. White, Lawrence J., *The Automobile Industry Since 1945*, Cambridge: Harvard University Press, 1971 pp. 19-39.

12. Rhys, R.G.D., *The Motor Industry: An Economic Survey*, London: Butterworth, 1972, pp. 79-89.

13. *Divco Corporation, Annual Report, 1947*, p. 2.

14. Interviews with Arnold N. Gentz, of Fraser, Michigan, December 2, 1995 (Divco employee from 1955 to 1963) and Clarence Gentz (telephone interview) Harrison Township, Michigan, December 8, 1995 (Divco employee 1940 to 1961).

15. Almanac Issue, 1950, *Automotive News*, p. 36.

16. Divco Corporation, "Notice of Special Meeting of Shareholders and Proxy Statement", proof of September 14, 1956, p. 3.

17. These concepts on vertical integration are elaborated upon in Langlois, Richard N. and Robertson, Paul L., "Explaining Vertical Integration: Lessons from the American Automobile Industry," *The Journal of Economic History*, vol. 49, no.2, June, 1989, pp. 361-375.

18. Divco Proxy, September 14, 1956, p. 3.

19. *Divco Corporation, Annual Report, 1947*, p. 15.

20. See *Annual Report to Stockholders, 1948*, Divco Corporation, Detroit, January 24, 1949, p. 3; and Divco ad, *The Milk Dealer*, September, 1948, p. 85.

21. "New Refrigerated Trucks for Retail Milk Delivery," *The Milk Dealer*, July, 1935, pp. 34-35.

22. "Refrigerated Bodies Have Hot Prospects," *Commercial Car Journal*, April, 1933, p. 14.

23. *Divco Corporation, Annual Report, 1949*, Detroit, January 23, 1950, pp. 4 and 12.

24. "Now, Refrigerated Divcos," advertisement, *The Milk Dealer*, January, 1954, p. 113.

25. *Divco Corporation, Annual Report to Stockholders, 1953*, Detroit, January 25, 1954. p. 4.

26. *Divco Corporation, Annual Report, 1953*, p. 12.

27. *Divco Corporation, Annual Report, 1953*, p. 4.

28. *Divco Corporation, Annual Report to Stockholders, 1951*, Detroit, January 23, 1952, p. 4.

29. *Divco Corporation, Annual Report, 1951*, p. 4.

30. *Divco Corporation, Annual Report, 1953*, p. 4.

31. *Divco Corporation Annual Report to Stockholders, 1952*, Detroit, January 26, 1953, p. 3.

32. *Divco Corporation, Annual Report, 1952*, p. 12.

33. "Divco offers the 'Dividend' for Multi-Purpose Delivery," *Commercial Car Journal*, vol. 90, no. 1, September, 1955, pp. 87 and 156.

34. "Divco 'Dividend Series' Truck," Sales literature, number 5074-55.

35. "Square-up Your Profit Picture with Divco's New Squared-up Body," ad in *The Milk Dealer*, May, 1955, p. 77.

36. Information in this chapter about the executive and administrative structure of Divco was obtained from corporate annual reports, *Moody's Manual of Investments*, for the 1943-1956 period, and the Divco Proxy Statement proof of September 14, 1956.

37. Parker, George W., "Alas, The Horse," *Detroit Free Press*, October 16, 1955, p. 2-13.

CHAPTER 5. The Divco-Wayne Corporation (1956-1967)

1. Bedingfield, Robert E., "Personality: A Gold Mine in a Storm Cellar," *New York Times*, May 8, 1960, Part III, p. 3, col. 3.

2. Bedingfield, p. 3, col. 3.

3. Divco Corporation, "Notice of Special Meeting of Shareholders, and Proxy Statement," proof of September 14, 1956, pp. 7-10.

4. Notice and Proxy Statement, September 14, 1956, pp. 7-8.

5. Notice and Proxy Statement, September 14, 1956, p. 2.

6. Bedingfield, p. 3, col. 3.

7. "Divco-Wayne Delivery," *Financial World*, vol. 118, August 15, 1962, p. 20.

8. Bedingfield, p. 3, col. 3.

9. Thompson, Kenneth A., "Divco Signs Merger Deal," *Detroit Free Press*, August 29, 1956.

10. Purchase Agreement between Divco Corporation and Wayne Works, Inc., August 27, 1956, p. 5.

11. *Financial World*, August 15, 1962, p. 20.

12. *Moody's Industrial Manual*, 1958, p. 237.

13. *Divco-Wayne Corporation Annual Report, 1958*, Richmond, Indiana, p. 25.

14. *Divco-Wayne Corporation Annual Report, 1962*, Richmond, Indiana, January 10, 1963, pp. 4-8.

15. George E. Muma obituary *Detroit News*, September 23, 1961; *Divco-Wayne Corporation Annual Report, 1959*, Richmond, Indiana.

16. *Divco-Wayne Corporation Annual Report, 1960*, Richmond, Indiana, p. 5.

17. "New Unit Bought by Divco-Wayne," *New York Times*, September 17, 1958, col. 2, p. 55.

18. *Divco-Wayne Corporation Annual Report, 1958*, p. 4.

19. Bedingfield, p. 3. col. 3, and *Divco-Wayne Corporation Annual Report, 1959*, Richmond, Indiana.

20. "Divco-Wayne Corp.," *New York Times*, January 3, 1962, p. 47, col. 1.

21. *Moody's Industrial Manual*, 1966, p. 562 and *Divco-Wayne Corporation Annual Report for the Fiscal Year Ended October 31, 1966*, January 9, 1967, p. 2.

22. *Divco-Wayne Annual Report*, 1960, p. 5.

23. *Introducing Divco-Wayne*, corporate profile brochure, Richmond, Indiana, 1966.

24. *Divco-Wayne Corporation Annual Report, 1966*, Richmond, Indiana, p. 5.

25. "Divco-Wayne Unveils New Bus for Schools, Small Cities," *Automotive Industries*, vol. 120, no. 6, March 15, 1959, p. 60.

26. For a more comprehensive analysis of the Studebaker-Packard corporation situation at the time of the merger discussions with Divco-Wayne, see: Ebert, Robert R., "On the Wings of Larks and Hawks: The Last Flight of Studebaker: 1956-1966," three part series in *The Bulb Horn* magazine of the Veteran Motor Car Club of America, vol. 52, nos. 3 and 4, vol. 53, no. 1, July-September, 1991, October-December, 1991, and January-March 1992 issues, respectively.

27. Bedingfield, p. 3, col. 3.

28. *Divco-Wayne Corporation Annual Report, 1966*, p. 5.

29. *Introducing Divco-Wayne*, p. 10.

30. Chapman, William Ray, Grosse Ile, Michigan, former chief engineer at Divco (1953-1968), letter to John S. Rienzo, Jr., Calverton, New York, February 18, 1997.

31. *Divco-Wayne Corporation Annual Report, 1963*, Richmond, Indiana, p. 5.

32. Purchase Agreement, p. 1.

33. Notice and Proxy Statement, proof of, September 14, 1956, p. 5.

34. Employees and relatives interviewed included the following: Clarence Gentz, Harrison Township, Michigan (worked at Divco in the press shop from 1940 to 1961) telephone interview, December 8, 1995. Arnold Gentz, Fraser, Michigan (worked at Divco in various production capacities from 1955 to 1963). Albert A. Kneale, Jr. and Mrs. Kneale, Royal Oak, Michigan (son and wife respectively of Albert A. Kneale, test driver for Divco and Vice President of UAW Local 889). Roy Sjoberg, Jr., Bloomfield Hills, Michigan (Vice President of Chrysler Corporation, and son of Roy Sjoberg who was Vice President of Divco sales and marketing from 1952-1960).

35. "Production Men Strike at Divco," *The Detroit News*, October 3, 1961, p. 16B.

36. Morris, Kenneth (former Co-Director of Region 1 of the United Auto Workers Union for the East End of Detroit and former member of the Executive Board of the U.A.W.); telephone interview with, September 11, 1996 at his U.A.W. office in Detroit, Michigan.

37. "Pact Ends Divco Strike," *Detroit Free Press*, January 9, 1962, p. 3.

38. *Divco-Wayne Corporation Annual Report, 1961*, January 25, 1962, pp. 2 and 6.

39. Data from "Summaries of Car and Truck Registrations," *Automotive Industries*, March 15, 1965, p. 109. (The source of the *Automotive Industries* data was R.L. Polk and Co.)

40. "The Power of a Six! The Economy of a Four!" Divco ad, *The Milk Dealer*, December, 1959, p. 55.

41. Information on new features for 1963 taken from "Divco Discloses Major Improvements in Truck Lines," *Commercial Car Journal*, vol. 107, no. 1, March, 1964, p. 159, and "6 Major Improvements," Divco ad in *The Milk Dealer*, March, 1963, p. 93.

42. Information on the Divco line for 1965 taken from "What's New in Trucks and Tractors," *Commercial Car Journal*, vol. 108, no.3, November, 1964, p. 258, and "4 new Divco 6-Wides outwork 5 ordinary milk trucks," Divco ad in *The Milk Dealer*, November, 1965, pp. 64-65.

43. Chapman, William R., letter of February 18, 1997 and Chapman, William Ray, Grosse Ile, Michigan letter to John S. Rienzo, Jr., Calverton, New York, April 3, 1997.

44. Chapman, William R., letters of February 18, 1997 and April 3, 1997.

45. *Divco-Wayne Corporation Annual Report, 1960*, p. 6.

46. Sjoberg, Roy H., Vice President of Sales and Marketing, Divco Truck Division, memo to Max V. Downing, February 15, 1967.

47. Sjoberg, Roy H., letter of February 15, 1967.

48. Harvey, Rampton W., Poulsbo, Washington, letter to John S. Rienzo, Jr., Calverton, New York, December 13, 1996.

49. *Divco-Wayne Corporation Annual Report, 1962*, p. 10.

50. Data from *Automotive Industries* annual statistical issues, March 15, 1962 and March 15, 1965.

51. Data from *Automotive Industries* annual statistical issues, March 15, 1962 and March 15, 1965.

52. *Divco-Wayne Annual Report, 1960*, p. 10.

53. *Divco Model 15 Instruction Book*, Detroit: Divco Corporation, November, 1953, p. 9 and ad in *Commercial Car Journal*, vol. 100, no. 6, February, 1961, pp. 86-87.

CHAPTER 6. America's Favorite Milk Truck

1. *Divco-Wayne Annual Report, 1958*, Warren, Michigan, pp. 16-17.

2. Divco Corporation, "Notice of Special Meeting of Shareholders and Proxy Statement," proof of September 14, 1956, p. 5.

3. Selitzer, Ralph, *The Dairy Industry in America*, New York: Dairy and Ice Cream Field and Books for Industry, 1976, pp. 116, 117, 209.

4. Statistical data on truck production, food prices and consumption, milk and other dairy product consumption and prices related to the dairy industry in this chapter are taken from the following sources: *Historical Statistics of the United States: Colonial Times to 1970*, Part 1, Washington D.C.: U.S. Department of Commerce, 1976, *Milk Facts*, U.S. Milk Industry Foundation, Washington, D.C.: 1993; *Agricultural Statistics*, U.S. Department of Agriculture, Washington D.C.: U.S. Government Printing Office, annual editions, 1936-1993; and "Calendar Year Truck and Buses Production by Makes" and "New Truck Registrations by Make and G.V.W.," *Automotive Industries* magazine, selected issues, 1937-1970.

5. "Must Milk Be Rationed?" *The Milk Dealer*, July, 1943, p. 33.

6. Morrow, Alexander, "The War's Impact on Milk Marketing," *The Journal of Marketing*, vol. 10, January, 1946, pp. 237. Note: Per capita Gross National Product in the United States declined from $847 in 1929 to $442 in 1933 (*Historical Statistics of the United States*, p. 224).

7. Selitzer, p. 211.

8. Anderson, Roice and Spencer, Leland (both of Cornell University), "Streamlining Our Milk Delivery System," *The Milk Dealer*, February, 1942, p. 2.

9. *Agricultural Statistics* (U.S.D.A.), selected editions.

10. Morrow, p. 238.

11. Anderson and Spencer, p. 22.

12. Morrow, p. 238.

13. Morrow, p. 242.

14. Bressler, R. G. Jr., E. O. Anderson, D. A. Clarke, Jr. and Bilenker, E. N., *Efficiency of Milk Marketing in Connecticut* (Storrs Agricultural Experiment Station, Bulletin 247, 1943), p. 18 (as reported in Morrow, p. 242).

15. Holm, Ward, "3-Day-A-Week Retail Delivery," *The Milk Dealer*, April, 1950, pp. 146-151. (Ward Holm was Secretary of the Columbus, Ohio, Milk Distributors Association.)

16. Morrow, p. 241.

17. Morrow, p. 241.

18. *Divco-Twin Truck Company, Annual Report to Stockholders, 1943*, Detroit, January 3, 1944.

19. *Divco Corporation, Annual Report to Stockholders, 1945*, Detroit, January 28, 1946.

20. Selitzer, p. 209.

21. U.S. Department of Agriculture, "Packaged Fluid Milk Sales in Federal Milk Order Markets by Size and Type of Containers and Distribution Method During November, 1991," Washington, D.C., U.S.D.A. Agricultural Marketing Service Bulletin AMA-553, p. 3. Precise historic statistical breakdowns of how milk has been retailed are difficult to ascertain. The U.S. Department of Agriculture did not start collecting data until 1963, and prior to 1977, surveys categorized methods of distribution other than home delivery as "wholesale" even though the milk may have been sold through a retail food company store (U.S.D.A., AMS—552, 1991, p. 5).

22. Selitzer, pp. 211-214.

23. Leland Spencer, "The Changing Picture of Fluid Milk Marketing," *The Milk Dealer*, February, 1937, pp. 84-85.

24. Albert M. Freiberg, "Milk Delivery: Necessity or Luxury?" *Harvard Business Review*, vol. 20, no. 1, 1941, pp. 116-123.

25. Freiberg, pp. 120-123.

26. Per capita disposable personal income in 1946 was $1132 and in 1966 it was $2604. Real (inflation adjusted) per capita disposable personal income in 1958 constant dollars was $1606 in 1946 and $2335 in 1966. See: *Historic Statistics of the United States: Colonial Times to 1970*, Part 1, Washington, D.C.: U.S. Department of Commerce, 1976, pp. 8, 224, 225.

27. "Selling Milk Through Stores," *The Milk Dealer*, August, 1947, p. 134.

28. "Delivered Price of Milk," *Historical Statistics of the United States*, p. 213. Retail store price (average, 25 cities), U.S. Department of Agriculture, Agricultural Statistics, 1966, Washington, D.C.: U.S. Government Printing Office, 1966, p. 396.

29. See for example, Hadary, Gideon, "Chocolate Milk Boosts Milk Consumption," *The Milk Dealer*, June, 1944, p. 30; "Chocolate Milk Drink," *The Milk Dealer*, May, 1943, pp. 29-30; "Who Drinks Orangeade and Why?" *The Milk Dealer*, March, 1938, p. 112; "Fresh Orange Juice Selling Big on Milk Routes," *The Milk Dealer*, April, 1955, pp. 46-47 and 77-80; "Ice Cream on Milk Routes," *The Milk Dealer*, August, 1949, pp. 44 and 105.

30. Neeley, George E. "Do Retail Quantity Discounts Work?" *The Milk Dealer*, August, 1956, pp. 63-67.

31. "Milkmen Reduce Home Milk Price," *The Milk Dealer*, September, 1954, p. 98.

32. Anastos, Chris. "Sale of Routes," *The Milk Dealer*, March, 1961, pp. 30, 31, 75, 80.

33. Anastos, pp. 30-31.

34. *U.S.D.A. Agricultural Marketing Services Bulletin 553*, Nov. 1991, p. 37.

35. "1990 U.S. Census Reveals Growth Trends: Suburbs Gain, but Central Cities Hold Their Own," *Landlines*, May 1993, published by the Lincoln Institute of Land Policy.

36. "Divco Milk Delivery Trucks," Condensed Catalog-A, Detroit, Michigan: Divco-Wayne Corporation, catalog TCP 357, 1957.

37. *Divco Corporation 1953 Annual Report to Stockholders*, Detroit, Michigan, Divco Corporation, p. 4.

38. *Divco-Wayne Corporation, 1960 Annual Report*, Richmond, Indiana, December 28, 1960, p. 6.

39. "Refrigerated Wholesale Delivery Truck," *Commercial Car Journal*, vol. 100, no. 1, January 1961, p. 114; and Chapman, William R., Gross Ile, Michigan, former Chief Engineer at Divco (1953-1968), letter to John S. Rienzo, Jr., Calverton, N.Y., April 11, 1997.

40. *Divco-Wayne Corporation Annual Report, 1960*, p. 6.

41. *Automotive Industries* magazine, selected issues, 1948-1970.

42. Nicol, John, President, *Annual Report to Stockholders, 1946*, Detroit: Divco Corporation, January 27, 1947, p. 2.

43. *Divco-Wayne Corporation Annual Report, 1958*, Richmond, Indiana, 1959, pp. 16-17.

44. *Automotive Industries*, March 15, 1959, p. 96.

45. Divco Corporation Notice of Special Meeting of Shareholders and Proxy Statement, proof of September 14, 1956, p. 6.

46. "Notice of Special Meeting and Proxy," proof of September 14, 1956, p. 5.

47. "Notice of Special Meeting and Proxy," proof of September 14, 1956, p. 6.

48. "Divco Offers the 'Dividend' for Multi-Purpose Delivery, "*Commercial Car Journal*, vol. 90, no. 1, September, 1955, pp. 87 and 156.

49. *Divco-Wayne Corporation Annual Report, 1959*, Richmond, Indiana, pp. 8, 17.

50. Interview with Arnold N. Gentz, of Fraser, Michigan, December 2, 1995 in Detroit, Michigan. (Divco employee from 1955 to 1963).

51. *Divco-Wayne Corporation Annual Report, 1959*, pp. 8 and 17.

52. *Divco-Wayne Corporation Annual Report for the fiscal year ended October 31, 1966*, Richmond, Indiana, February 28, 1967, pp. 1 and 10.

CHAPTER 7. Divco on the Block

1. "Divco Has Begun Talks to Sell its Truck Unit," The *Wall Street Journal*, December 7, 1966, p. 2, col. 3.

2. "Divco-Wayne Directors Vote Against Backing Boise-Cascade's Offer," The *Wall Street Journal*, August 17, 1967, p. 4, col. 3.

3. "Merger Is Slated By Boise Cascade, Divco-Wayne," *Wall Street Journal*, June 20, 1967, p. 2, col. 1.

4. *Wall Street Journal*, August 17, 1967, p. 4, col. 3.

5. "Divco-Wayne Board Votes Improved Terms for Proposed Merger Into Boise Cascade," *Wall Street Journal*, October 2, 1967, p. 8, col. 3.

6. Barmash, Isadore, "At Beck: Acquisition Indiges-tion," *New York Times*, August 30, 1970, sec. III, p. 11, col. 1.

7. "Chairman Resigns at Beck Industries," *New York Times*, October 3, 1970, p. 45, col. 1.

8. Dorfman, Dan, "Heard on the Street," *Wall Street Journal*, November 24, 1970, p. 39, col. 3.

9. "Newton Glekel Buys 22% of Hygrade Food Shares," *New York Times*, December 9, 1968, p. 73, col. 2.

10. "American Book Names Director to Its Board," *New York Times*, July 25, 1968, p. 50, col. 2.

11. Raymont, Henry, "New Daily to Run Opinion Features," *New York Times*, February 13, 1968, p. 46.

12. "Companies Take Merger Actions," *New York Times*, November 6, 1969, pp. 67 and 69.

13. Dorfman, p. 39.

14. "Drimmer Bid Fails, First Surety Says," *New York Times*, December 19, 1972, p. 70, col. 4.

15. "Indian Head to Acquire Transportation Division," *Wall Street Journal*, October 15, 1968, p. 9. col. 3.

16. Way, Glenn W., President and Walter Kimball, General Plant Manager, of Correct Manufacturing Co., Delaware, Ohio, interview by Robert R. Ebert, December 17, 1976.

17. Chapman, William Ray, Grosse Ile, Michigan, former chief engineer of Divco Corporation, letter to John S. Rienzo, Jr., Calverton, New York, February 18, 1997.

18. Way and Kimball interview, December 17, 1976.

19. Hoefferle Truck Sales, Inc. vs. Divco-Wayne Corporation, et al.; August Schmidt Company vs. Boise-Cascade Corporation; Eastland Truck Sales, Inc. vs. Boise-Cascade Corporation; and Jack Fogelman and Norma Fogelman vs. Boise-Cascade Corporation, Nos. 74-1481, 74-1765 to 74-1769, United States Courts of Appeals, Seventh Circuit, decision written by Circuit Court Judge Bauer in 523 *Federal Court Reporter, 2d Series*, 523 F2d 543 (1975), pp. 546-547.

20. Myers, Joseph Thomas II, Owner, Davey Drill Company of Kent, Ohio, and son of Joseph T. Myers, telephone interview, November 13, 1996; Holing, James B. ed., *Portage Heritage*, Kent, Ohio: Portage County Historical Society, 1957, p. 214; and Grisner, Karl H. *The History of Kent*, 1st ed., Kent, Ohio: Record Publishing Co., 1932, pp. 187-193.

21. Myers interview and letter to John S. Rienzo, Jr. from Jim Stimac, Chrysler Historical Foundation volunteer, Highland Park, Michigan, April 24, 1997.

22. Way, Glenn W., letter to Devine, Millimet, Stahl and Branch (attorneys), Manchester, New Hampshire, October 8, 1979, p. 4, and *Federal Reporter* 523 F2d 543 (1975), pp. 543-547.

Chapter 8. Divco in Delaware

1. Way, Glenn W., letter to Devine, Millimet, Stahl and Branch (attorneys), Manchester, New Hampshire, October 8, 1979, p. 4.

2. Way, Glenn W., President, and Kimball, Walter, General Plant Manager of Correct Manufacturing Co. Delaware, Ohio, interview by Robert R. Ebert, December 17, 1976.

3. Way and Kimball interview and plant tour, December 17, 1976.

4. Humes, Harry A., Delaware, Ohio, letter to Robert R. Ebert, July 1, 1996. Mr. Humes was chief financial officer for Hughes-Keenan Corporation, the parent firm owned by Glenn W. Way.

5. Humes, Harry A., Delaware, Ohio, letter to Robert R. Ebert, July 12, 1996.

6. Beard, Duane, former Accountant and Controller for Correct Manufacturing; Owens, Robert, former Supervisor of the Fabricating Department, Correct Manufacturing; Sealey, Robert, former Divco line and Sky-Worker line Supervisor for Correct Manufacturing; Stegner, James A., former Superintendent of Sky-Worker production, Correct Manufacturing; group interview by Robert R. Ebert, February 3, 1996, Delaware, Ohio.

7. Hume letter of July 1, 1996.

8. Fischer, Philip B., General Manager, Divco Truck Division, Divco-Wayne Corporation and G. W. Way, President, Transairco; letter to all Divco Service Parts Dealers, September 11, 1968.

9. Edwards, Charles E., *Dynamics of the United States Automobile Industry*, Columbia, South Carolina: University of South Carolina Press, 1965, p. 123.

10. Sjoberg, Roy H., letter to Divco Dealers, Detroit, Michigan, Divco-Wayne Corporation, August 3, 1967; and Answer Brief of August Schmidt Company, Eastland Truck Sales, Inc. et al., Plaintiffs—Cross-Appellees and J. A. Fogelman Truck and Sales Service, Plaintiff—Appellee, and Reply Brief of Hoefferle Truck Sales, Inc., August Schmidt Company and Eastland Truck Sales, Inc., et al., Plaintiffs—Appellants; Hoefferele Truck Sales, Inc. (No. 74-1481) vs. Boise-Cascade Corporation; August Schmidt Company (Nos. 74-1765 and 74-1766) vs. Boise-Cascade Corporation, Eastland Truck Sales, Inc., et al., (Nos. 74-1767, 74-1768) vs. Boise-Cascade Corporation; J. A. Fogelman Truck Sales and Service (No. 74-1769) vs. Boise-Cascade Corporation, in the United States Court of Appeals for the Seventh Circuit, On Appeal from the United States District Court for the Northern District of Illinois, Northern Division, No. 74-1481 (Consolidated), pp. 22-23.

11. Hoefferle, Schmidt, Eastland, Fogelman vs. Boise-Cascade, No. 74-1481, p. 21.

12. Hoefferele, Schmidt, Eastland, Fogelman vs. Boise-Cascade, No. 74-1481, p. 14; and *Federal Court Reporter, 2d Series*, 523 F2d 543 (1975) p. 546.

13. *Federal Court Reporter, 2d Series*, 523 F2d 543 (1975) pp. 546-547.

14. Hoefferle, Schmidt, Eastland, Fogelman vs. Boise-Cascade, No. 74-1481, p. 20.

15. *Federal Court Reporter, 2d Series*, 523 F2d 543 (1975), p. 547.

16. *Federal Court Reporter, 2d Series*, 523 F2d, 543 (1975), p. 547.

17. *Federal Court Reporter, 2d Series*, 523 F2d, 543 (1975), pp. 550-551.

18. *Federal Court Reporter, 2d Series*, 523 F2d, 543 (1975), pp. 549-552.

19. *Federal Court Reporter, 2d Series*, 523 F2d, 543 (1975), p. 550.

20. Hocfferle, Schmidt, Eastland, Fogelman vs. Boise-Cascade, No. 74-1481, p. 5.

21. Way, Glenn W., letter to Devine, Millimet, Stahl, and Branch (attorneys), Manchester, New Hampshire, October 8, 1979, and "Industrialist Glenn Way Dies at 87," *Delaware Gazette*, November 22, 1988, p. 1, and "To All Hughes-Keenan Dealers and Sales Representatives," letter of May 7, 1971 from A. J. Andreoli, Chairman of the Board of Transairco.

22. Mansfield, Edwin, *Microeconomic Theory/Applications* 8th ed., New York: W.W. Norton, 1994, pp. 238-240.

23. Way and Kimball Interview, December 17, 1976.

24. Rhys, D. G., *The Motor Industry: An Economic Survey*. London: Butterworth, 1972, p. 56.

25. Snyder, C. Jim, "Service Managers," *Divco Service Bulletin* 70-4, November 18, 1970 to all Divco dealers.

26. Way, G. W., President, Correct Manufacturing Corporation, Delaware, Ohio, letter to Robert R. Ebert, Baldwin-Wallace College, August 3, 1980.

27. Way, G. W., President, Transairco and The Divco Truck Company, Delaware, Ohio, "To All Divco Dealers," May 3, 1969.

28. "To All Hughes Keenan Dealers and Sales Representatives," Transairco, Inc., Delaware, Ohio, Memo of May 7, 1971, from A. J. Andreoli.

29. Craig, L.E. Jr. Vice President, Marketing, Transairco, Inc., Delaware, Ohio "To All Divco Dealers and Vanette Agents," March 16, 1971, and letter to Divco Dealers signed by James W. McNamee, Manufacturing Manager, Thomas Burke, Controller and George Foster, Sales Director, Automotive Division, Divco Truck Co., Delaware, Ohio, April 11, 1972.

30. McNamee, Burke, Foster, letter to Divco Dealers, April 11, 1972.

31. Way, Glenn W., "To All Divco Dealers: SUBJECT: Prices for the Start of Production in 1973," letter of March 13, 1973.

32. Foster, George D., Sales Director, Automotive Division of Transairco, to Divco Dealers, February 21, 1972.

33. Kimball, W. A., letters to "All Divco Dealers," March 1, 1975 and July 10, 1975.

34. Way and Kimball interview, December 17, 1976, and Beard, Owens, Sealey, Stegner interview, February 3, 1996.

35. Way and Kimball interview, December 17, 1976.

36. Way and Kimball interview, December 17, 1976.

37. Way and Kimball interview, December 17, 1976.

38. "Divco Snub-nosed Retail Delivery Trucks," Models 206 and 200, and Models 306 and 300, literature published by the Divco Truck Company, Delaware, Ohio.

39. Insulation information related by Robert Sealey and Duane Beard in Beard, Owens, Sealey, and Stegner interview.

40. Way, letter to Ebert, August 3, 1980 and Beard, Owens, Sealey and Stegner interview.

41. *Branham's Automobile Reference Book*, Chicago: Branham Printing Company, 1986.

42. *Branham's Automobile Reference Book*, Chicago: Branham Printing Company, 1971.

43. Way and Kimball interview, December 17, 1976.

44. Way, Alton of Clarksville, Tennessee, son of Glenn W. Way, telephone interview, January 12, 1996.

45. Way, Alton interview.

46. Beard, Owens, Sealey, and Stegner interview.

47. Beard, Owens, Sealey, and Stegner interview.

48. Way and Kimball interview, December 17, 1976.

49. Way letter to Devine, Millimet, Stahl and Branch, attorneys, October 8, 1979.

50. Way letter to Devine, Millimet, Stahl and Branch, attorneys, October 8, 1979.

51. Correct Manufacturing Corp., United States Bankruptcy Court, Southern District of Ohio, Eastern Division, Case No. 2-86-00096, Voluntary Case: Debtor's Petition, January 10, 1986, Exhibit B.

52. Correct Manufacturing Bankruptcy Petition, January 10, 1986.

53. Correct Manufacturing Bankruptcy Petition, January 10, 1986, Schedule A-3.

54. Correct Manufacturing Bankruptcy Petition, Summary of Debts and Property.

55. Staats, Larry, Columbus, Ohio, letter to Robert R. Ebert, February 8, 1996.

56. Alton Way, son of Glenn Way, and Duane Beard, James Stegner, Robert Sealey, and Robert Owens were in agreement on the amount the auction raised. (Alton Way interview and Beard, Owen, Sealey, Stegner interview.)

57. Beard, Owen, Sealey, Stegner interview.

58. Alton Way interview.

59. Staats, Larry, Columbus, Ohio, letter to Robert R. Ebert, letter of January 30, 1996 and Beard, Owen, Sealey, Stegner interview.

60. Beard, Owen, Sealey, Stegner interview.

61. Correct Manufacturing Bankruptcy Petition, "Statement of Executory Contracts."

62. Beard, Owen, Sealey, Stegner interview.

CHAPTER 9. Divco in Retrospect

1. Weingart, Wally, Willowbrook, Illinois, telephone interview with Robert R. Ebert, November 25, 1996.

2. Gentz, Arnold N., former Divco Production employee, Fraser, Michigan; interviewed by Robert R. Ebert, December 2, 1995.

3. Abell, Carl, Medina, Ohio; interview with Robert R. Ebert, August 22, 1995.

4. Christiansen, John; Christiansen Dairy Company, North Providence, Rhode Island, telephone interview by Robert R. Ebert, November 22, 1995.

5. Armstrong, Robert C., Jr., President, Munroe Dairy, East Providence, Rhode Island, letter from, October 20, 1995.

6. Bergmann, Richard, "Divcos Press on in D.C." *Divco News*, official publication of the Divco Club of America, no.20, June, 1995, pp. 4-5; and "Bergmann's Bail Out," *Divco News*, no. 25, June, 1996, p. 11.

7. Theodore, Ted J., Special Assistant to the Vice-President for Advancement of Baldwin-Wallace College, Berea, Ohio, interviewed by Robert R. Ebert and Nicole R. Price in Berea, Ohio, November 4, 1996.

8. Degyansky, Eugene, Parma, Ohio (retired Lakewood, Ohio, school teacher), interviewed by Robert R. Ebert and Nicole R. Price in Berea, Ohio, November 14, 1996.

9. Beard, Duane, former Accountant and Controller for Correct Manufacturing; Owens, Robert, former Supervisor of the Fabricating Department, Correct Manufacturing; Sealy, Robert, former Divco line and Sky-Worker line Supervisor for Correct Manufacturing; Stegner, James A., former Supervisor of Sky-Worker production, Correct Manufacturing; group interview with Robert R. Ebert, February 3, 1996, Delaware, Ohio.

In this index, an "APP" designation after an entry indicates reference to the appropriate appendix to the book.

INDEX

INDEX

INDEX

Stutz *(continued)*
  liquidation of and Pak-Age-Car, 28
Suburbanization, milk delivery and, 86
Suppliers, to Divco Corporation, 54, 55
Tanks, military parts for, 61
Taylor, Edward R.
  board member of Divco, 64
  director of Divco-Wayne Corporation, 67
The Hole, Hoover Road plant and, 115
Theodore, Ted J., Divco truck driver for
  Producers Dairy, 115
Thorne, Niblack, Thorne Motor Corporation
  and, 26, 27
Thorne Trucks, 23, 24, 26, 27, 115
  competitor of Divco, 28
  gas-electric delivery truck, 26
Thorne, Ward, Thorne Motor Corporation
  and, 27
Three-point control, Divco Model B's and, 27
Transairco Corporation, 97
  Aldrich Company and, App. H
  Andre Andreoli and, App. H
  Aqua-Heat and, App. H
  Associated Dayton Equities and, App. H
  Associated Equities, Inc. and, App. H
  Correct Manufacturing and, App. H
  Curtis Air Conditioning Company and,
    App. H
  Divco Truck Company and, 102
  Glenn Way and, 101, App. H
  Hughes Keenan Corporation and, App. H
  production of Divco parts and, 98
  Roustabout Cranes and, App. H
  Rybolt Heater Company and, App. H
  sale of Divco operations to Glenn Way,
    104
  United States Air Conditioning and,
    App. H
Transverse aisle, and Model H Divco, 9
Tri-City Divco, 74
  Dividend Series and, 89
Truck Engineering Company, Divco alleges
  patent infringement by, 39
Truck Manufacturers, of multi-stop delivery
  trucks, 22
Truck operations, costs of, 15
Truck vs. Horse costs,
  Commercial Car Journal study of, 16
  Horse and Mule Association and, 16, 18,
    20
Trucks, multi-stop, advantages, of, 21
Twenty-fifth anniversary, of Divco
  Corporation, 61
Twin Coach, 64
  delivery truck division sold to Divco-
    Twin, 28
  Flxible Company and, 95
  Highway Products and, 95
  organized by Fageol Brothers, 28
  partner for Divco, 29
  patents held by, App. F
Twin Coach Company, Continental-Divco
  and, 14
Twin Coach delivery trucks, 30
  Carl and Sherry Abell and, 30
  Helms Bakery and, 30

Twin Coach style, discontinued by Divco-
  Twin, 30
Twin Coach trucks, 23, 24
Twin-Pines Dairy, milk route leasing and, 86
U.S. District Court, of Northern District of
  Illinois, 98
United Auto Workers
  Local 576 and Divco, 69
  strike against Divco, 1961, 69
United Dairy Workers, 86
United Parcel Service, Divco trucks and, 87
United Plant Guards of America, Local 114
  and Divco, 69
United States Air Conditioning Company
  Glenn Way and, App. H
  Hughes Keenan Corporation and, App. H
  Roustabout Cranes and, App. H
  Transairco and, App. H
Universal Sales, Vanette bodies and, 104
University of Michigan, 11
Urban crowding, and horse-drawn milk wag-
  ons, 21
Val-U-Van, Divco prototype, 87
Vanette, 97
  Glenn Way and, 101, 102
  production discontinued, 105
  prototype of, 105
  truck body builder, 88
Vorys, Sater, Seymour, and Pease, attorneys
  and Correct Manufacturing bankruptcy,
  114
Vought Industries, purchased by Divco-
  Wayne, 68
Wages, of milk truck drivers, 81
Walker trucks, competitor of Divco, 23, 24,
  28, 115
Walker Dynamotive trucks, gas-electric deliv-
  ery trucks, 25
Walker Vehicle Company
  accused of patent infringement by Ward,
    25
  C-T Electric Truck Co., absorption of, 25
  division of Yale and Towne, 26
  Dynamotive truck, 26
  patent pool entered into with Divco, 25
Walker, David, and Wayne Works, 67
War production, Divco subcontractor to
  Curtiss-Wright, 41
War Production Board, 41
War reconversion, Divco plans and opera-
  tions, 45
Ward Motor Vehicle Company, accuses Divco
  of patent infringement, 24, 25
Ward Trucks
  electric delivery trucks, 23, 24, 28
  competitor of Divco, 24
Ward, Charles A., patents issued to, 24
Way, Alton
  Albetway Corporation and, 114
  operations of Correct manufacturing and,
    113
Way, Betty, Albetway Corporation and, 114
Way, Glenn W.
  Burkett Closed Body Co. and, App. H
  business background of, App. H

children of, 114
Correct Manufacturing and, App. H
determination of, 97
Divco production and, 111
Divco Truck Company and, 102
Gerstenslager Company and, App. H
Hughes Keenan Corporation, App. H
industrialist, 101
operations of Correct Manufacturing and,
  113
Postal van bodies and, 95
problems of parts supply and, 103
purchase of Divco from Transairco and,
  104
Roustabout Cranes and, App. H
sale of Divco to Transairco and Glenn
  Way, 98
Sky-Worker and, 101
Transairco and purchase of Divco, 95
Transairco and, 113
Transairco Corporation and, App. H
United States Air Conditioning and, App.
  H
Vanette and, 101
Wayne Division, school buses and, 66, 68
Wayne Works
  financial result of, 66
  history of, 65
  merger with Divco, 65
  purchased by Divco, conditions of, 67
  purchased by Glekel and Drimmer, 65
Weiland, C.J., and Sons Dairy, refrigerated
  trucks, 57
Weingart, Wally, Divco truck driver, 115
Welles Corporation Limited
  Canadian market and, 69
  division of Divco-Wayne, 68
  postal van bodies and, 95
White Horse Delivery Truck
  as competitor of Divco, 28, 31
  as serious competitor for Divco, 23
  Franklin engine and, 23
  licenses Divco patents, 39, 40
  of White Motor Company, 23
  PDQ trucks and, 23, 88
  sales of, 23
  White Horse delivery truck, 23
White, Lawrence, efficient motor vehicle pro-
  duction and, 49
Whitney, Eddy R.
  C-T Electric Co. and, 25
  reissue patent, alleged infringement of,
    38, 39
  Walker/Divco patent pool and, 25
William, Frank A., board member of Divco,
  64
Wilson, Ira Dairy, milk route leasing and, 86
Windsor, Ontario, Divco-Wayne subsidiary
  and, 68
Women, labor force participation of and
  Divco, App. G
World War II, 20, 28, 82, 115
  milk delivery and, 83, 84
  production for by Divco-Twin, 41
Yale and Towne Manufacturing, owned
  Walker Vehicle Company, 26

INDEX